S0-BAN-810

Croatia

AUSTRIA

HUNGARY

100 Kilometers

100 Miles

Drava

Maribor

Ptuj

Varaždin

Pécs

Bled

Ljubljana

SERBIA

Zagreb

SLOVENIA

Samobor

CROATIA

Sava

Osijek

Vukovar

SLAVONIA

ITALY

Trieste

Piran

Opatija

Motovun

Poreč

Karlovac

Rijeka

ISTRIA

Slunj

Krk

Senj

Plitvice Lakes

National Park

BOSNIA-

HERZEGOVINA

Rovinj

Pula

Cres

Otočac

KVARNER GULF

Rab

Brijuni

Islands

Pag

Zadar

Knin

Sarajevo

Dugi

Otok

Šibenik

Adriatic

Trogir

Split

Mostar

Makarska

Medugorje

MONTE-

NEGRO

Hvar

Hvar

Neum

DALMATIAN COAST

Korčula

Ploče

Korčula

Ston

Trebinje

Kotor

Mljet

Dubrovnik

Sea

Cavtat

Cetinje

ITALY

Budva

Bay of

Kotor

Sveti

Stefan

INTRODUCTION

This Snapshot guide, excerpted from my guidebook *Rick Steves' Croatia & Slovenia*, introduces you to Croatia's single best destination, the "Pearl of the Adriatic"—Dubrovnik. This magnificent medieval city, encircled by a stout wall and poking proudly into the sea, comes with an epic history and plenty of ways to idle away your vacation days. Climb steep steps to the top of the city's imposing stone walls, and stroll high above Dubrovnik's patchwork of red roof tiles. Promenade down the inviting main drag, dropping into an eclectic smattering of fine museums—history, art, folk life, war photography, and the Jewish and Orthodox faiths. Hit the beach and go for a swim in the crystal-clear waters of the Adriatic.

While there are many island and resort-town side-trips from Dubrovnik, this book emphasizes a diverse pair of neighboring countries that offer a more culturally stimulating look at the region. Mostar, a leading city of Bosnia-Herzegovina, is a fascinating combination of Ottoman (Turkish) history, Muslim faith, welcoming locals, lingering war damage, and inspiring postwar reconciliation. Rugged, scenic Montenegro, just south of Dubrovnik, is an emerging Mediterranean hotspot—especially the historic old town of Kotor—but deep in its mountains, you'll find echoes of a bygone mountain kingdom.

To help you have the best trip possible, I've included the following topics in this book:

• **Planning Your Time,** with advice on how to make the most of your limited time

• **Orientation,** including tourist information (abbreviated as TI), tips on public transportation, local tour options, and helpful hints

• **Sights** with ratings:

▲▲▲—Don't miss

▲▲—Try hard to see

▲—Worthwhile if you can make it

No rating—Worth knowing about

• **Sleeping** and **Eating,** with good-value recommendations in every price range

• **Connections,** with tips on driving, buses, and boats

The **Understanding Yugoslavia** chapter offers a simplified explanation of the history of this complex part of Europe.

Practicalities, near the end of this book, has information on money, phoning, accommodations, transportation, and other helpful hints, plus Croatian survival phrases.

To travel smartly, read this little book in its entirety before you go. It's my hope that this guide will make your trip more meaningful and rewarding. Traveling like a temporary local, you'll get the absolute most out of every mile, minute, and dollar.

Sretan put—happy travels!

Rick Steves

DUBROVNIK

DUBROVNIK

Dubrovnik is a living fairy tale that shouldn't be missed. It feels like a small town today, but 500 years ago, Dubrovnik was a major maritime power, with the third-biggest navy in the Mediterranean. Still jutting confidently into the sea and ringed by thick medieval walls, Dubrovnik deserves its nickname: the Pearl of the Adriatic. Within the ramparts, the traffic-free Old Town is a fun jumble of quiet, cobbled back lanes; low-impact museums; narrow, steep alleys; and kid-friendly squares. After all these centuries, the buildings still hint at old-time wealth, and the central promenade (Stradun) remains the place to see and be seen. If I had to pick just one place to visit in Croatia, this would be it.

The city's charm is the sleepy result of its no-nonsense past. Busy merchants, the salt trade, and shipbuilding made Dubrovnik rich. But the city's most valued commodity was always its freedom—even today, you'll see the proud motto *Libertas* displayed all over town (see *"Libertas"* sidebar).

Dubrovnik flourished in the 15th and 16th centuries, but an earthquake destroyed nearly everything in 1667. Most of today's buildings in the Old Town are post-quake Baroque, although a few palaces, monasteries, and convents displaying a rich Gothic-Renaissance mix survive from Dubrovnik's earlier Golden Age. Dubrovnik remained a big tourist draw through the Tito years, bringing in much-needed hard currency from Western visitors. Consequently, the city never acquired the hard socialist patina of other Yugoslav cities (such as the nearby Montenegrin capital Podgorica, then known as "Titograd").

As Croatia violently separated from Yugoslavia in 1991, Dubrovnik became the only coastal city to be pulled into the

DUBROVNIK

Libertas

Libertas—liberty—has always been close to the heart of every Dubrovnik citizen. Dubrovnik was a proudly independent republic for centuries, even as most of Croatia became Venetian and then Hungarian. Dubrovnik believed so strongly in *libertas* that it was the first foreign state in 1776 to officially recognize an upstart, experimental republic called the United States of America.

In the Middle Ages, the city-state of Dubrovnik (then called Ragusa) bought its independence from whichever power was strongest—Byzantium, Venice, Hungary, the Ottomans—sometimes paying off more than one at a time. Dubrovnik's ships flew whichever flags were necessary to stay free, earning the nickname "Town of Seven Flags." It was sort of a Hong Kong of the Middle Ages—a spunky, trading-oriented statelet that maintained its sovereignty while being completely surrounded by an often-hostile mega-state (in Dubrovnik's case, the Ottoman Empire). As time went on, Europe's big-league nations were glad to have a second major seafaring power in the Adriatic to balance the Venetian threat; Dubrovnik emerged as an attractive alternative at times when Venetian ports were blockaded by the Ottomans. A free Dubrovnik was more valuable than a pillaged, plundered Dubrovnik.

In 1808, Napoleon conquered the Adriatic and abolished the Republic of Dubrovnik. After Napoleon was defeated, the fate of the continent was decided at the Congress of Vienna. But Dubrovnik's delegate was denied a seat at the table. The more powerful nations, no longer concerned about Venice and fed up after years of being sweet-talked by Dubrovnik, were afraid that the delegate would play old alliances off each other to re-establish an independent Republic of Dubrovnik. Instead, the city became a part of the Habsburg Empire and entered a long period of decline.

Libertas still hasn't died in Dubrovnik. In the surreal days of the early 1990s, when Yugoslavia was reshuffling itself, a movement for the creation of a new Republic of Dubrovnik gained some momentum (led by a judge who, in earlier times, had convicted others for the same ideas). Another movement pushed for Dalmatia to secede as its own nation. But now that the dust has settled, today's locals are content and proud to be part of an independent Republic of Croatia.

fighting (see "The Siege of Dubrovnik" sidebar). Imagine having your youthful memories of good times spent romping in the surrounding hills replaced by visions of tanks and warships shelling your hometown. The city was devastated, but Dubrovnik has been repaired with amazing speed. The only physical reminders of the war are lots of new, bright-orange roof tiles. Locals, relieved the fighting is over but forever hardened, are often willing to talk openly about the experience with visitors—offering a rare opportunity to grasp the harsh realities of war from an eyewitness perspective.

Though the war killed tourism in the 1990s, today the crowds are most decidedly back—even exceeding prewar levels. In fact, Dubrovnik's biggest downside is the overwhelming midday crush of multinational tourists who converge on the Old Town when their cruise ships dock. These days the city's economy is based almost entirely on tourism, and most locals have moved to the suburbs so they can rent their Old Town apartments to travelers. All of this can make the Old Town feel, at times, like a very pretty but soulless theme park. Dubrovnik lacks the gritty real-world vibe of Split or the charming local vitality of Ljubljana. But, like Venice, Dubrovnik rewards those who get off the beaten path and stick around beyond the normal midday cruise-ship window. Europeans set up here for a full week or two to explore the entire region, and even busy Americans might want to build some slack into their Dubrovnik time for a wide array of worthwhile side-trips.

Planning Your Time

While Dubrovnik's museums are nothing special, the town is one of those places that you never want to leave. The real attraction here is the Old Town and its relaxing, breezy ambience. While Dubrovnik could easily be "seen" in a day, a second or third day to unwind (or even more time, for side-trips) makes the long trip here more worthwhile.

To hit all the key sights in a single day, start at the Pile Gate, just outside the Old Town. Walk around the city's walls to get your bearings (before it gets too hot and crowded), then work your way down the main drag (following my "Strolling the Stradun" self-guided walk). As you explore, drop in at any museums or churches that appeal to you. To squeeze the most into a single day (or with a second day), hit the beach or consider a boat excursion from the Old Port (Lokrum Island, just offshore, requires the least brainpower).

Dubrovnik also makes an excellent home base for day trips into the surrounding area, including a dizzying array of island

DUBROVNIK

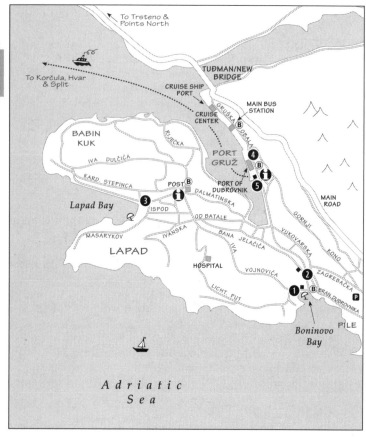

getaways, plus a pair of particularly striking international destinations: Bosnia-Herzegovina's Mostar and Montenegro's Bay of
Kotor. I enjoy staying three or four nights, for maximum side-
tripping flexibility.

Orientation to Dubrovnik

(area code: 020)
Nearly all of the sights worth seeing are in Dubrovnik's traffic-free,
walled **Old Town** (Stari Grad) peninsula. The main pedestrian
promenade through the middle of town is called the **Stradun;**
from this artery, the Old Town climbs steeply uphill in both
directions to the walls. The Old Town connects to the mainland
through three gates: the **Pile Gate,** to the west; the **Ploče Gate,**
to the east; and the smaller **Buža Gate,** at the top of the stepped
lane called Boškovićeva. The **Old Port** (Gradska Luka), with lei-

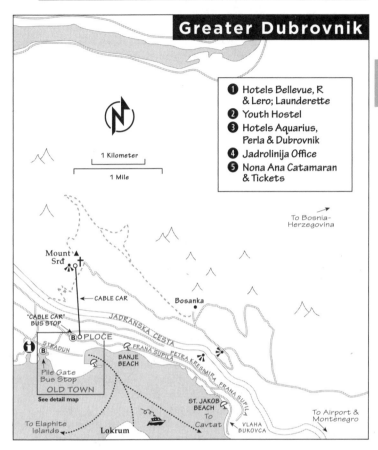

Greater Dubrovnik

1. Hotels Bellevue, R & Lero; Launderette
2. Youth Hostel
3. Hotels Aquarius, Perla & Dubrovnik
4. Jadrolinija Office
5. Nona Ana Catamaran & Tickets

1 Kilometer

1 Mile

To Bosnia-Herzegovina

Mount Srđ

CABLE CAR

Bosanka

"CABLE CAR" BUS STOP

JADRANSKA CESTA

PLOCE

STRADUN

FRANA SUPILA

PETRA KRESIMIRA

FRANA SUPILA

BANJE BEACH

Pile Gate Bus Stop

OLD TOWN

See detail map

ST. JAKOB BEACH

To Cavtat

To Airport & Montenegro

To Elaphite Islands

Lokrum

VLAHA BUKOVCA

sure boats to nearby destinations, is at the east end of town. While greater Dubrovnik has about 50,000 people, the local population within the Old Town is just a few thousand in the winter—and even smaller in summer, when many residents move out to rent their apartments to tourists.

The **Pile** (PEE-leh) neighborhood, a pincushion of tourist services, is just outside the western end of the Old Town (through the Pile Gate). In front of the gate, you'll find the main TI, ATMs, a post office, taxis, buses (fanning out to all the outlying neighborhoods), a cheap Konzum grocery store, and the Atlas Travel Agency (described later, under "Helpful Hints"). Just off this strip are some good *sobe* (rooms in private homes—described under "Sleeping in Dubrovnik"). This is also the starting point for my "Strolling the Stradun" self-guided walk.

A mile or two away from the Old Town are beaches peppered with expensive resort hotels. The closest area is **Boninovo Bay** (a

20-minute walk or 5-minute bus trip from the Old Town), but most cluster on the lush **Lapad Peninsula** to the west (a 15-minute bus trip from the Old Town); I've recommended accommodations in each of these areas. Across the bay from the Lapad Peninsula is **Port Gruž,** with the main bus station, ferry terminal, and cruise-ship port.

Tourist Information

Dubrovnik's main TI is just outside the Old Town's **Pile Gate,** at the far end of the big terrace with the modern video-screens sculpture (July-Aug daily 8:00-22:00; June and Sept daily 8:00-21:00; May and Oct daily 8:00-20:00; Nov-April Mon-Sat 8:00-19:00, Sun 8:00-16:00; Brsalje 5, tel. 020/312-011, www.tzdubrovnik.hr). There are also locations at **Port Gruž,** across the street from the Jadrolinija ferry dock (June-Sept daily 8:00-21:00; May and Oct daily 8:00-20:00; Nov-April Mon-Fri generally 9:00-15:00, Sat 9:00-14:00, closed Sun; Gruška obala, tel. 020/417-983); in the **Lapad** resort area, at the head of the main drag (May-Oct daily 8:00-20:00, until 21:00 in July-Aug; closed Nov-April; Šetalište Kralja Zvonimira 25, tel. 020/437-460); and at the arrivals area of the **airport.**

All the TIs are government-run and legally can't sell you anything except a Dubrovnik Card—but they can answer questions and give you a copy of the free town map and two similar information booklets: the annual *Dubrovnik Riviera* and the monthly *The Best in Dubrovnik* (with a current schedule of events and performances); both contain helpful maps, bus and ferry schedules, museum hours, specifics on side-trip destinations, and more. If you need a room and the TI isn't busy, they might be willing to unofficially call around to find a place for you.

Sightseeing Pass: The heavily promoted **Dubrovnik Card** covers local public transportation; admission to the City Walls (one time only), Rector's Palace, Rupe Museum, and a few other minor sights; and various discounts around town. If you're here for three days and plan to do a lot of sightseeing and take the bus a few times, this may add up—do the math (130 kn/24 hours includes unlimited transit, 180 kn/3 days includes 10 transit rides, 220 kn/7 days includes 20 transit rides, sold at TIs and many sights and hotels).

Arrival in Dubrovnik

As is the case throughout Croatia, you'll be met at the boat dock or bus station by locals trying to get you to rent a room *(soba)* at their house. If you've already reserved elsewhere, honor your reservation; if not, consider the offer (but be very clear on the location before you accept—many are nowhere near the Old Town).

Dubrovnik Essentials

English	Croatian	Pronounced
Old Town	Stari Grad	STAH-ree grahd
Old Port	Stara Luka	STAH-rah LOO-kah
Pile Gate	Gradska Vrata Pile	GRAHD-skah VRAH-tah PEE-leh
Ploče Gate	Gradska Vrata Ploče	GRAHD-skah VRAH-tah PLOH-cheh
Main Promenade	Stradun	STRAH-doon
Adriatic Sea	Jadran	YAH-drahn

By Bus: Dubrovnik's **main bus station** (Autobusni Kolodvor) is just beyond the ferry terminal along the Port Gruž embankment (about 2.5 miles northwest of the Old Town). It's straightforward and user-friendly, with pay toilets, baggage storage, and a helpful bus information window. To reach the Old Town's Pile Gate, walk straight ahead through the bus stalls, then bear right at the main road to the city bus stop, where you can hop on a bus (#1, #1a, #1b, or #1c) to the Pile stop. A taxi from the main bus station to the Old Town and most accommodations runs about 75 kn.

Some buses (especially southbound regional buses, such as those to Cavtat) originate at the main bus station, but also use another stop, much handier to the Old Town. The **"cable car" bus stop** (a.k.a. "fire station" bus stop) is just uphill from the Buža Gate, overlooking the old wall, right next to the bottom station of the cable car up to Mount Srđ. From this bus stop, simply walk downhill (and through the pedestrian underpass)—you'll be inside the Old Town walls within a few minutes.

By Car Ferry or Catamaran: The big car ferries currently arrive at Port Gruž, two miles northwest of the Old Town. On the road in front of the ferry terminal, you'll find a bus stop (#1, #1a, #1b, and #1c go to the Old Town's Pile Gate; wait on the embankment side of the street) and a taxi stand (figure 70 kn to the Old Town and most accommodations). Across the street is the Jadrolinija office (with an ATM out front) and a TI. You can book a private room *(soba)* at Atlas Travel Agency (room-booking desk in boat terminal building, May-Sept only) or at Gulliver Travel Agency (behind TI). The fast *Nona Ana* catamaran from Mljet and Korčula also arrives near this big ferry dock.

By Cruise Ship: Some ships anchor just offshore from the Old Port, then send their passengers into the Old Town on tenders. Others put in at Port Gruž, just beyond the bus station. To reach the Old Town, take a public bus or pay 80 kn for a taxi (described

Dubrovnik at a Glance

▲▲▲**Stradun Stroll** Charming walk through Dubrovnik's vibrant Old Town, ideal for coffee, ice cream, and people-watching. **Hours:** Always open. See page 15.

▲▲▲**Town Walls** Scenic mile-long walk along top of 15th-century fortifications encircling the city. **Hours:** July-Aug daily 8:00-19:30, progressively shorter hours off-season until 10:00-15:00 in mid-Nov-mid-March. See page 24.

▲▲▲**Mount Srđ** Napoleonic fortress above Dubrovnik with spectacular views and a modest museum to the recent war. **Hours:** Mountaintop—always open; cable car—daily June-Aug 9:00-24:00, April-May and Sept-Oct 9:00-20:00, Feb-March and Nov 9:00-17:00, Dec-Jan 9:00-16:00; museum—same hours as cable car except closes at 22:00 in summer. See page 39.

▲**Franciscan Monastery Museum** Tranquil cloister, medieval pharmacy-turned-museum, and a century-old pharmacy still serving residents today. **Hours:** Daily April-Oct 9:00-18:00, Nov-March 9:00-17:00. See page 29.

▲**Rector's Palace** Sparse antiques collection in the former home of rectors who ruled Dubrovnik in the Middle Ages. **Hours:** Daily May-Oct 9:00-18:00, Nov-April 9:00-16:00. See page 30.

▲**Cathedral** Eighteenth-century Roman Baroque cathedral and treasury filled with unusual relics, such as a swatch of Jesus' swaddling clothes. **Hours:** Church—daily 8:00-20:00, treasury—generally open same hours as church, both have shorter hours off-season. See page 32.

▲**Dominican Monastery Museum** Another relaxing cloister with precious paintings, altarpieces, and manuscripts. **Hours:** Daily May-Sept 9:00-18:00, Oct-April 9:00-17:00. See page 33.

▲**Synagogue Museum** Europe's second-oldest synagogue and Croatia's only Jewish museum, with 13th-century Torahs

earlier, under "By Bus").

By Plane: Dubrovnik's small airport (Zračna Luka) is near a village called Čilipi, 13 miles south of the city. A Croatia Airlines bus meets arriving flights for most major airlines at the airport, and brings you to the main bus station (35 kn, 40 minutes; may also stop near the Old Town—ask driver or airport TI). Legitimate cabbies charge around 220 kn for the ride between the airport and the center (though some cabbies charge as much as 300 kn; con-

and Holocaust-era artifacts. **Hours:** May-mid-Nov daily 10:00-20:00; mid-Nov-April Mon-Fri 10:00-13:00, closed Sat-Sun. See page 36.

▲**War Photo Limited** Thought-provoking photographic look at contemporary warfare. **Hours:** June-Sept daily 10:00-22:00; May and Oct Tue-Sun 10:00-16:00, closed Mon; closed Nov-April. See page 36.

▲**Serbian Orthodox Church and Icon Museum** Active church serving Dubrovnik's Serbian Orthodox community and museum with traditional religious icons. **Hours:** Church—daily May-Sept 8:00-14:00 & 16:00-21:00, until 19:00 in shoulder season, until 17:00 in winter; museum—May-Oct Mon-Sat 9:00-13:00, closed Sun; Nov-April Mon-Fri 9:00-13:00, closed Sat-Sun. See page 37.

▲**Rupe Granary and Ethnographic Museum** Good folk museum with tools, jewelry, clothing, and painted eggs above immense underground grain stores. **Hours:** Wed-Mon 9:00-16:00, closed Tue. See page 38.

Maritime Museum Contracts, maps, paintings, and models from Dubrovnik's days as a maritime power and shipbuilding center. **Hours:** Flex with demand, usually March-Oct Tue-Sun 9:00-18:00, until 16:00 in Nov-Feb, closed Mon year-round. See page 35.

Aquarium Tanks of local sea life housed in huge, shady old fort. **Hours:** Daily July-Aug 9:00-21:00, progressively shorter hours off-season until 9:00-13:00 Nov-March. See page 35.

Institute for the Restoration of Dubrovnik Photos and videos of the recent war and an exhibit on restoration work. **Hours:** Completely unpredictable—just drop by and see if it's open. See page 36.

sider arranging your transfer in advance with one of the drivers, or through your *sobe* host). Airport info: tel. 020/773-333, www.airport-dubrovnik.hr.

To get *to* the airport, you can take the same Croatia Airlines bus, which typically leaves from Dubrovnik's main bus station 1.5 hours before each Croatia Airlines or Austrian Airlines flight, or two hours before other airlines' international flights (the schedule is posted the day before—ask at the TI). It's possible that the bus may also stop at a point closer to the Old Town (maybe at the Pile Gate, or possibly at the Buža Gate above the Old Town). As of this writing, this has not been decided—ask at the TI to see if it can save you some time.

Bad-Weather Warning: If you're considering flying into or out of Dubrovnik, be aware that the airport is located right in the blast zone of the fierce Bora winds that periodically howl along the Dalmatian Coast (especially in the late fall). It's not uncommon for flights coming into Dubrovnik to be diverted to Split instead, with passengers forced to take a dull five-hour bus journey to their intended destination. Departing flights are usually less affected (though disruptions to incoming planes could, obviously, cause delays for departures as well). Personally, I've flown out of Dubrovnik a dozen times without incident, but it's not unheard-of for travelers to be inconvenienced by this.

Nearby: If you have time to kill at the airport, you can go spelunking in the karstic **Đurović Cave,** which was recently discovered beneath the runway and opened to the public. It's filled with a "skycellar," allowing you to sample local wines in an underground cavern while waiting for your flight...no joking (40 kn to enter, 75 kn to taste up to 10 wines, sporadic hours; as you face the terminal, go to the right end and buzz the bell, or enter through the cafeteria).

By Car: Coming from the north, you'll drive over the supermodern Tuđman Bridge (which most locals, mindful of their former president's tarnished legacy, call simply "the New Bridge"). Immediately after crossing the bridge, you have two options: To get to the main bus station, ferry terminal (with some car-rental drop-off offices nearby), and Lapad Peninsula, take the left turn just after the bridge, wind down to the waterfront, then turn left and follow this road along the Port Gruž embankment. Or, to head for the Old Town, continue straight after the bridge. You'll pass above the Port Gruž area, then take the right turn-off marked *Dubrovnik* (with the little bull's-eye). You'll go through a tunnel, then turn left for *Centar,* and begin following the brown signs for *Grad* (Old Town); individual big hotels are also signed from here. Turn right to get to the Buža Gate at the top of the Old Town; first you'll pass the Old Town parking garage (described next), then wind up just above the walls (with more parking options—also described next). From this point, the direction you choose determines which one-way loop you'll be stuck on. Turning right takes you to the Pile Gate, then back up out of town toward Boninovo Bay and Lapad; turning left takes you the pretty Viktorija area, then (after looping down again) to the Ploče Gate.

If you're sleeping in or near the Old Town, **parking** is tricky. The handiest place to park long-term is the Old Town garage, which you'll pass on the right as you head toward the Old Town (15 kn/hour, 180 kn/day, half-price Oct-May). From here, it's about a 10-minute downhill walk to the Old Town, or you can take a shuttle bus (2/hour, free if you're paying to park here). If you'd like to be closer to the Old Town, you can take your chances on finding a spot—either on the street directly behind and above the town walls (pay at meter), or in the convenient but often-crammed pay lot nicknamed "the tennis court," just behind the wall (10 kn/hour). Another option is to drive to this area near the Old Town to unload your bags, then leave your car at the Old Town garage (or a cheaper, more distant one) for the duration of your visit. When in doubt, ask your *sobe* host or hotel for parking tips.

If you're sleeping at Lapad or Boninovo Bay, you'll have an easier time finding parking at or near your hotel—ask.

Helpful Hints

Festivals: Dubrovnik is most crowded during its Summer Festival, a month and a half of theater and musical performances held annually from July 10 to August 25 (www.dubrovnik-festival .hr). This is quickly followed by the "Rachlin & Friends" classical music festival in September (www.julianrachlin.com). For other options, see "Entertainment in Dubrovnik," later.

Crowd-Beating Tips: Dubrovnik has been discovered—especially by cruise ships (nearly 800 of which visit each year, bringing a total of around 900,000 passengers). Cruise-ship crowds descend on the Old Town on most summer days, roughly between 8:30 and 14:00 (the streets are most crowded 9:00-13:00). In summer, try to avoid the big sights—especially walking around the wall—during these peak times, and hit the beach or take a siesta midday, when the town is hottest and most crowded. On very busy days, as many as 9,000 cruise-ship day-trippers deluge Dubrovnik (three big ships' worth). If you're caught off-guard, it can be miserable. For others, it's entertaining to count the dozens of tour guides toting numbered paddles through the Old Town, and to watch the blocky orange tenders going back and forth to the ships moored offshore.

No Euros: Dubrovnik's merchants can be stubborn about accepting only kunas—no euros. (While it's technically illegal for vendors to accept any payment other than kunas, this is rarely enforced.) Even some of the top sights—including the City Walls and the cable car to Mount Srđ—accept only kunas (or, sometimes, credit cards). Even if you're in town for just a few hours, visit an ATM to avoid hassles when it comes time to pay.

Wine Shop: For the best wine-tasting selection in a cool bar atmosphere, don't miss **D'Vino Wine Bar**. If you want to shop rather than taste, **Vinoteka Miličić** offers a nice variety of local wines; wry Dolores can explain your options, though she does tend to push Miličić wines (daily June-Aug 9:00-23:00, April-May and Sept-Oct 9:00-20:00, Nov-March 9:00-16:00, near the Pile end of the Stradun, tel. 020/321-777).

Internet Access: Most accommodations in Dubrovnik offer free Wi-Fi, and several cafés and bars around town provide Wi-Fi for customers. In the Old Town, the modern **Netcafé** has several speedy terminals and pay Wi-Fi right on Prijeko street, the "restaurant row" (daily 9:00-24:00, Prijeko 21, tel. 020/321-025).

English Bookstore: The **Algoritam** shop, right on the Stradun, has a wide variety of guidebooks, nonfiction books about Croatia and the former Yugoslavia, novels, and magazines—all in English (July-Aug Mon-Sat 9:00-23:00, Sun 10:00-13:00 & 18:00-22:00; June and Sept Mon-Sat 9:00-21:00, Sun 10:00-14:00; shorter hours off-season; Placa 8, tel. 020/322-044).

Laundry: Hotels charge a mint to wash your clothes; *sobe* hosts are cheaper, but often don't have the time (ask). The handy, fun, retro, self-service **Sanja and Rosie's Launderette** is just outside the Ploče Gate (cross the bridge and look left; 50-kn wash, 30-40-kn dry, clear English instructions, machines take bills, daily 8:00-22:00, 100-kn drop-off service available Mon-Sat before 14:00, put od Bosanke 2, mobile 099-254-6959, www.dubrovniklaundry.com). Two full-service launderettes are near the hotels at **Boninovo Bay**, a 20-minute uphill walk or five-minute bus trip from the Pile Gate: one at Pera Čingrije 8 (145-kn wash and dry in about 3 hours, no self-service, Mon-Fri 9:00-13:00 & 15:00-18:00, Sat 9:00-15:00, closed Sun, shorter hours off-season, across from the big seafront Hotel Bellevue, tel. 020/333-347), and another a few steps toward the main road at bana Jelačića 1 (120 kn to wash and dry up to an 11-pound load, same-day service possible if you bring it in by 10:00, open Mon-Fri 8:00-20:00, Sat 9:00-14:00, closed Sun, mobile 091-190-0888).

Car Rental: The big international chains, such as **Avis** (tel. 020/313-633), have offices both at the airport and near the Port Gruž embankment where the big boats come in. In addition, the many travel agencies closer to the Old Town also have a line on rental cars. Figure €50-60 per day, including taxes, insurance, and unlimited mileage (at the bigger chains, there's usually no extra charge for drop-off elsewhere in Croatia). Be sure the agency knows if you're crossing a border (such as Bosnia-Herzegovina or Montenegro) to ensure you have the proper paperwork.

Travel Agency: You'll see travel agencies all over town. At any of them, you can buy seats on an excursion, rent a car, book a room, buy Jadrolinija ferry tickets, and pick up a pile of brochures. The most established company is **Atlas,** with an office just outside the Pile Gate from the Old Town—though the location might change (June-Sept Mon-Sat 8:00-21:00, Sun 8:00-13:00; Oct-May Mon-Sat 8:00-20:00, closed Sun; down the little alley at Sv. Đurđa 4, otherwise look for signs to new location around the bus-stop area, tel. 020/442-574, fax 020/323-609, www.atlas-croatia.com, atlas.pile@atlas.hr).

Best Views: Walking the **Old Town walls** late in the day, when the city is bathed in rich light, is a treat. The cable car up to **Mount Srđ** provides bird's-eye panoramas over the entire region, from the highest vantage point without wings. The **Fort of St. Lawrence,** perched above the Pile neighborhood cove, has great views over the Old Town. A stroll up the road east of the city walls offers nice views back on the Old Town (best light early in the day). Better yet, if you have a car, head south of the city in the morning for gorgeously lit Old Town views over your right shoulder; various turn-offs along this road are ideal photo stops. The best one, known locally as the **"panorama point,"** is where the road leading up and out of Dubrovnik meets the main road that passes above the town (look for the pull-out on the right, with tour buses). Even if you're heading north, in good weather it's worth a quick detour south for this view.

Getting Around Dubrovnik

If you're staying in or near the Old Town, everything is easily walkable. But those sleeping on Boninovo Bay or the Lapad Peninsula will want to get comfortable using the buses. Once you understand the system, commuting to the Old Town is a breeze.

By Bus: Libertas runs Dubrovnik's public buses. Tickets, which are good for an hour, are cheaper if you buy them in advance from a newsstand or your hotel (10 kn, ask for *autobusna karta*, ow-toh-BOOS-nah KAR-tah) than if you buy them from the bus driver (12 kn). A 24-hour ticket costs 30 kn (only sold at special bus-ticket kiosks, such as the one near the Pile Gate bus stop).

When you enter the bus, validate your ticket in the machine next to the driver (insert it with the orange arrow facing out). Because most tourists can't figure out how to validate their tickets, it can take a long time to load the bus (which means drivers are understandably grumpy, and locals aren't shy about cutting in line).

All buses stop near the Old Town, just in front of the Pile Gate (buy tickets at the newsstand or bus-ticket kiosk right by the stop). From here, they fan out to just about anywhere you'd want to go (hotels on Boninovo Bay, Lapad Peninsula, and the ferry terminal and main bus station). You'll find bus schedules and a map in the TI booklet (for more information, visit www.libertas dubrovnik.hr).

By Taxi: Taxis start at 25 kn, then charge 8 kn per kilometer. The handiest taxi stand for the Old Town is just outside the Pile Gate. The biggest operation is Radio Taxi (tel. 0800-0970).

Tours in Dubrovnik

Walking Tours—Two companies—**Dubrovnik Walking Tours** and **Dubrovnik Walks**—offer similar one-hour walking tours of the Old Town daily at 10:00 and usually also at 18:00 (90 kn, also other departures and topics—look for fliers at TI). I'd skip these tours—they're pricey and brief, touching lightly on the same information explained in this chapter.

Local Guide—For an in-depth look at the city, consider hiring your own local guide. **Štefica Curić** is a sharp professional guide who offers a great by-the-book tour and an insider's look at the city (500 kn/2 hours, mobile 091-345-0133, www.dubrovnikprivate guide.com, dugacarapa@yahoo.com). If Štefica is busy, she can refer you to another good guide for the same price. **Roberto de Lorenzo** and his mother **Marija Tiberi** are both warm people enthusiastic about telling evocative stories from medieval Dubrovnik, including some off-the-beaten-path stops tailored to your interests (480 kn/2 hours, mobile 091-541-6637, bobdel70@yahoo.com). The TI can also suggest guides.

Bus-plus-Walking Tours—Two big companies (**Atlas** and **Elite**) offer expensive tours of Dubrovnik (about 250 kn, 2 hours).

From Dubrovnik

Hire Your Own Driver—I enjoy renting my own car to see the sights around Dubrovnik (see "Helpful Hints," earlier). But if you're more comfortable having someone else do the driving, consider hiring a driver. While the drivers listed here are not official tour guides, they speak great English and offer ample commentary as you roll, and can help you craft a good day-long itinerary to Mostar, Montenegro, or anywhere else near Dubrovnik (typically departing around 8:00 and returning in the early evening). They're flexible about tailoring the tour to your interests: Because there are lots of options en route to either Mostar or Montenegro, do your homework so you can tell them what you'd like to see (and not see). Or you can just leave it up to them and go along for the ride.

Friendly **Pepo Klaić,** a veteran of the recent war, is enjoyable to get to know and has a knack for making the experience both informative and meaningful (€250/day, €125 for half-day trip to nearer destinations, airport transfer for about €30—cheaper than a taxi, these prices for up to 4 people—more expensive for bigger group, mobile 098-427-301, www.dubrovnikshoretrip.com, pepo klaic@yahoo.com). For €70, Pepo can drive you to the fortress at Mount Srđ up above the Old Town, with sweeping views of the entire area (about 1-1.5 hours round-trip). **Petar Vlašić** does similar tours for similar prices, and specializes in wine tours to the Pelješac Peninsula, with stops at various wineries along the way (€30 airport transfers, €190-200 for 2-person trip to Pelješac wineries, €230 to Mostar including guide, €250 to Montenegro including local guide and boat to Our Lady of the Rock, these prices for 1-3 people—more for larger groups, mobile 091-580-8721, www.dubrovnikrivieratours.com, meritum@du.t-com.hr). **Pero Carević,** who runs the recommended Villa Ragusa guest house, also drives travelers on excursions (similar prices, mobile 098-765-634, villa.ragusa@du.t-com.hr). If your destination is Mostar, like-able Bosnian driver **Ermin Elezović** will happily come pick you up for less than the Dubrovnik-based drivers (for up to 3 people: €100 for one-way transfer from Dubrovnik to Mostar, €150 for an all-day excursion with stops en route, €200 for round-trip to Mostar with same-day return to Dubrovnik).

Self-Guided Walk

▲▲▲Strolling the Stradun

Running through the heart of Dubrovnik's Old Town is the 300-yard-long Stradun promenade—packed with people and lined with sights. This walk offers an ideal introduction to Dubrovnik's charms. It takes about a half-hour, not counting sightseeing stops.

• *Begin at the busy square in front of the west entrance to the Old Town, the Pile (PEE-leh) Gate.*

Pile Neighborhood

This bustling area is the nerve center of Dubrovnik's tourist indus-try—it's where the real world meets the fantasy of Dubrovnik (for details on services offered here, see "Orientation to Dubrovnik," earlier). Near the modern, mirrors-and-TV-screens monument (which honors the "Dubrovnik Defenders" who protected the city during the 1991-1992 siege) is a leafy café terrace. Wander over to the edge of the terrace and take in the imposing walls of the Pearl of the Adriatic. The huge, fortified peninsula just outside the city walls is the **Fort of St. Lawrence** (Tvrđava Lovrijenac), Dubrovnik's oldest fortress and one of the top venues for the Dubrovnik Summer Festival. Shakespearean plays are often per-

formed here, occasionally starring Goran Višnjić, the Croatian actor who became an American star on the TV show *ER*. You can climb this fortress for great views over the Old Town (30 kn, or covered by same ticket as Old Town walls on the same day).

• *Cross over the moat (now a shady park) to the round entrance tower in the Old Town Wall. This is the...*

Pile Gate (Gradska Vrata Pile)

Just before you enter the gate, notice the image above the entrance of **St. Blaise** (Sveti Vlaho in Croatian) cradling Dubrovnik in his arm. You'll see a lot more of Blaise during your time here—we'll find out why later on this walk.

Inside the outer wall of the Pile Gate and to the left, a white **map** shows where each bomb dropped on the Old Town during

the siege. Once inside town, you'll see virtually no signs of the war—demonstrating the townspeople's impressive resilience in rebuilding so well and so quickly.

Passing the rest of the way through the gate, you'll find a lively little square surrounded by landmarks. To the left, a steep stairway leads up to the imposing **Minčeta Tower**. It's possible to enter here to begin Dubrovnik's best activity, walking around the top of the wall (described later, under "Sights in Dubrovnik")—but this walk ends near a better entry point.

Next to the stairway is the small **Church of St. Savior** (Crkva Svetog Spasa). Appreciative locals built this votive church to thank God after Dubrovnik made it through a 1520 earthquake. When the massive 1667 quake destroyed the city, this church was one of the only buildings left intact. And during the recent war, the church survived another close call when a shell exploded on the ground right in front of it (you can still see faint pockmarks from the shrapnel).

The big building on the left just beyond the small Church of St. Savior is the **Franciscan Monastery Museum**. This building, with a delightful cloister and one of Europe's oldest pharmacies, is worth touring (described later).

The giant, round structure in the middle of the square is

DUBROVNIK

Onofrio's Big Fountain (Velika Onofrijea Fontana). In the Middle Ages, Dubrovnik had a complicated aqueduct system that brought water from the mountains seven miles away. The water

ended up here, at the town's biggest fountain, before continuing through the city. This plentiful supply of water, large reserves of salt (a key source of Dubrovnik's wealth, from the town of Ston), and a massive granary (now the Rupe Granary and Ethnographic Museum, described later) made little, independent Dubrovnik very siege-resistant.

Tucked across the square from the church is the **Visia Dubrovnik Multimedia Museum,** showing a badly produced 3-D film about the city's history that isn't worth your 35 minutes or 75 kn (schedule posted at entry). In the evening, the theater shows first-run 3-D movies.

• *When you're finished taking in the sights on this square, continue along...*

The Stradun

Dubrovnik's main promenade—officially called the Placa, but better known as the Stradun—is alive with locals and tourists alike. This is the heartbeat of the city: an Old World shopping mall by day and sprawling cocktail party after dark, when everybody seems to be doing the traditional evening stroll—flirting, ice-cream-licking, flaunting, and gawking. A coffee and some of Europe's best

people-watching in a prime Stradun café is one of travel's great $3 bargains.

When Dubrovnik was just getting its start in the seventh century, this street was a canal. Romans fleeing from the invading Slavs lived on the island of Ragusa (on your right), and the

Slavs settled on the shore. In the 11th century, the canal separating Ragusa from the mainland was filled in, the towns merged, and a unique Slavic-Roman culture and language blossomed. While originally much more higgledy-piggledy, this street was rebuilt in the current, more straightforward style after the 1667 earthquake.

During your time in Dubrovnik, you'll periodically hear the rat-a-tat-tat of a drum echoing through the streets from the Stradun. This means it's time to head for this main drag to get

DUBROVNIK

Dubrovnik's Old Town

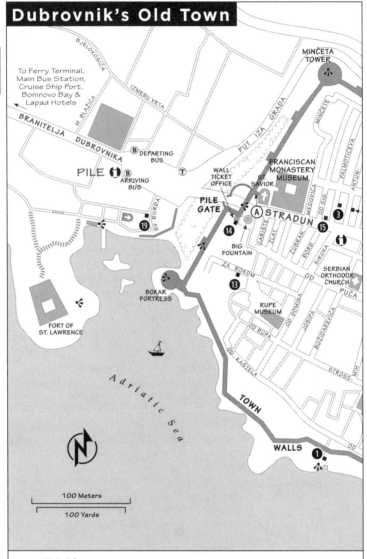

To Ferry Terminal,
Main Bus Station,
Cruise Ship Port,
Boninovo Bay &
Lapad Hotels

MINČETA
TOWER

BJELOKOSIĆA

IZMEĐU VRTA

M. BLAŽIĆA

BRANITELJA

DUBROVNIKA

DEPARTING
BUS

PILE

ARRIVING
BUS

WALL
TICKET
OFFICE

FRANCISCAN
MONASTERY
MUSEUM

ST.
SAVIOR

PILE
GATE

STRADUN

PALMOTIĆEVA

ANTUN.

MINČETE

PUT IZA GRADA

OD SIG.

MEDOVIĆA

GARIŠTE

ZLAT.

CUBRAN.

DORĐ.

SIROKA

SERBIAN
ORTHODOX
CHURCH

PUČA

BIG
FOUNTAIN

ZA ROKOM

OD

BOKAR
FORTRESS

RUPE
MUSEUM

OD DOMINA

OD RUPA

JOSIPA

BOŽIDAREVIĆA

STROSS.

MIH

FORT OF
ST. LAWRENCE

OD KAŠTELA

Adriatic Sea

TOWN

WALLS

OD

100 Meters

100 Yards

Nightlife

1 Cold Drinks "Buža" II
2 Cold Drinks "Buža" I
3 D'Vino Wine Bar
4 Jazz Caffè Troubadour
5 Nonenina Cocktail Bar
6 The Gaffe Irish Pub

7 Sky Bar
8 Africa Nightclub
9 Gil's Cocktail Bar
10 Revelin Dance Club
11 To EastWest Dance Club

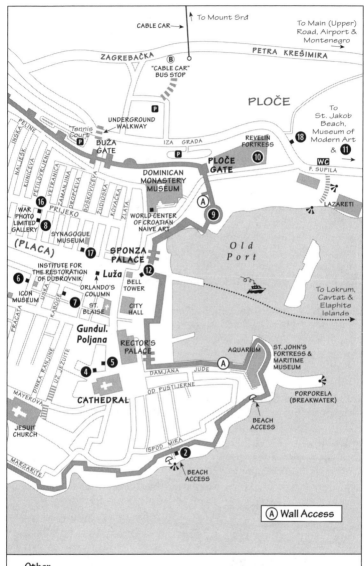

To Mount Srd

CABLE CAR

To Main (Upper)
Road, Airport &
Montenegro

ZAGREBAČKA

(B)
"CABLE CAR"
BUS STOP

PETRA KREŠIMIRA

PLOČE

P

UNDERGROUND
WALKWAY

Tennis
Court

P

BUŽA
GATE

IZA GRADA

P

REVELIN
FORTRESS

To
St. Jakob
Beach,
Museum of
Modern Art
&

18

10

WC

DOMINICAN
MONASTERY
MUSEUM

PLOČE
GATE

(A)

9

F. SUPILA

LAZARETI

PELINE

NALJEŠK

KUNIČEVA

PETILOVRIJENCI

ŽVETRANIĆA

ZAMANJINA

PROPUČEVA

BOŠKOVIĆEVA

KOVAČKA

ŽIDIOSKA

ZLATA

16

PRIJEKO

WAR
PHOTO
LIMITED
GALLERY

8

SYNAGOGUE
MUSEUM

17

WORLD CENTER
OF CROATIAN
NAIVE ART

SPONZA
PALACE

12

*Old
Port*

(PLACA)

INSKA

INSTITUTE FOR
THE RESTORATION
OF DUBROVNIK

6

Luža

BELL
TOWER

To Lokrum,
Cavtat &
Elaphite
Islands

ICON
MUSEUM

USKA

KABOGE

ORLANDO'S
COLUMN

7

ST.
BLAISE

CITY
HALL

PRACATA

DIRKA RANJINE

MAYEROVA

*Gundul.
Poljana*

RECTOR'S
PALACE

UZ JEZUITE

5

4

CATHEDRAL

DAMJANA
JUDE

OD PUSTIJERNE

AQUARIUM

(A)

ST. JOHN'S
FORTRESS &
MARITIME
MUSEUM

PORPORELA
(BREAKWATER)

JESUIT
CHURCH

MARGARITE

ISPOD MIKA

BEACH
ACCESS

2

BEACH
ACCESS

(A) **Wall Access**

Other

12 Sloboda Cinema
13 Jadran Cinema
14 Visia Dubrovnik (3-D Movies)
15 Vinoteka Miličić Wine Shop
16 Netcafé (Internet)

17 Algoritam Bookshop
18 Launderette
19 Atlas Travel Agency

DUBROVNIK

a glimpse of the colorfully costumed **"town guards"** parading through (and a cavalcade of tourists running alongside them, trying to snap a clear picture). You may also see some of these characters standing guard outside the town gates. It's all part of the local tourist board's efforts to make their town even more atmospheric.

• *Branching off from this promenade are several museums and other attractions. At the end of the Stradun is a passageway leading to the Ploče Gate. Just before this passage is the lively Luža Square. Its centerpiece is...*

Orlando's Column (Orlandov Stup)

Columns like this were typical of towns in northern Germany. Dubrovnik erected the column in 1417, soon after it had shifted allegiances from the oppressive Venetians to the Hungarians. By putting a northern European symbol in the middle of its most prominent square, Dubrovnik decisively distanced itself from Venice. Whenever a decision was made by the Republic, the town crier came to Orlando's Column and announced the news. The step he stood on indicated the importance of his message—the higher up, the more important the news. It was also used as the pillory, where people were publicly punished. The thin line on the top step in front of Orlando is exactly as long as the statue's forearm. This mark was Dubrovnik's standard measurement—not for a foot, but for an "elbow."

• *Now stand in front of Orlando's Column and orient yourself with a...*

Luža Square Spin-Tour

Orlando is looking toward the **Sponza Palace** (Sponza-Povijesni Arhiv). This building, from 1522, is the finest surviving example of Dubrovnik's Golden Age in the 15th and 16th centuries. It's a combination of Renaissance (ground-floor arches) and Venetian Gothic (upstairs windows). Houses up and down the main promenade used to look like this, but after the 1667 earthquake, they

were replaced with boring uniformity. This used to be the customs office *(dogana),* but now it's an exhaustive archive of the city's history, with temporary art exhibits and a war memorial. The poignant **Memorial Room of Dubrovnik Defenders** (on the left as you enter) has photos of dozens of people from Dubrovnik who were killed fighting Yugoslav forces in 1991. A TV screen and images near the ceiling show the devastation of the city. Though the English descriptions are pointedly—if unavoidably—slanted to the Croat perspective, it's compelling to look in the eyes of the brave young men who didn't start this war...but were willing to finish it (free, long hours daily in peak season, shorter hours off-season). Beyond the memorial room, the impressive **courtyard,** which generally displays temporary exhibits, is worth a peek (25 kn, generally free after-hours).

To the right of Sponza Palace is the town's **Bell Tower** (Gradski Zvonik). The original dated from 1444, but it was rebuilt when it started to lean in the 1920s. The big clock may be an octopus, but only one of its hands tells time. Below that, the golden circle shows the phase of the moon. At the bottom, the old-fashioned digital readout tells the hour (in Roman numerals) and the minutes (in five-minute increments). At the top of each hour (and again three minutes later), the time is clanged out on the bell up top by two bronze bell-ringers, Maro and Baro. (If this all seems like a copy of the very similar clock on St. Mark's Square in Venice, locals are quick to point out that this clock predates that one by several decades.) The clock still has to be wound every two days. Notice the little window between the moon phase and the "digital" readout: The clock-winder opens this window to get some light. The Krasovac family was in charge of winding the clock for generations (1877-2005). During the 1991-1992 siege, their house was destroyed—with the winding keys inside. For days, the clock bell didn't run. But then, miraculously, the keys were discovered lying in the street. The excited Dubrovnik citizens came together in this square and cheered as the clock was wound and the bell chimed, signaling to the soldiers surrounding the city that they hadn't won yet.

It's possible to climb up to the **gallery** next to the tower for a fine view of the Stradun, but only in the evening (July-Aug nightly 20:00-23:00, spring and fall nightly 19:00-21:00 or 22:00, closed in winter) and—as of this writing—only if you have a Dubrovnik Card. Even if you don't have the card, you can try asking nicely (the entrance is in the passageway just to the left of the tower).

The big building to the right of the Bell Tower is the **City Hall** (Vijećnica). Next to that is **Onofrio's Little Fountain** (Mala Onofrijea Fontana), the little brother of the one at the other end of the Stradun. Beyond that is the **Gradska Kavana,** or "Town Café." This hangout—historically Dubrovnik's favorite spot for gossiping and people-watching—has pricey drinks and seating all the way through the wall to the Old Port. Just down the street from the Town Café is the Rector's Palace, and then the cathedral (for more on each, see "Sights in Dubrovnik").

Behind Orlando is **St. Blaise's Church** (Crkva Sv. Vlaha), dedicated to the patron saint of Dubrovnik. You'll see statues

DUBROVNIK

The Siege of Dubrovnik

In June 1991, Croatia declared independence from Yugoslavia. Within weeks, the nations were at war (for more on the war, see the Understanding Yugoslavia chapter). Though warfare raged in the Croatian interior, nobody expected that the bloodshed would reach Dubrovnik.

As refugees from Vukovar (in northeastern Croatia) arrived in Dubrovnik that fall, telling horrific stories of the warfare there, local residents began fearing the worst. Warplanes from the Serb-dominated Yugoslav People's Army buzzed threateningly low over the town, as if to signal an impending attack.

Then, at 6:00 in the morning on October 1, 1991, Dubrovnik residents awoke to explosions on nearby hillsides. The first attacks were focused on Mount Srđ, high above the Old Town. First the giant cross was destroyed, then a communications tower (both have been rebuilt and are visible today). This first wave of attacks cleared the way for Yugoslav land troops—mostly Serbs and Montenegrins—who surrounded the city. The ragtag, newly formed Croatian army quickly dug in at the old Napoleonic-era fortress at the top of Mount Srđ, where just 25 or 30 soldiers fended off a Yugoslav takeover of this highly strategic position.

At first, shelling targeted military positions on the outskirts of town. But soon, Yugoslav forces began bombing residential neighborhoods, then the Pearl of the Adriatic itself: Dubrovnik's Old Town. Defenseless townspeople took shelter in their cellars, and sometimes even huddled together in the city wall's 15th-century forts. It was the first time in Dubrovnik's long history that the walls were actually used to defend against an attack.

Dubrovnik resisted the siege better than anyone expected. The Yugoslav forces were hoping that residents would flee the town, but the people of Dubrovnik stayed.  Though severely outgunned and outnumbered, Dubrovnik's defenders managed to hold the fort atop Mount Srđ, while Yugoslav forces controlled the nearby mountaintops. All supplies had to be carried up to the fort by foot or by donkey. Dubrovnik wasn't prepared for war, so its citizens had to improvise their defense. Many brave young locals lost their lives when they slung old hunting rifles over their shoulders and, under cover of darkness, climbed the hills above Dubrovnik to meet Yugoslav soldiers face-to-face.

After eight months of bombing, Dubrovnik was liberated by the Croatian army, which attacked Yugoslav positions from the north. By the end of the siege, 100 civilians were dead, as well as more than 200 Dubrovnik citizens who lost their lives actively fighting for their hometown (much revered today as "Dubrovnik Defenders"); in the greater Dubrovnik area, 420 "Defenders" were killed, and another 900 wounded. More than two-thirds of Dubrovnik's buildings had been damaged, and more than 30,000 people had to flee their homes—but the failed siege was finally over.

Why was Dubrovnik—so far from the rest of the fighting—dragged into the conflict? Yugoslavia wanted to catch the city and surrounding region off-guard, gaining a toehold on the southern Dalmatian Coast so they could push north to Split. They also hoped to ignite pro-Serb passions in the nearby Serb-dominated areas of Bosnia-Herzegovina and Montenegro. But perhaps most of all, Yugoslavia wanted to hit Croatia where it hurt—its proudest, most historic, and most beautiful city, the tourist capital of a nation dependent on tourism. (It seems their plan backfired. Locals now say, "When Yugoslavia attacked Dubrovnik, they lost the war"—because images of the historic city under siege swayed international public opinion *against* Yugoslavia.)

The war initially devastated the tourist industry. Now, to the casual observer, Dubrovnik seems virtually back to normal. Aside from a few pockmarks and bright, new roof tiles, there are scant reminders of what happened here two decades ago. But even though the city itself has been repaired, the people of Dubrovnik are forever changed. Imagine living in an idyllic paradise, a place that attracted and awed visitors from around the world...and then watching it gradually blown to bits. It's understandable if Dubrovnik's citizens are a little less in love with life than they once were.

It's clear that in the case of this siege, the Croats of Dubrovnik were the largely innocent victims of a brutal surprise attack. But keep in mind the larger context of the war: The cousins of these Croats, who were defending the glorious monument that is Dubrovnik, bombarded another glorious monument—the Old Bridge of Mostar (see page 149). It's just another reminder that the "good guys" and "bad guys" in these wars are far from clear-cut.

Dubrovnik has several low-key attractions related to its recent war, including the museum in the ruined fortress atop Mount Srđ, the Memorial Room of Dubrovnik Defenders in the Sponza Palace on Luža Square, and the Institute for the Restoration of Dubrovnik. Another sight, War Photo Limited, expands the scope to war photography from around the world.

DUBROVNIK

and paintings of St. Blaise all over town, always holding a model of the city in his left hand. According to legend, a millennium ago St. Blaise came to a local priest in a dream and warned him that the up-and-coming Venetians would soon attack the city. The priest alerted the authorities, who prepared for war. Of course, the prediction came true. St. Blaise has been a Dubrovnik symbol—and locals have resented Venice—ever since.

• *Your tour is finished. From here, you've got plenty of sightseeing options (all described next, under "Sights in Dubrovnik"). As you face the Bell Tower, you can go up the street to the right to reach the Rector's Palace and cathedral; you can walk through the gate straight ahead to reach the Old Port; or you can head through the gate and jog left to find the Dominican Monastery Museum. Even more sights—including an old synagogue, an Orthodox church, two different exhibits of war photography, and the medieval granary—are in the steep streets between the Stradun and the walls.*

Sights in Dubrovnik

Nearly all of Dubrovnik's sights are inside the Old Town's walls.

Combo-Tickets: The Rector's Palace, Maritime Museum, and Rupe Granary and Ethnographic Museum—which normally cost 40 kn apiece—are covered by a combo-ticket (55 kn to visit any two, 70 kn to visit all three, tickets sold at all three sights, valid for three days). The TI's Dubrovnik Card—which covers the same three sights, plus the City Walls and a few lesser attractions—can also be a good deal for busy sightseers (see "Tourist Information," earlier).

▲▲▲Town Walls (Gradske Zidine)

Dubrovnik's single best attraction is strolling the scenic mile-and-a-quarter around the city walls. As you meander along this lofty perch—with a sea of orange roofs on one side, and the actual sea on the other—you'll get your bearings and snap pictures like mad of the ever-changing views. Bring your map, which you can use to pick out landmarks and get the lay of the land.

Cost: 70 kn to enter walls, also includes the St. Lawrence Fort outside the Pile Gate (kunas or credit cards only—no euros).

Hours: July-Aug daily 8:00-19:30, progressively shorter hours off-season until mid-Nov-mid-March 10:00-15:00. Since the hours change with the season, confirm them by checking signs posted at the entrance (essential if you want to time your wall walk to avoid the worst crowds—explained below). The posted closing time indicates when the walls shut down, *not* the last entry—ascend well before this time if you want to make it all the way around. (If you want to linger, begin at least an hour ahead; if you're speedy, you can ascend 30 minutes before closing time.) Attendants begin circling the walls about 30 minutes after the posted closing time to lock the gates. There's talk of someday illuminating the walls at

night, in which case the hours would be extended until after dark.

Entrances and Strategies: There are three entry points for the wall, and wall-walkers are required to proceed counterclockwise. The best plan is to begin at the far side of the Old Town, using the entrance **near the Ploče Gate** and Dominican Monastery. This entrance is the least crowded, and you'll tackle the steepest part (and enjoy the best views) first, as you climb up to the landward side of the wall with magnificent views across the entire Old Town and the Adriatic. If you're wiped out, overheated, or fed up with crowds after that, you can bail out halfway (at the Pile Gate), having seen the best—or you can continue around the seaward side. The other two entrances are **just inside the Pile Gate** (by far the most crowded; for this location only, you must buy your tickets at the desk across the square; if you begin here, you'll reach the Minčeta Tower—with the steepest ascent and best views—last) and **near St. John's Fort** overlooking the Old Port (next to the Maritime Museum).

Crowd Control: Because this is Dubrovnik's top attraction, it's extremely crowded. Your best strategy is to avoid the walls during the times when the cruise ships are in town. On days when the walls open at 8:00, try to get started around that time. The walls are the most crowded from about 8:30 until 11:00, when the cruise ships are docked. There's generally an afternoon lull in the crowds (11:00-15:00), but that's also the hottest time to be atop the walls. Crowds pick up again in the late afternoon (starting around 15:00), peaking about an hour before closing time (18:30 in high season). So your peak-season options are either early, crowded, or hot; the ticket-takers told me that, all things considered, they'd ascend either at 8:00 or 30-60 minutes before closing.

Tips: Speed demons with no cameras can walk the walls in about an hour; strollers and shutterbugs should plan on longer. Because your ticket is electronically scanned as you enter, you can't leave and re-enter the wall later; you have to do it all in one go. If you have a Dubrovnik Card—even a multiple-day one—you can only use it to ascend the walls once.

Warning: The walls can get deliriously hot—all that white stone and seawater reflect blazing sunshine something fierce, and there's virtually no shade. It's essential to bring sunscreen, a hat, and water. Take your time: There are several steep stretches, and you'll be climbing up and down the whole way around. A few scant shops and cafés along the top of the wall (mostly on the sea side) sell water and other drinks, but it's safest to bring what you'll need with you.

Audioguide: You can rent a 40-kn audioguide, separate from the admission fee, for a dryly narrated circular tour of the walls (look for vendors near the Pile Gate entrance—not available at other entrances). But I'd rather just enjoy the views and lazily pick out the landmarks with my map.

Background: There have been walls here almost as long as there's been a Dubrovnik. As with virtually all fortifications on the Croatian Coast, these walls were beefed up in the 15th century, when the Ottoman navy became a threat. Around the perimeter are several substantial forts, with walls rounded so that cannonballs would glance off harmlessly. These stout forts intimidated would-be invaders during the Republic of Dubrovnik's Golden Age, and protected residents during the 1991-1992 siege.

◐ Self-Guided Tour: It's possible to just wander the walls and snap photos like crazy as you go. And trying to hew too closely to guided commentary kind of misses the point of being high above the Dubrovnik rooftops. But this brief tour will help give you bearings to what you're seeing, as you read Dubrovnik's unique and illustrious history into its street plan.

Part 1—Ploče Gate to Pile Gate: Begin by ascending near the **Ploče Gate** (go through the gate under the Bell Tower, walk along the stoutly walled passageway between the port and the Dominican Monastery, and look for the wall entrance on your right). Buy your ticket, head up, turn left, and start walking counterclockwise, with Mount Srđ and the cable car on your right. Passing the Dominican Monastery's fine courtyard on the left, you're walking above what was the poorest part of medieval Dubrovnik, the domain of the craftsmen—with narrow, stepped lanes that had shops on the ground floor and humble dwellings up above.

As you walk, keep an eye on the different-colored **rooftops** for an illustration of the damage Dubrovnik sustained during the 1991-1992 siege. It's easy to see that nearly two-thirds of Dubrovnik's roofs were replaced after the bombings (notice the new, bright-orange tiles—and how some buildings salvaged the old tiles, but have 20th-century ones underneath). The pristine-seeming Old

Town was rebuilt using exactly the same materials and methods with which it was originally constructed.

As the level path you're on becomes stepped, you are rewarded with higher and higher views. Nearing the summit, you pass a juice bar (you can use the WCs if you buy a drink). At the very top, you enjoy the best possible view of the Old Town—you can see the rooftops, churches, and the sea. For an even better view, if you have the energy, huff up the steep stairs to the (empty) **Minčeta**

Tower. From either viewpoint, observe the valley-like shape of

Dubrovnik. It's easy to imagine how it began as two towns—one where you are now, and the other on the hilly island with the church spires across the way—originally separated by a seawater canal. Notice the relatively regular, grid-like pattern of houses on this side, but the more higgledy-piggledy arrangement on the far side (a visual clue that the far side is older).

The sports court at your feet is a reminder that Dubrovnik is a living city—though it's not as vibrant as it once was. While officially 2,000 people live within these walls, most locals estimate the real number at about half that; the rest rent out their homes to tourists. And with good reason: Imagine the challenges that come with living in such a steep medieval townscape well into the 21st century. Delivery trucks rumble up and down the Stradun early each morning, and you'll see hardworking young men delivering goods on hand carts throughout the day. Looking up at the fortress atop Mount Srđ—seemingly custommade for keeping an eye on a large swathe of coastline—the strategic position of Dubrovnik is clear. Independent Dubrovnik was not just this walled city, but an entire region.

Now continue downhill (you've earned it) until you get to the flat stretch. If you're bushed and ready to head back to town, you can turn left and head downstairs to the exit—but be aware that once you leave, you can't re-enter on the same ticket. Better yet, carry on straight for part 2.

Part 2—Pile Gate to Old Port: Pause to enjoy the full frontal view of the **Stradun,** barreling right at you. In the Middle Ages, lining this drag were the merchants, and before that, this was a canal. At your feet is Onfrio's Big Fountain, which supplied water to a thirsty town. From here, you can see a wide range of

church steeples representing the cosmopolitan makeup of a thriving medieval trade town (from left to right): Dominican, Franciscan (near you), the town Bell Tower, St. Blaise's (the round dome—hard to see from here), Serbian Orthodox, Cathedral, and (high on the hill) Jesuit. Sit and watch the river of humanity, flowing constantly up and down one of Europe's finest main streets.

Carry on through the guard tower and along the wall, climbing uphill again. On the right across the little cove is the **Fort of St. Lawrence,** which worked in concert with these stout walls to make Dubrovnik virtually impenetrable. Climbing higher and looking to your left, into town, you'll see that this area is still damaged—not from the 1991-1992 siege, but from the 1667 earthquake. Notice that, unlike the extremely dense construction on the poorer far side of town, this area has more breathing space—and even some gardens. Originally this was also densely populated, but after the quake, rather than rebuild, the wealthy folks who lived here decided to turn some former homes into green space. Grates cover the openings to old wells and grain stores that once supplied homes here—essential for surviving a siege.

As the walkway levels out, you pass a bar with drinks; more (with WCs) are coming up. Farther along, at the picturesque little turret, are gift shops and WCs. Looking down to your right (outside the wall), you'll begin to see tables and umbrellas clinging to the rocks at the base of the wall. This is the recommended Cold Drinks "Buža" II, the best spot in town for a scenic drink. On

the horizon is the isle of Lokrum and—often—cruise ships at anchor, sending their passengers to and fro on tenders. After passing Buža, look down on the left to see the local kids' makeshift soccer pitch, wedged between the walls— the best they can do in this vertical town. Soon you'll see the "other"

Buža (technically Buža I) ahead; nearby, notice the little statue of St. Blaise, Dubrovnik's patron, enjoy some shade under the turret.

Rounding the bend, you see the facade of the Jesuit church. Notice that the homes in this area are much larger. These are aristocratic palaces—VIPs wanted to live as close as possible to the Cathedral and Rector's Palace, which are just below—and this also happens to be the oldest part of town, where "Ragusa" was born on a steep offshore island.

Continue around the wall, passing another snack bar (with WCs) and more ruined houses. From the high plateau, you have another opportunity to head down into town. (In the little plant-filled square at the bottom of these stairs is a cute little cat hospice, with a donation box for feeding some homeless feline residents.) But the final stretch of our wall walk is shorter than the other two, and mostly level.

Part 3—Old Port to Ploče Gate: Continuing along the wall, you'll pass near the entrance to the skippable Maritime Museum, then walk along the top of the wall overlooking the Old Port. Imagine how this heavily fortified little harbor (facing away from Dubrovnik's historic foes, the Venetians) was busy with trade in the Middle Ages. Today it's still the economic lifeline for town—watch the steady stream of cruise-ship tenders injecting dose after dose of tourist cash into town. As you curl around the far side of the port, you'll see the inviting outdoor tables of Gil's, a cocktail bar/restaurant catering to high-rolling yachters. While it looks appealing, it's a very exclusive place that frowns on would-be visitors who dress like normal people. Gussied-up jet-set diners enjoy coming here for good but extremely expensive designer fare. (One local told me, "The food is great—just eat a hamburger before you go.")

Just past Gil's, you come to the stairs back down to where you started this wall walk. Nice work. Now head on down and reward yourself with an ice-cream cone...and some shade.

The "Other" Wall Climb: Your ticket for the Old Town Walls also includes the Fort of St. Lawrence just outside the Old Town (valid same day only). If you've already bought a 30-kn ticket there, show it when buying your main wall ticket and you'll pay only the difference.

Near the Pile Gate

This museum is just inside the Pile Gate.

▲**Franciscan Monastery Museum (Franjevački Samostan-Muzej)**—In the Middle Ages, Dubrovnik's monasteries flourished. While all you'll see here are a fine cloister and a one-room museum in the old pharmacy, it's a delightful space. Enter through the gap between the small church and the big monastery. Just inside the door (before the ticket-seller), a century-old pharmacy still serves residents.

Explore the peaceful, sun-dappled **cloister.** Examine the capitals at the tops of the 60 Romanesque-Gothic double pillars. Each one is different. Notice that some parts of the portals inside the courtyard are made with a lighter-colored stone—these had to be repaired after being hit during the 1991-1992 siege. The damaged 19th-century frescoes along the tops of the walls depict the life of St. Francis, who supposedly visited Dubrovnik in the early 13th century.

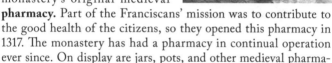

In the far corner stands the monastery's original medieval **pharmacy.** Part of the Franciscans' mission was to contribute to the good health of the citizens, so they opened this pharmacy in 1317. The monastery has had a pharmacy in continual operation ever since. On display are jars, pots, and other medieval pharma-

cists' tools. The sick would come to get their medicine at the little window (on left side), which limited contact with the pharmacist and reduced the risk of passing on disease. Around the room, you'll also find some relics, old manuscripts, and a detailed painting of early 17th-century Dubrovnik.

The adjoining **church** (enter next door) has a fine Baroque interior.

Cost and Hours: 30 kn, daily April-Oct 9:00-18:00, Nov-March 9:00-17:00, Placa 2, tel. 020/321-410, www.malabraca.hr.

Near Luža Square

These sights are at the far end of the Stradun (nearest the Old Port). As you stand on Luža Square facing the Bell Tower, the Rector's Palace and cathedral are up the wide street called Pred Dvorom to the right, and the Dominican Monastery Museum is through the gate by the Bell Tower and to the left.

▲**Rector's Palace (Knežev Dvor)**—In the Middle Ages, the Republic of Dubrovnik was ruled by a rector (similar to a Venetian doge), who was elected by the nobility. To prevent any one person from becoming too powerful, the rector's term was limited to one month. Most rectors were in their 50s—near the end of the average life span and when they were less likely to shake things up. During his term, a rector lived upstairs in this palace. Because it's been plundered twice (most recently by Napoleon's forces, who stole all the furniture), this empty-feeling museum isn't as interesting as most other European palaces. What little you'll see was donated by local aristocrats to flesh out the pathetically empty complex. The palace collection, which requires a ticket and has good English explanations, is skippable, but it does offer a glimpse of Dubrovnik in its glory days. Even if you pass on the interior, the palace's exterior and courtyard are viewable at no charge.

Cost and Hours: 40 kn, covered by 55-kn or 70-kn combo-ticket, daily May-Oct 9:00-18:00, Nov-April 9:00-16:00, some posted English information, 6-kn English booklet is helpful, Pred Dvorom 3, tel. 020/322-096.

Visiting the Palace: The **exterior** is decorated in the Gothic-Renaissance mix (with particularly finely carved capitals) that was so common in Dubrovnik before the 1667 earthquake. Above the entrance is the message *Obliti privatorum publica curate*—loosely translated, "Forget your personal affairs and concern yourself with the affairs of state." This was a bold statement in a feudal era before democracy, when aristocrats were preoccupied exclusively with their self-interests.

Standing at the main door, you can generally get a free look at the palace's impressive **courtyard**—a venue for the Summer Festival, hosting music groups ranging from the local symphony to the Vienna Boys' Choir. In the courtyard (and also visible from the door) is the only secular statue created during the centuries-long Republic. Dubrovnik republicans, mindful of the dangers of hero-worship, didn't believe that any one citizen should be singled out. They made only one exception—for Miho Pracat (a.k.a. Michaeli Prazatto), a rich citizen who donated vast sums to charity and willed a fleet of ships to the city. But notice that Pracat's statue is displayed in here, behind closed doors, not out in public.

If you pay to go **inside,** you'll start on the ground-floor, where you'll see dull paintings, the green-stucco courtroom (with explanations of the Republic's unique governmental system), and one of the palace's highlights, the original bronze bell-ringers from the town Bell Tower (named Maro and Baro). Like antique robots (from the Renaissance, c. 1470), these eerily lifelike sculptures could pivot at the waist to ring the bell. Then you'll see some iron chests (including a few with elaborate locking mechanisms) before entering some old prison cells, which supposedly were placed

DUBROVNIK

within earshot of the rector's quarters, so he would hear the moans of the prisoners...and stay honest. Leaving the prison, you'll enter the courtyard described earlier, where you can get a better look at the Pracat statue.

On the mezzanine level (stairs near the main entrance, above the prison), you'll find a decent display of furniture, a wimpy gun exhibit, votive offerings (mostly silver), a ho-hum coin collection, and an interesting painting of "Ragusa" in the early 17th century—back when it was still bisected by a canal.

Head back down to the courtyard and go to the upper floor (using the staircase across from mezzanine stairs, near the Pracat statue—notice the "hand" rails). Upstairs, you'll explore old apartments that serve as a painting gallery. The only vaguely authentic room is the red room in the corner, decorated more or less as it was in 1500, when it was the rector's office. Mihajlo Hamzić's exquisite *Baptism of Christ* painting, inspired by Italian painter Andrea Mantegna, is an early Renaissance work from the "Dubrovnik School" (see "Dominican Monastery Museum" listing, later).

▲**Cathedral (Katedrala)**—Dubrovnik's original 12th-century cathedral was funded largely by the English King Richard the Lionhearted. On his way back from the Third Crusade, Richard was shipwrecked nearby. He promised God that if he survived, he'd build a church on the spot where he landed—which happened to be on Lokrum Island, just off-

shore. At Dubrovnik's request, Richard agreed to build his token of thanks inside the city instead. It was the finest Romanesque church on the Adriatic...before it was destroyed by the 1667 earthquake. This version is 18th-century Roman Baroque.

Cost and Hours: Church—free, daily 8:00-20:00; treasury—15 kn, generally open same hours as church; both have shorter hours off-season.

Touring the Cathedral: Inside, you'll find a painting from the school of Titian *(Assumption of the Virgin)* over the stark contemporary altar, and a quirky treasury *(riznica)* packed with 187 relics. Examining the treasury collection, notice that there are three locks on the treasury door—the stuff in here was so valuable, three different VIPs (the rector, the bishop, and a local aristocrat) had to agree before it could be opened. On the table near the door are several of St. Blaise's body parts (pieces of his arm, skull, and leg—all encased in gold and silver). In the middle of the wall directly opposite the door, look for the crucifix with a piece of the True Cross. On a dig in Jerusalem, St. Helen (Emperor Constantine's mother) discovered what she believed to be the cross that Jesus was crucified on. It was brought to Constantinople, and the Byzantine czars doled out pieces of it to Balkan kings. Note the folding three-paneled altar painting (underneath the cross). Dubrovnik ambassadors packed this on road trips (such as their annual trip to pay off the Ottomans) so they could worship wherever they traveled.

On the right side of the room, the silver casket supposedly holds the actual swaddling clothes of the Baby Jesus (or, as some locals call it somewhat less reverently, "Jesus' nappy"). Dubrovnik bishops secretly passed these clothes down from generation to generation...until a nun got wind of it and told the whole town. Pieces of the cloth were cut off to miraculously heal the sick, especially new mothers recovering from a difficult birth. No matter how often it was cut, the cloth always went back to its original form. Then someone tried to use it on the wife of a Bosnian king. Since she was Muslim, it couldn't help her, and it never worked again. True or not, this legend hints at the prickly relationships between faiths (not to mention the male chauvinism) here in the Balkans.

▲**Dominican Monastery Museum (Dominikanski Samostan-Muzej)**—You'll find many of Dubrovnik's art treasures—paintings, altarpieces, and manuscripts—gathered around the peaceful Dominican Monastery cloister inside the Ploče Gate. Historically, this was the church for wealthy people, while the Franciscan Church (down at the far end of the Stradun) was for poor people. Services were staggered by 15 minutes to allow servants to drop off their masters here, then rush down the Stradun for their own service.

Cost and Hours: 20 kn, art buffs enjoy the 50-kn English book, daily May-Sept 9:00-18:00, Oct-April 9:00-17:00.

Touring the Museum: Turn left from the entry and work your way clockwise around the cloister. The room in the far corner contains paintings from the **"Dubrovnik School,"** the Republic's circa-1500 answer to the art boom in Florence and Venice. Though the 1667 earthquake destroyed most of these paintings, about a dozen survive, and five of those are in this room. Don't miss the triptych by Nikola Božidarović with St.

Blaise holding a detailed model of 16th-century Dubrovnik (left panel)—the most famous depiction of Dubrovnik's favorite saint. You'll also see reliquaries shaped like the hands and feet that they hold.

Continuing around the courtyard, duck into the next room. Here you'll see a painting by **Titian** depicting St. Blaise, Mary Magdalene, and the donor who financed this work.

At the next corner of the courtyard is the entrance to the striking **church** at the heart of this still-active monastery. Step inside. The interior is decorated with modern stained glass, a fine 13th-century stone pulpit that survived the earthquake (reminding visitors of the intellectual approach to scripture that character-

ized the Dominicans), and a precious 14th-century Paolo Veneziano crucifix hanging above the high altar. The most memorable piece of art in the church is the *Miracle of St. Dominic,* showing the founder of the order bringing a child back to life (over the altar to the right, as you enter). It was painted in the Realist style (late 19th century) by Vlaho Bukovac.

World Center of Croatian Naive Art—Just inside the entrance to the Dominican Monastery complex, look left to find this Croatian naive art center. The gallery displays and sells works of this little-known art movement. In addition to some less-impressive starving artists, the gallery has some pieces by movement founder Ivan Generalić (priced at €15,000), Ivan Večenaj, and Mijo Kovačić. If you're not going to the excellent Croatian Museum of Naive Art in Zagreb, this is a good chance to get a peek at this unique art form.

Cost and Hours: Free, Mon-Sat 10:00-18:00, closed Sun, 4 Sv. Dominika, tel. 020/321-565.

Museum of Modern Art (Umjetnička Galerija)—While salty old Dubrovnik and modern art don't quite seem to go together, the city has a fine modern art gallery a 10-minute walk outside the Ploče Gate. You'll see a permanent collection with 20th-century Croatian art (including some paintings by local artist Vlaho Bukovac—whose home in Cavtat offers a more intimate look at his life and works), as well as changing exhibits.

Cost and Hours: 30 kn, Tue-Sun 10:00-20:00, closed Mon, put Frana Supila 23, tel. 020/426-590, www.ugdubrovnik.hr.

Near the Old Port (Stara Luka)

The picturesque Old Port, carefully nestled behind St. John's Fort, faces away from what was Dubrovnik's biggest threat, the  Venetians. At the port, you can haggle with captains selling excursions to nearby towns and islands and watch cruise-ship passengers coming and going on their tenders. The long seaside building across the bay on the left is the Lazareti, once the medieval quarantine house. In those days, all visitors were locked in here for 40 days before entering town. (Today it hosts folk-dancing shows—described later, under "Entertainment in Dubrovnik.") A bench-lined harborside walk leads around the fort to a breakwater, providing a peaceful perch. From the breakwater, rocky beaches curl around the outside of the wall.

Maritime Museum (Pomorski Muzej)—By the 15th century, when Venice's nautical dominance was on the wane, Dubrovnik emerged as a maritime power and the Mediterranean's leading shipbuilding center. The Dubrovnik-built "argosy" boat (from "Ragusa," an early name for the city) was the Cadillac of ships, even mentioned by Shakespeare. This small museum traces the history of Dubrovnik's most important industry with contracts, maps, paintings, and models—all well-described in English. The main floor takes you through the 18th century, and the easy-to-miss upstairs covers the 19th and 20th centuries. Boaters will find the museum particularly interesting.

Cost and Hours: 40 kn, covered by 55-kn or 70-kn combo-ticket, 5-kn English booklet, hours flex on demand—usually March-Oct Tue-Sun 9:00-18:00, until 16:00 in Nov-Feb, closed Mon year-round, upstairs in St. John's Fort, at far/south end of Old Port, tel. 020/323-904.

Aquarium (Akvarij)—Dubrovnik's aquarium, housed in the cavernous St. John's Fort, is an old-school place, with 31 tanks on one floor. A visit here allows you a close look at the local marine life and provides a cool refuge from the midday heat.

Cost and Hours: 40 kn, kids-15 kn, English descriptions, daily July-Aug 9:00-21:00, progressively shorter hours off-season until 9:00-13:00 Nov-March, ground floor of St. John's Fort, enter from Old Port, tel. 020/323-484.

Between the Stradun and the Mainland

These two museums are a few steps off the main promenade toward the mainland.

▲**Synagogue Museum (Sinagoga-Muzej)**—When the Jews were forced out of Spain in 1492, a steady stream of them passed through here en route to today's Turkey. Finding Dubrovnik to be a flourishing and relatively tolerant city, many stayed. Žudioska ulica ("Jewish Street"), just inside Ploče Gate, became the ghetto in 1546. It was walled at one end and had a gate (which would be locked at night) at the other end. Today, the same street is home to the second-oldest continuously functioning synagogue in Europe (after Prague's), which contains Croatia's only Jewish museum. The top floor houses the synagogue itself. Notice the lattice windows that separated the women from the men (in accordance with Orthodox Jewish tradition). Below that, a small museum with good English descriptions gives meaning to the various Torahs (including a 14th-century one from Spain) and other items—such as the written orders *(naredba)* from Nazi-era Yugoslavia, stating that Jews were to identify their shops as Jewish-owned and wear armbands. (The Ustaše—the Nazi puppet government in Croatia—interned and executed not only Jews and Roma/Gypsies, but also Serbs and other people they considered undesirable.) Of Croatia's 24,000 Jews, only 4,000 survived the Holocaust. Today Croatia has about 2,000 Jews, including a dozen Jewish families who call Dubrovnik home.

Cost and Hours: 20 kn, 10-kn English booklet; May-mid-Nov daily 10:00-20:00; mid-Nov-April Mon-Fri 10:00-13:00, closed Sat-Sun; Žudioska ulica 5, tel. 020/321-028.

▲**War Photo Limited**—If the tragic story of wartime Dubrovnik has you in a pensive mood, drop by this gallery with images of warfare from around the world. The brainchild of Kiwi-turned-Croatian photojournalist Wade Goddard, this thought-provoking museum attempts to show the ugly reality of war through raw, often disturbing photographs taken in the field. You'll find well-displayed exhibits on two floors; a small permanent exhibit depicts the wars in the former Yugoslavia through photography and video footage. Each summer, the gallery also houses various temporary exhibits. Note that the focus is not solely on Dubrovnik, but on war anywhere and everywhere.

Cost and Hours: 30 kn; June-Sept daily 10:00-22:00; May and Oct Tue-Sun 10:00-16:00, closed Mon; closed Nov-April; Antuninska 6, tel. 020/322-166, www.warphotoltd.com.

Between the Stradun and the Sea

Institute for the Restoration of Dubrovnik (Zavod za Obnovu Dubrovnika)—This small photo gallery considers the eight-month siege of Dubrovnik from late 1991 to mid-1992 (see "The Siege of Dubrovnik" sidebar, earlier). You'll see images of bombed-out Dubrovnik, each one juxtaposed with an image of the same building after it was rebuilt, as well as rotating exhibits about efforts to restore Dubrovnik to its pre-siege glory. The photos are too few, but still illuminating. The highlight of the exhibit is a video showing a series of breathless news reports from a British journalist stationed here during the siege. As you watch shells devastating this glorious city, and look in the eyes of its desperate citizens at their darkest hour, you might just begin to grasp what went on here not so long ago.

Cost and Hours: Free, completely unpredictable hours—just drop by and see if it's open, a half-block off the Stradun at Miha Pracata, tel. 020/324-060.

▲**Serbian Orthodox Church and Icon Museum (Srpska Pravoslavna Crkva i Muzej Ikona)**—Round out your look

at Dubrovnik's major faiths (Catholic, Jewish, and Orthodox) with a visit to this house of worship—one of the most convenient places in Croatia to learn about Orthodox Christianity. Remember that people from the former Yugoslavia who follow the Orthodox faith are, by definition, ethnic Serbs. With all the (perhaps understandably) hard feelings about the recent war, this church serves as an important reminder that all Serbs aren't bloodthirsty killers.

Dubrovnik never had a very large Serb population (an Orthodox church wasn't even allowed inside the town walls until the mid-19th century). During the recent war, most Serbs fled, created new lives for themselves elsewhere, and saw little reason to return. But some old-timers remain, and Dubrovnik's dwindling, aging Orthodox population is still served by this **church.** The candles stuck in the sand (to prevent fire outbreaks) represent prayers: The ones at knee level are for the deceased, while the ones higher up are for the living. The gentleman selling candles encourages you to buy and light one, regardless of your faith, so long as you do so with the proper intentions and reverence.

A few doors down, you'll find the **Icon Museum.** This small collection features 78 different icons (stylized paintings of saints, generally on a golden background—a common feature of Orthodox churches) from the 15th through the 19th centuries, all identified in English. In the library—crammed with old shelves holding some 12,000 books—look for the astonishingly detailed calendar, with portraits of hundreds of saints. The gallery on the ground floor, run by Michael, sells original icons and reproductions (open longer hours than museum).

Cost and Hours: Church—free but donations accepted, good

The Serbian Orthodox Church

The emphasis of this book is on the Catholic areas of the former Yugoslavia, but don't overlook the rich diversity of faiths in this region. Dubrovnik's Serbian Orthodox church, as well as Orthodox churches in Kotor, Montenegro; Sarajevo, Bosnia-Herzegovina; and Ljubljana, Slovenia; offer invaluable opportunities to learn about a faith that's often unfamiliar to American visitors.

As you explore an Orthodox church, keep in mind that these churches carry on the earliest traditions of the Christian faith. Orthodox and Catholic Christianity came from the same roots, so the oldest surviving early-Christian churches (such as the stave churches of Norway) have many of the same features as today's Orthodox churches.

Notice that there are no pews. Worshippers stand through the service, as a sign of respect (though some older parishioners sit on the seats along the walls). Women stand on the left side, men on the right (equal distance from the altar—to represent that all are equal before God). The Orthodox Church uses essentially the same Bible as Catholics, but it's written in the Cyrillic alphabet, which you'll see displayed around any Orthodox church. Following Old Testament Judeo-Christian tradition, the Bible is kept on the altar behind the iconostasis, the big screen in the middle of the room covered with curtains and icons (golden

20-kn English book explains church and museum; daily May-Sept 8:00-14:00 & 16:00-21:00, until 19:00 in shoulder season, until 17:00 in winter; short services daily at 8:30 and 19:00, longer liturgy Sun 9:30-11:00; museum—10 kn; May-Oct Mon-Sat 9:00-13:00, closed Sun; Nov-April Mon-Fri 9:00-13:00, closed Sat-Sun, Od Puča 8, tel. 020/323-283.

▲Rupe Granary and Ethnographic Museum (Etnografski Muzej Rupe)—This huge, 16th-century building was Dubrovnik's biggest granary, and today houses the best folk museum I've seen in Croatia. *Rupe* means "holes"—and it's worth the price of entry just to peer down into these 15 cavernous underground grain stores, designed to maintain the perfect temperature to preserve the seeds (63 degrees Fahrenheit). When the grain had to be dried, it was moved upstairs—where today you'll find a surprisingly well-presented Ethnographic Museum, with tools, jewelry, clothing, instruments, painted eggs, and other folk artifacts from Dubrovnik's colorful history. Borrow the free English information guide at the entry. The museum hides several blocks uphill from the main promenade, toward the sea (climb up Široka—the widest side street from the Stradun—which becomes Od Domina on the way to the museum).

paintings of saints), which separates the material world from the spiritual one. At certain times during the service, the curtains or doors are opened so the congregation can see the Holy Book.

Unlike the decorations in many Catholic churches, Orthodox icons are not intended to be lifelike. Packed with intricate symbolism, and cast against a shimmering golden background, they're meant to remind viewers of the metaphysical nature of Jesus and the saints rather than of their physical form, which is considered irrelevant. You'll almost never see a statue, which is thought to overemphasize the physical world...and, to Orthodox people, feels a little too close to violating the commandment, "Thou shalt not worship graven images." Orthodox services generally involve chanting (a dialogue that goes back and forth between the priest and the congregation), and the church is filled with the evocative aroma of incense.

The incense, chanting, icons, and standing up are all intended to heighten the experience of worship. While many Catholic and Protestant services tend to be more of a theoretical and rote consideration of religious issues (come on—don't tell me you've never dozed through the sermon), Orthodox services are about creating a religious experience. Each of these elements does its part to help the worshipper transcend the physical world and join in communion with the spiritual one.

Cost and Hours: 40 kn, covered by 55-kn or 70-kn combo-ticket, Wed-Mon 9:00-16:00, closed Tue, od Rupa 3, tel. 020/323-013.

Above Dubrovnik

▲▲▲**Mount Srđ**—After adding Dubrovnik to his holdings, Napoleon built a fortress atop the hill behind the Old Town to

keep an eye on his new subjects (in 1810). During the city's 20th-century tourism heyday, a cable car was built to effortlessly whisk visitors to the top so they could enjoy the fine views from the fortress and the giant cross nearby. Then, when war broke out in the 1990s, Mount Srđ (pronounced like "surge") became a crucial link in the defense of Dubrovnik—the only high land that locals were able to hold. The fortress was shelled and damaged, and the cross and cable car were destroyed. Minefields and unexploded ordnance left the hilltop a dangerous no-man's land. But more recently, the mountain's fortunes have reversed. The landmines have been removed, and in 2010, the cable car was rebuilt to once again connect Dubrovnik's Old Town to its mountaintop. Visitors head to the top both for the spectacular sweeping views and for the ragtag museum about the war.

Warning: While this area has officially been cleared of landmines, nervous locals remind visitors that this was once a war zone. Be sure to stay on clearly defined paths and roads.

Getting There: The **cable car** is easily the best option for reaching the summit of Mount Srđ (80 kn round-trip, 50 kn one-way, kunas or credit cards only—no euros; 2/hour—generally departing at :00 and :30 past each hour, maybe more frequent with demand, 3-minute ride; daily June-Aug 9:00-24:00, April-May and Sept-Oct 9:00-20:00, Feb-March and Nov 9:00-17:00, Dec-Jan 9:00-16:00; doesn't run in Bora wind or heavy rain, last ascent 30 minutes before closing, tel. 020/325-393, www.dubrovnikcablecar.com). The lower station is just above the Buža Gate at the top of the Old Town (from the main drag, huff all the way to the top of Boškovićeva, exit through gate, and climb uphill one block, then look right). You may see travel agencies selling tickets elsewhere in town, but there's no advantage to buying them anywhere but here.

If you have a **car,** you can drive up. From the high road above the Old Town, watch for the turnoff to Bosanka, which leads you to that village, then up to the fortress and cross—follow signs for *Srđ* (it's twisty but not far—figure a 20-minute drive from the Old Town area). If you're coming south from the Old Town, once you reach the main road above, you'll have to turn left and backtrack a bit to reach the Bosanka turnoff. A **taxi** to the top is needlessly expensive (figure €50-70 round-trip, including some waiting time at the top); this is worthwhile only if you hire recommended driver Pepo Klaić to take you to the summit while sharing his firsthand experiences defending the fortress (€70, listed on next page). For **hikers,** a switchback trail (used to supply the fortress during the siege) connects the Old Town to the mountaintop—but it's very steep and provides minimal shade. (If you're in great shape and it's not too hot, you could ride the cable car up, then hike down.)

Mountaintop: From the top cable-car station, head up the stairs to the panoramic terrace. The bird's-eye **view** is truly spectacular, looking straight down to the street plan of Dubrovnik's Old Town. From this lofty perch, you can see north to the Dalmatian islands (the Elaphite archipelago, Mljet, Korčula, and beyond); south

to Montenegro; and east into Bosnia-Herzegovina. Gazing upon those looming mountains that define the border with Bosnia-Herzegovina—which, centuries ago, was also the frontier of the huge and powerful Ottoman Empire—you can appreciate how impressive it was that stubborn little Dubrovnik managed to remain independent for so much of its history.

The **cross** was always an important symbol in this very Catholic town. After it was destroyed, a temporary wooden one was erected to encourage the townspeople who were waiting out the siege below. During a visit in 2003, Pope John Paul II blessed the rubble from the old cross; those fragments are now being used in the foundations of the city's newest churches.

To reach the museum in the old fortress, walk behind the cable-car station along the rocky red soil.

Fort and Museum: The Napoleonic-era Fort Imperial (Trđava Imperijal) houses the **Dubrovnik During the Homeland War (1991-1995) Museum** (20 kn, 40-kn booklet, same hours as cable car except closes at 22:00 in summer). Photos, video clips, documents, and artifacts tell the story (with English descriptions) of the overarching war with Yugoslavia and how the people defended this fortress. The descriptions are too dense and detailed for casual visitors, but you'll see lots of photos and some actual items used in the fighting: primitive, rusty rifles (some dating from World War II) that the Croatians used for their improvised defense, and mortar shells and other projectiles that Yugoslav forces hurled at the fortress and the city. Look for the wire-guided Russian rockets. After being launched at their target, the rockets would burrow into a wall, waiting to be detonated once their operators saw the opportunity for maximum destruction. You'll also learn how a squadron of armed supply ships became besieged Dubrovnik's only tether to the outside world.

While the devastation of Dubrovnik was disturbing, this museum could do a far better job of fostering at least an illusion of impartiality. Instead, descriptions rant one-sidedly against "Serbian and Montenegrin aggression" and the "Serbian imperialist war," and the exhibits self-righteously depict Croats exclusively as victims (which was basically true here in Dubrovnik, but ignores Croat atrocities elsewhere). All of this serves only to trivialize and distract from the human tragedy of this war.

After seeing the exhibit, climb up a few flights of stairs to the **rooftop** for the view. The giant communications tower overhead flew the Croatian flag during the war, to inspire the besieged residents below. You might see some charred trees around here—these were claimed not by the war, but more recently, by forest fires. (Fear of landmines and other explosives prevented locals from fighting the wildfires as aggressively as they might otherwise, making these fires more dangerous than ever.)

Eating: Boasting undoubtedly the best view in Dubrovnik, **Restaurant/Snack Bar Panorama** has reasonable prices and drop-dead, astonishing views over the rooftops of the Old Town and to the most beautiful parts of three different countries (25-35-kn drinks, 55-70-kn cocktails, 10-kn ice cream, 27-kn cakes, 65-90-kn pastas, 85-145-kn main dishes, open same hours as cable car).

Activities in Dubrovnik

Swimming and Sunbathing—If the weather's good and you've had enough of museums, spend a sunny afternoon at the beach.

There are no sandy beaches on the mainland near Dubrovnik, but there are lots of suitable pebbly options, plus several concrete perches. The easiest and most atmospheric place to take a dip is right off the Old Town. From the Old Port and its breakwater, uneven steps clinging to the outside of the wall lead to a series of great sunbathing and swimming coves (and even a showerhead sticking out of the town wall). Another delightful rocky beach hangs onto the outside of the Old Town's wall (at the bar called Cold Drinks "Buža" I). Locals prefer to swim on Lokrum Island, because there are (relatively) fewer tourists there. Other convenient public beaches are Banje (just outside Ploče Gate, east of Old Town) and the beach in the middle of Lapad Bay (near Hotel Kompas).

My favorite hidden beach—**St. Jakob**—takes a lot longer to reach, but if you're up for the hike, it's worth it to escape the crowds. Figure about a 25-minute walk (each way) from the Old Town. Go through the Ploče Gate at the east end of the Old Town, and walk along the street called Frana Supila as it climbs uphill above the waterfront. At Hotel Argentina, take the right (downhill) fork and keep going

on Vlaha Bukovca. Eventually you'll reach the small church of St. Jakob. You'll see the beach—in a cozy protected cove—far below. Curl around behind the church and keep an eye out for stairs going down on the right. Unfortunately, these stairs are effectively unmarked, so it might take some trial and error to find the right ones. (If you reach the rusted-white gateway of the old communist-era open-air theater, you've gone too far.) Hike down the very steep stairs to the gentle cove, which has rentable chairs and a small restaurant for drinks (and a WC). Enjoy the pebbly beach and faraway views of Dubrovnik's Old Town.

Sea Kayaking—Paddling a sleek kayak around the outside of Dubrovnik's imposing walls is a memorable experience. Several outfits in town offer half-day tours (most options 250-350 kn); popular itineraries include loops along the City Walls, to secluded beaches, and around Lokrum island. As this scene is continually evolving, look for fliers locally.

Shopping in Dubrovnik

Most souvenirs sold in Dubrovnik—from lavender sachets to plaster models of the Old Town—are pretty tacky. Whatever you buy, prices are much higher along the Stradun than on the side streets.

A classy alternative to the knickknacks is a type of local jewelry called *Konavoske puce* ("Konavle buttons"). Sold as earrings,

 pendants, and rings, these distinctive and fashionable filigree-style pieces consist of a sphere with several small posts. Though they're sold around town, it's least expensive to buy them on Od Puča street, which runs parallel to the Stradun two blocks toward the sea (near the Serbian Orthodox Church). The high concentration of jewelers along this lane keeps prices reasonable. You'll find the "buttons" in various sizes, in both silver (affordable) and gold (pricey).

You'll also see lots of jewelry made from red coral, which can only be legally gathered in small amounts from two small islands in northern Dalmatia. If you see a particularly large chunk of coral, it's likely imported. To know what you're getting, shop at an actual jeweler instead of a souvenir shop.

Gift-Shop Chains: Several pleasant gift shops in Dubrovnik (with additional branches throughout Dalmatia) hawk fun, if sometimes made-in-China, items. Look for these chains, which are a bit classier than the many no-name shops around town: **Aqua**

DUBROVNIK

sells pleasant nautical-themed gifts, blue-and-white-striped sailor shirts, and other gear. **Bonbonnière Kraš** is Croatia's leading chocolatier, selling a wide array of tasty candies.

Entertainment in Dubrovnik

Musical Events

Dubrovnik annually hosts a full schedule of events for its Summer Festival (July 10-Aug 25, www.dubrovnik-festival.hr). Lovers of classical music enjoy the "Rachlin & Friends" festival in September (www.julianrachlin.com). But the town also works hard to offer traditional music outside of festival time. Spirited folk-music concerts are performed for tourists twice weekly in the Lazareti (old quarantine building) just outside the Old Town's Ploče Gate (100 kn, usually at 21:30). About one night per week through the winter, you can watch the Dubrovnik Symphony Orchestra (usually at the Rector's Palace in good weather, or Dominican Monastery in bad weather). And since Dubrovnik is trying to become a year-round destination, the city also offers tourist-oriented musical events most nights throughout the winter (often at a hotel). For the latest on any of these festivals and concerts, check the events listings in the *Best in Dubrovnik* brochure, or ask the TI.

Also consider the folk dancing and market each Sunday morning at Čilipi, a small town near the airport. Dubrovnik-based companies offer excursions that include transportation there and back (230 kn).

Nightlife

Dubrovnik's Old Town is one big, romantic parade of relaxed and happy people out strolling. The main drag is brightly lit and packed with shops, cafés, and bars, all open late. This is a fun scene. And if you walk away from the crowds or out on the port, you'll be alone with the magic of the Pearl of the Adriatic. Everything feels—and is—very safe after dark.

If you're looking for a memorable bar after dark, consider these:

▲▲▲**Drinks with a View**—Cold Drinks "**Buža**" offers, without a doubt, the most scenic spot for a drink. Perched on a cliff above the sea, clinging like a barnacle to the outside of the city walls, this is a peaceful, shaded getaway from the bustle of the Old Town... the perfect place to watch cruise ships disappear into the horizon.

Buža means "hole in the wall"—and that's exactly what you'll have to go through to get to this place. There are actually two different Bužas, with separate owners. My favorite is Buža II (which is actually the older and bigger of the pair). Filled with mellow tourists and bartenders pouring wine from tiny screw-top bottles into plastic cups, Buža II comes with castaway views and Frank Sinatra ambience. This is supposedly where Bill Gates hangs out when he visits Dubrovnik

(25-40-kn drinks, summer daily 9:00-into the wee hours, closed mid-Nov-Jan). Buža I, with a different owner, is more casual, plays hip rather than romantic music, and has concrete stairs leading down to a beach on the rocks below (18-45-kn drinks). If one Buža is full, check the other one.

Getting There: Both Bužas are high above the bustle of the main drag, along the seaward wall. To reach them from the cathedral area, hike up the grand staircase to St. Ignatius' Church, then go left to find the lane that runs along the inside of the wall. To find the classic Buža II, head right along the lane and look for the *Cold Drinks* sign pointing to a literal hole in the wall. For the hipper Buža I, go left along the same lane, and locate the hole in the wall with the *No Toples No Nudist* graffiti.

Wine-Tasting—**D'Vino Wine Bar,** just a few steps off the main drag, has a relaxed atmosphere and a knowledgeable but unpretentious approach—making it the handiest place in Dalmatia to taste and learn about Croatian wines. Run by gregarious Aussie-Croat Sasha, this cozy bar (with a few outdoor tables) sells more than 60 wines by the glass and lots more by the bottle. The emphasis is on Croatian wines by small-production wineries, but they also have a few international vintages. Each wine is well-described on the menu, and the staff is happy to guide you through your options— just tell them what you like (18-80-kn glasses—most around 25-35 kn, 50-kn wine flights; light food—70-kn 2-person cheese plate, 90-kn antipasti plate; daily 10:30-2:00 in the morning, possibly less in winter, Palmotićeva 4a, tel. 020/321-130, www.dvino.net). Sasha takes wine-lovers on all-day wine tours to the Pelješac Peninsula; also ask about his wine dinners.

Cocktails and People-Watching—**Jazz Caffè Troubadour** is a cool place, originally owned by a former member of the Dubrovnik Troubadours—Croatia's answer to the Beatles (or, perhaps more accurately, the Turtles). On balmy evenings, 50 chairs with tiny tables are set up theater-style in the dreamy alley facing the musicians. Step inside to see old 1970s photos of the band (50-60-kn cocktails, daily 9:00-24:00, happy hour 14:00-19:00 with 20-kn drinks, live jazz nightly from about 20:30, often live piano at other times, next to cathedral at Bunićeva Poljana 2).

The square just around the corner from Troubadour, alongside the cathedral, is another happening nightspot. Several cafés that ring the square have outdoor seating, filling the entire space with a convivial hubbub of people out enjoying the al fresco ambience.

Nonenina, a few steps from the cathedral on Pred Dvorom, is an outdoor lounge with big, overstuffed chairs at a fine vantage point for people-watching. They brag that they serve 180 different types of cocktails (55-80 kn, also 35-45-kn beers, daily 9:00-2:00 in the morning, shorter hours off-season, across from Rector's Palace).

The Gaffe Irish Pub, with a nice pubby interior and a small courtyard, is a rollicking spot to drain a pint and watch some rugby (Miha Pracata 4, mobile 098-196-2149, see full listing under "Eating in Dubrovnik," later).

Nightclubs—Dubrovnik has a variety of nightclubs. The streets branching off from the Stradun are lined with several options with drinks and pumping music, including **Sky Bar** (toward the water on Marojice Kaboge) and **Africa** (toward the mountain at Vetranićeva 3). Just follow the beat.

More places are near or just beyond the Ploče Gate at the east end of town. Head under the Bell Tower, then up the street past the Dominican Monastery. You'll pass the hole-in-the-wall entrance (right) for the snobby, upscale **Gil's** cocktail bar and "pop lounge" (www.gilsdubrovnik.com). Then, after crossing the bridge, look (on the left) for the entrance to **Revelin**—a dance club that fills one of the city wall's fortress towers (nightly 22:00-6:00, www.revelinclub-dubrovnik.com). Then head out and up the street until you reach Banje Beach, half of which is occupied by the **EastWest** dance club (www.ew-dubrovnik.com). Note that some of these are more exclusive and may charge admission on weekends.

Movies

The Old Town has a trio of movie theaters showing American blockbusters (usually in English with Croatian subtitles, unless the film's animated or for kids). The **Sloboda** cinema, right under the Bell Tower on Luža Square, is nothing special. But in good weather, head for the fun outdoor **Jadran** cinema, where you can lick ice cream (B.Y.O.) while you watch a movie with a Dubrovnik-mountaintop backdrop. This is a cheap, casual, and very Croatian scene, where people smoke and chat, and the neighbors sit in their windowsills to watch the movie (most nights in summer only, shows begin shortly after sundown; in the Old Town near the Pile

Gate). For first-run 3-D movies, head to the **Visia Dubrovnik Multimedia Museum** just inside the Pile Gate (tel. 020/324-714, www.visiadubrovnik.com).

Sleeping in Dubrovnik

You basically have two options in Dubrovnik: a centrally located room in a private home *(soba)*; or a resort hotel on a distant beach, a bus ride away from the Old Town. Since Dubrovnik hotels are generally a poor value, I highly recommend giving the *sobe* a careful look.

Be warned that the Old Town is home to many popular discos. My listings are quieter than the norm, but if you're finding a place on your own, you may discover you have a late-night soundtrack—particularly if you're staying near the Stradun.

No matter where you stay, prices are much higher mid-June through mid-September, and highest in July and August. Reserve ahead for these peak times, especially during the Summer

Sleep Code

(5 kn = about $1, €1 = about $1.40, country code: 385, area code: 020)

S = Single, **D** = Double/Twin, **T** = Triple, **Q** = Quad, **b** = bathroom. The modest tourist tax (about 7 kn per person, per night) is not included in these rates. Hotels generally accept credit cards and include breakfast in their rates, while most *sobe* accept only cash and don't offer breakfast. While rates are listed in euros, you'll pay in kunas. Unless otherwise noted, everyone listed here speaks English.

Rates: If I've listed two sets of rates for an accommodation, I've noted when the second rate applies (generally off-season, Oct-May); if I've listed three sets of rates, separated by slashes, the first is for peak season (July-Aug), the second is for shoulder season (May-June and Sept-Oct), and the third is for off-season (Nov-April). The dates for seasonal rates vary by hotel, and prices can change without notice; verify the hotel's current rates online or by email. For other updates, see www.ricksteves.com/update.

Price Ranges: To help you sort easily through these listings, I've divided the accommodations into three categories based on the price for a double room with bath in peak season:

$$$ Higher Priced—Most rooms €95 or more.
  $$ Moderately Priced—Most rooms between €55-95.
    $ Lower Priced—Most rooms €55 or less.

DUBROVNIK

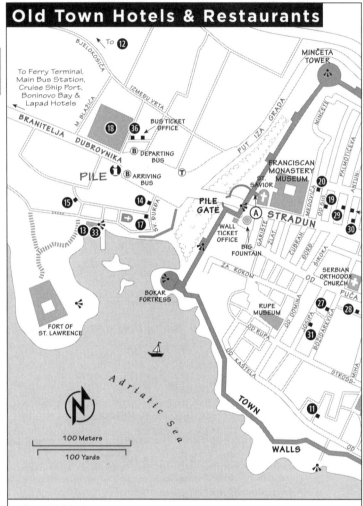

Old Town Hotels & Restaurants

Accommodations

1. Villa Ragusa & Apts. Paviša
2. Apartments Martecchini
3. Raič Apartments
4. Plaza Apartments
5. Minerva Apartments
6. Karmen Apartments
7. Apartments Amoret (3)
8. Apartments Placa
9. Garden Cottage
10. Renata Zijadić Rooms
11. Fresh Sheets Hostel
12. To Jadranka Benussi Rooms
13. Rest. Orhan Guest House
14. Nedjeljka Benussi Rooms
15. Paulina Čumbelić Rooms
16. Villa Adriatica
17. Atlas Travel Agency
18. Hilton Imperial Dubrovnik
19. Hotel Stari Grad

DUBROVNIK

To Mount Srd

CABLE CAR →

To Main (Upper) Road, Airport & Montenegro

ZAGREBAČKA

PETRA KREŠIMIRA

"CABLE CAR" BUS STOP

PLOČE

To St. Jakob Beach, Museum of Modern Art & Viktorija Apartments

UNDERGROUND WALKWAY

Tennis Court

BUŽA GATE

IZA GRADA

REVELIN FORTRESS

WC

F. SUPILA

PLOČE GATE

LAZARETI

DOMINICAN MONASTERY MUSEUM

PRIJEKO

WAR PHOTO LIMITED GALLERY

SYNAGOGUE MUSEUM

(PLACA)

Old Port

SPONZA PALACE

BELL TOWER

ORLANDO'S COLUMN

Luža

ST. BLAISE

CITY HALL

To Lokrum, Cavtat & Elaphite Islands

ICON MUSEUM

Gundul. Poljana

RECTOR'S PALACE

AQUARIUM

ST. JOHN'S FORTRESS & MARITIME MUSEUM

CATHEDRAL

DAMJANA

JUDE

OD PUSTIJERNE

PORPORELA (BREAKWATER)

JESUIT CHURCH

BEACH ACCESS

MAYEROVA

MARGARITE

ISPOD MIRA

BEACH ACCESS

(A) Wall Access

Eateries

20 Nishta Restaurant
21 Dalmatino & The Gaffe Irish Pub
22 Konoba Kamenice
23 Lokanda Peskarija
24 Lady Pi-Pi
25 Oliva Pizzeria
26 Tabasco Pizzeria
27 Spaghetteria Toni

28 Taj Mahal Restaurant
29 Buffet Škola
30 Dolce Vita Ice Cream
31 Sugar & Spice
32 Pupica
33 Orhan Restaurant
34 Komarda Restaurant
35 Produce Market
36 Konzum Groceries (2)
37 Dubrava Bistro

Festival (July 10-Aug 25 every year). Most accommodations pre-fer to list their rates in euros (and I've followed suit), but you'll pay in kunas.

Sobe (Private Rooms): A Dubrovnik Specialty

In Dubrovnik, you'll almost always do better with a *soba* than with a hotel. All of my favorite *sobe* are run by friendly English-speaking Croatians and are inside or within easy walking distance of the Old Town. There's a range of places, from simple and cheap rooms where you'll share a bathroom, to downright fancy places with private facilities, air-conditioning, kitchenettes, and satel-lite TV, where you can be as anonymous as you like. Most *sobe* don't include breakfast, so I've listed some suggestions later, under "Eating in Dubrovnik."

Book direct, using the email addresses I've listed for each place—middleman agencies (including booking websites) tack on fees, making it more expensive for both you and your host. Note that many Dubrovnik *sobe* hosts might ask you to send them a deposit to secure your reservation. Sometimes they'll accept your credit-card number; others might want you to mail them a check or traveler's check (the better option) or wire them the money (which can be expensive). While it's a bit of a hassle, this request is rea-sonable and part of the experience of sleeping at a *soba*. Remember that you'll usually need to pay your bill in cash (kunas), not with a credit card.

In the Old Town, Above the Stradun Promenade

These are some of my favorite accommodations in Dubrovnik. All are located at the top of town, high above the Stradun, and all are excellent values. The first three are within a few steps of each other, along a little block dubbed by some "Rickova ulica." If you don't mind the very steep hike up, you'll find this to be a wonderful enclave of hospitality. When one of these places is full, they work together to find space for you. The last two listings are a few blocks over, and nearly as nice (and equally steep). Because all of these hosts live off-site, be sure to let them know when you'll arrive so they can let you in.

$$ Villa Ragusa, offers my favor-ite rooms for the price in the Old Town. Pero and Valerija Carević have renovated a 600-year-old house at the top of town that was damaged during the war. The five comfortable, modern rooms come with atmospheric old wooden beams, antique furniture, and thoughtful touches. There are three doubles with bathrooms (including a top-floor room with breathtaking Old Town views for no extra charge—request when you reserve) and two singles that share a bathroom (S-€40/€35/€25, Db-€80/€70/€50, €8 breakfast can be eaten here or at nearby Stradun café, cash only, air-con, lots of stairs with no elevator, free Wi-Fi, Žudioska ulica 15, tel. 020/453-834, mobile 098-765-634, www.villaragusa-dubrovnik.com, villa.ragusa@du.t-com.hr). Pero offers his guests airport transfers for a reasonable €30, and can drive you on an all-day excursion (such as to Montenegro or Mostar) for €250—if you can split this cost with other guests, it's a good value (same price for up to 6 people).

$$ Apartments Paviša, next door to Villa Ragusa and run by Pero and Davorka Paviša, has three good, older-feeling rooms at the top of the Old Town (Db-€100/€70/€50, 10 percent discount if you book direct with this book, no breakfast, cash only, air-con, lots of stairs, free Wi-Fi, Žudioska ulica 19, mobile 098-427-399 or 098-175-2342, www.apartmentspavisa.com, davorka.pavisa @du.t-com.hr). They have two more rooms in the **Viktorija** neighborhood, about a 20-minute mostly uphill walk east of the Old Town. While it's a long-but-scenic walk into town, the views from these apartments are spectacular (same prices as in-town rooms, Frana Supila 59, bus stop nearby). Pero and Davorka also manage **Apartments Martecchini,** three units a bit closer to the main drag in the Old Town (small apartment-€100/€70/€50, bigger apartment-€110/€80/€50, biggest apartment-€120/€90/€60; 10 percent discount if you book direct with this book, prices depend on size and views, no breakfast, cash only, air-con, free Wi-Fi, www .apartmentsmartecchini.com).

$$ Ivana and Anita Raič are sisters renting three new-feeling apartments with kitchenettes and air-conditioning (Db-€90/€70/€50-60, no extra charge for 1- or 2-night stays, no breakfast, cash only, air-con, free Wi-Fi, Žudioska ulica 16, Ivana's mobile 098-996-0858, Anita's mobile 091-537-6035, www .apartments-raic.com, ivanaraic@gmail.com).

$$ Plaza Apartments, run by Lidija and Maro Matić, rents three clean, well-appointed apartments on a plant-filled lane—the steepest and most appealing stretch of stairs leading up from the Stradun. Lidija's sweet personality is reflected in the cheerful rooms, which are a great value if you don't mind the hike (Db-€75/€60/€55, cheaper Nov-April, these special prices for Rick Steves readers, no breakfast, cash only, air-con, free Wi-Fi, climb the stairs past Dolce Vita gelato shop to Nalješkovićeva 22, tel. 020/321-493, mobile 091-517-7048, www.dubrovnik-online.com /apartment_plaza, lidydu@yahoo.com).

$$ Minerva Apartments has two cozy ground-floor units near the top of a similar lane, in the home of Dubravka Vidosavljević-

Vučić (Db-€80/€75/€65, cheaper Nov-April, cash only, no break-fast, air-con, free Wi-Fi, washing machine, Antuninska 14, mobile 091-252-9677, duvivu@gmail.com).

In the Old Town, near the Cathedral and St. John's Fort

The following places are south of the Stradun, mostly clustering around the cathedral and St. John's Fort, at the end of the Old Port. To find the Karmen and Zijadić apartments from the cathe-dral, walk toward the big fort tower along the inside of the wall (follow signs for *akvarji*).

$$$ Apartments Amoret, run by Branka Dabrović and her husband Ivica, are in all the guidebooks. The pricey but comfortable apartments, with furnishings that are a step up from the norm, are in three different buildings: two over Amoret Restaurant in front of the cathedral (at Restićeva 2); eight more sharing an inviting ter-race on a quiet, untouristy lane a few blocks east (at Dinka Ranjine 5); and three more nearby (at Ilije Sarake 4). All three classes of apartments are comparably good; in every case, the furnishings are a tasteful mix of traditional and modern. Since Branka and Ivica don't live on-site, arrange a meeting time and place when you reserve ("regular" apartments-€100/€90/€80; "standard" apart-ments-€120/€110/€100; "superb" apartments-€140/€130/€110; cheaper Nov-April, 30 percent more for 1-night stays, 20 percent more for 2-night stays, 10 percent more for 3-night stays, no break-fast, cash only, air-con, free Wi-Fi, mobile 091-530-4910, tel. & fax 020/324-005, www.dubrovnik-amoret.com, dubrovnik@post .t-com.hr).

$$ Karmen Apartments are well-run by a Brit named Marc and his Croatian wife Silva, who offer four apartments just inside the big fort. The prices are very high, and they're in all the guide-books, but the apartments are big, well-equipped, and homey-feel-ing, each with a bathroom and kitchen. The decor is eclectic but tasteful, and Marc and Silva are good hosts, with a virtual mini-museum of historic Dubrovnik maps and documents in the stair-well (smaller apartment-€90/€70, mid-sized apartment-€135/€108, bigger apartment-€155/€110; higher price is for May-Sept, less Dec-March, usually 3-night minimum, no breakfast, cash only, air-con, free Wi-Fi, near the aquarium at Bandureva 1, tel. 020/323-433, mobile 098-619-282, www.karmendu.com, marc.van-bloemen @du.t-com.hr).

$$ Apartments Placa (PLAH-tsah; not to be confused with Plaza Apartments, described earlier) is run by Tonči (TOHN-chee). He rents three apartments with some antique furnishings and some modern, overlooking the market square in the heart of the Old Town. You might get some early-morning noise from the market set-up, but the double-paned windows help, and the location is wonderfully central. Since Tonči lives elsewhere, clearly communicate your arrival time (Db-€90/€80/€70, cheaper Nov-April, no breakfast, cash only, no extra charge for 1- or 2-night stays, several flights of stairs, air-con, free Wi-Fi, Gundulićeva poljana 5, mobile 091-721-9202, www.dubrovnik-online.com /apartments_placa, tonci.korculanin@du.t-com.hr).

$$ Garden Cottage is exactly that: a small freestanding house nestled in a very rare patch of green. It's a peaceful oasis smack-dab in the heart of the bustling city (just off the plaza in front of the Jesuit church). Roberto and his mother Marija (also recommended tour guides) live in an old Dubrovnik mansion with a fine little garden, and they've converted the old laundry building into a simple rental apartment that sleeps up to four people. When you book this place, you're also renting the entire garden for your own use...very cool, particularly in a city with virtually no green space (€80/€70/€60 per night for 4 or more nights, €90/€80/€70 per night for 2-3 nights, €100/€90/€80 for 1 night, extra bed-€15, cash only, air-con, washing machine, kitchenette, mobile 091-541-6637, bobdel70@yahoo.com).

$$ Renata Zijadić, a friendly mom who speaks good English, offers four well-located rooms with slanting floors, funky colors, and over-the-top antique furniture. A single and a double (both with great views) share one bathroom; another double features an ornate old cabinet and its own bathroom; and the top-floor apartment comes with low ceilings and fine vistas (S-€30/€28, D-€50/€45, Db-€60/€50, apartment-€85/€75, second price is for June and Sept, cheaper Oct-May, no extra charge for 1- or 2-night stays, no breakfast, cash only, all rooms have air-con except the single, free Wi-Fi; follow signs for wall access and walk up the steps marked *ulica Stajeva* going over the street to find Stajeva 1; tel. 020/323-623, www.dubrovnik-online.com/house_renata, renatadubrovnik@yahoo.com).

$ Fresh Sheets, a bright, stylish, and appealingly funky hostel run by a fun-loving Canadian-Croatian couple, is your best youth hostel option in the Old Town. The 22 bunks (two 8-bed dorms, one 4-bed dorm, and a double room) sit above a tight but enjoyable common area. Located at the very top of Dubrovnik just inside the town walls, it's a steep hike up from the main drag, but worth it if you enjoy youthful backpacker bonding (€22-33/bunk in a dorm, €25-38/person in a private room, likely closed Nov-March, free breakfast, free Internet access and Wi-Fi, lockers, kitchen, Svetog Šimuna/Smokvina 15, mobile 091-799-2086, www.freshsheets hostel.com, beds@igotfresh.com).

In the Pile Neighborhood, Just Outside the Old Town

There's a concentration of good *sobe* just outside the Old Town's Pile Gate. The Pile (PEE-leh) neighborhood offers all the conve-niences of the modern world (gro-cery store, bus stop, post office, travel agency, etc.), just steps from Dubrovnik's magical Old Town. The first place is up the hill (away from the water) from the Pile Gate's bus stop; the rest cluster around a quiet, no-name cove near

Restaurant Orhan. From the bus stop area in front of Pile Gate, various lanes lead down toward this cove.

$$ Jadranka and Milan Benussi, a middle-aged professional couple, rent four rooms in a quiet, traffic-free neighborhood. Their delightful stony-chic home, complete with a leafy terrace, is a steep 10-minute hike above the Old Town—close enough to be convenient, but far enough to take you away from the bustle and into a calm residential zone. Jadranka speaks good English, enjoys visiting with her guests, and gives her place a modern Croatian class unusual for a *soba*. This is one of your best values and most comfortable home bases in Dubrovnik, if you don't mind the walk (small Db-€60/€55, big Db-€70/€65, small apartment-€90/€85, big apartment with balcony-€100/€95, cheaper Oct-May, 20 per-cent more for stays less than 4 nights, no breakfast, cash only, air-con, kitchenettes, free Wi-Fi, Miha Klaića 10, tel. 020/429-339, mobile 098-928-1300, www.dubrovnik-benussi.com, jadranka @dubrovnik-benussi.com). To find the Benussis, go to the big Hilton Hotel just outside the Pile Gate (across from the TI). Walk up the little stepped lane called Marijana Blažića at the upper-left corner of the Hilton cul-de-sac. When that lane dead-ends, go left up ulica Don Iva Bjelokosića (more steps) until you see a little church on the left. The Benussis' house is just before this church.

$$ Restaurant Orhan Guest House allows hotel anonymity at *sobe* prices. Its 11 basic, old-fashioned, ramshackle rooms—in a couple of different buildings around the corner from the restau-rant—are well-located and quiet, with modern bathrooms. As the rooms are an afterthought to the restaurant, don't expect a warm welcome (Sb or Db-€60-75/€40, includes breakfast, cash only, air-con, free Wi-Fi, Od Tabakarije 1, tel. & fax 020/414-183, www .restaurant-orhan.com, restoran.orhan@yahoo.com). Their restau-rant is also a good spot for a scenic meal (described later, under "Eating in Dubrovnik").

$$ Nedjeljka Benussi, the sister-in-law of Jadranka Benussi (listed earlier), rents three modern, spacious, straightforward rooms sharing two bathrooms and a pretty view (D-€70/€55, T-€80/€75, cheaper Dec-March, same price for 1-night stays, no breakfast, cash only, fans but no air-con, Sv. Đurđa 4, tel. 020/423-062, mobile 098-170-5699).

$ Paulina Čumbelić is a kind, gentle woman renting four old-fashioned rooms in her homey, clean, and peaceful house (S-€30/€27, D-€50/€40, T-€60/€55, 20 percent more for 1- or 2-night stays, no breakfast, cash only, closed in winter, can be noisy outside, Od Tabakarije 2, tel. 020/421-327, mobile 091-530-7985).

Beyond the Ploče Gate, East of the Old Town

To reach these options, you'll go through the Ploče Gate and walk along the road stretching east from the Old Town (with fine views back on the Old Port). This area is shared by giant waterfront luxury hotels and residential areas, so it has a bit less character than the Pile and Old Town listings (which I prefer).

$$ Apartments Paviša has two fine apartments in the Viktorija neighborhood about a 20-minute walk or short bus ride from town.

$$ Villa Adriatica has four old-fashioned rooms above a travel agency and a family home just outside the Ploče Gate, a few steps from the Old Town. The rooms are antique-furnished, but have modern bathrooms, TVs, and air-conditioning. While impersonal and a lesser value than my other listings, it's worth considering just for the huge, shared terrace with priceless Old Port views, plus a common living room and kitchen furnished with museum-piece antiques. Teo manages the rooms; ask for him at the Perla Adriatic travel agency, just outside the Ploče Gate (Db-€85-95/€80-90/€75-85, cheaper Nov-April, price depends on size and view, 20 percent more for 1- or 2-night stays, no breakfast, cash only, air-con, free Wi-Fi in some areas, Frana Supila 4, mobile 098-334-500, tel. 020/411-962, fax 020/422-766, www.villa-adriatica.net, booking @villa-adriatica.net, Tomšić family).

Sobe-Booking Websites and Agencies

Several websites put you in touch with Dubrovnik's *sobe* and apartments. Of course, you'll save yourself and your host money if you book direct, but these sites are convenient. For example, www .dubrovnikapartmentsource.com, run by an American couple, offers a range of carefully selected, well-described accommodations. You can browse a variety of options, then reserve your choice and pay a nonrefundable deposit by credit card. Another, bigger operation—with a wider selection but less personal attention—is www.adriatica.net; international sites such as www.booking.com are another good option.

If you arrive without a reservation and the TI isn't too busy, they might be able to call around and find you a *soba* for no charge. Otherwise, just about any travel agency in town can help you, on the spot or in advance...for a fee. **Atlas** is the biggest company (figure Db-€55-60 and apartment-€75-100 in June-Sept, €15-20 less in shoulder season).

Hotels

If you must stay in a hotel, you have only a few good options. There are just two hotels inside the Old Town walls—and one of them charges $500 a night (Pucić Palace, www.thepucicpalace.com). Any big, resort-style hotel within walking distance of the Old Town will run you at least €200. These inflated prices drive most visitors to Boninovo Bay or the Lapad Peninsula, a bus ride west of the Old Town. In the mass-tourism tradition, many European visitors choose to take the half-board option at their hotel (i.e., dinner in the hotel restaurant). This can be convenient and a good value—especially considering the relatively low quality of Dubrovnik's restaurants (explained later, under "Eating in Dubrovnik")—but the Old Town is a much more atmospheric place to dine.

In and near the Old Town

$$$ Hilton Imperial Dubrovnik, sitting regally just outside the Pile Gate, is the closest big hotel to the Old Town. This grand 19th-century building was recently overhauled to create 147 plush rooms. If you want predictable Hilton comfort at outlandish prices a short walk from the Old Town, this is the place (Db-€300, less off-season, €55 extra for sea view, €65 extra for balcony but no view, €120 extra for balcony and view, most rates include breakfast but not the 10 percent tax, elevator, air-con, pay Wi-Fi in lobby and pay cable Internet in rooms, parking-€27/night, $7 bottles of water at the reception desk, Marijana Blažića 2, tel. 020/320-320, fax 020/320-220, www.hilton.com, sales.dubrovnik@hilton.com).

$$$ Hotel Stari Grad knows it's the only real hotel option inside the Old Town—and charges accordingly. It has eight modern yet nicely old-fashioned rooms a half-block off the Old Town's main drag. The rooftop terrace enjoys an amazing view over orange tiles. This place books up fast, so reserve early (Sb-€180/€134/€99, Db-€240/€192/€140, no extra charge for 1- or 2-night stays, includes breakfast, air-con, lots of stairs with no elevator, free Wi-Fi, Od Sigurate 4, tel. 020/322-244, fax 020/321-256, www.hotelstarigrad.com, info@hotelstarigrad.com).

Near Boninovo Bay

Boninovo Bay (boh-NEE-noh-voh) is your best bet for an affordable and well-located hotel. Above this bay are Dubrovnik's only three-star hotels within walking distance of the Old Town (not to mention the city's only official youth hostel). These places offer slightly better prices and closer proximity to the Old Town than the farther-out Lapad Bay resorts. They're on or near the water, but don't have views of the Old Town (which is around the bend). Boninovo Bay is an uphill 20-minute walk or five-minute bus ride from the Old Town (straight up Branitelja Dubrovnika). Once you're comfortable with the buses, the location is great: Any bus that leaves the Pile Gate stops first at Boninovo Bay. You'll see the bay on your left as you climb the hill, then get off at the stop after the traffic light (or stay on bus #4, which stops even closer to the hotels). To reach the hotels from the Boninovo bus stop, go up Pera Čingrije (the busy road running along the top of the cliff overlooking the sea). There's a super little bakery, Pekarnica Klas, on the right (across the street from Hotel Bellevue).

$$$ Hotel Bellevue has a striking location, with its back against the cliff rising up from Boninovo Bay and an elevator plunging directly to its own pebbly beach. Completely gutted and rebuilt just a few years ago, its 91 top-notch rooms—all but two with sea views, many with balconies—offer upscale wood-grain elegance (standard Db-generally €250/€220, less Nov-April, very flexible rates, €50 more for balcony, air-con, elevator, free Internet access and Wi-Fi, Pera Čingrije 7, tel. 020/330-000, fax 020/330-100, www.hotel-bellevue.hr, welcome@hotel-bellevue.hr).

$$$ Hotel R, a homey enclave with just 10 rooms, feels friendlier and less greedy than all the big resort hotels. Well-run by the Rešetar family, it's a good small-hotel value (Sb-€72/€56/€50, Db-€110/€86/€77, closed Nov-Easter, 10 percent more for balcony, half-board-€13, air-con, free Wi-Fi, just beyond the big Hotel Lero at Iva Vojnovića 16, tel. 020/333-200, fax 020/333-208, www.hotel-r.hr, helpdesk@hotel-r.hr).

$$$ Hotel Lero, 250 yards up the street from the bus stop, has 140 recently renovated rooms and a fine outdoor pool. Choose between so-so sea views with some road noise, or quieter back rooms (soft rates, but generally Sb-€110/€85, Db-€140/€106, cheaper mid-Oct-April; in busy times, you may be quoted more than these rates—try asking for a better deal; "superior" rooms with balcony not worth the extra €30/person, air-con, elevator, pay Internet access, free Wi-Fi, half-board-€6, Iva Vojnovića 14, tel. 020/341-333, fax 020/332-123, www.hotel-lero.hr, sales@hotel-lero.hr).

$ Dubrovnik's official **Youth Hostel** is quiet, modern, and well-run by proud manager Laura. It's institutional, with 82 beds in 19 fresh, woody dorms and few extra hostel amenities (bunk in 4- to 6-bed dorm-€18/€17/€16, cheaper Nov-March, €1.50 more for nonmembers, includes sheets, includes breakfast, no air-con in rooms, free Internet access, no Wi-Fi; reception open daily June-Oct 7:00-3:00 in the morning, Nov-May 8:00-14:00 &

18:00-20:00; 2:00 a.m. curfew in summer, none in winter; up the steps at ulica bana Jelačića 15-17 to ulica Vinka Sagrestana 3, tel. 020/423-241, fax 020/412-592, www.hfhs.hr, dubrovnik@hfhs.hr). From the Boninovo bus stop, go down Pera Čingrije toward Hotel Bellevue, but take the first right uphill onto ulica bana Jelačića and look for signs up to the hostel on your left, on ulica Vinka Sagrestana. Several houses nearby rent rooms to those who prefer a double...and pick off would-be hostelers as they approach.

In Lapad

For a real resort-style vacation (at premium prices), many travelers call the touristy area around Lapad (LAH-pahd) Bay home. The main drag running through the middle of this scene, called Šetalište Kralja Zvonimira, is a nicely pedestrianized people zone buzzing with tourists, restaurants, cafés, and mild diversions. From the bus stop, the main drag leads to a pleasant pebble beach good for swimming and a romantic bayside path. While I much prefer sleeping near the Old Town, this is an appealing place to be on vacation (even if the Old Town weren't just a short bus ride away). To get here from the Old Town's Pile Gate, pile onto bus #6 with all the other tourists and get off at the Pošta Lapad stop (poorly marked—after bus turns left away from the big harbor, watch for low-profile yellow *pošta* sign on left; 4-6 buses/hour until 24:30, 15 minutes). A taxi costs about 60 kn.

$$$ Small Hotels in Lapad: In this area, I like three newish, interchangeable small hotels. While not affiliated with each other, each one has similar amenities—air-con, elevator (except Hotel Dubrovnik), Internet access either in lobby or in room—and similar prices (roughly Db-€160/€140/€110, but prices are very soft and can flex with demand, season, and length of stay; check online for the latest, and ask for a deal when you reserve). **Hotel Aquarius,** hiding a block off the main drag, has 24 comfortable, plush-feeling rooms and an inviting terrace out front (Mata Vodopića 8, tel. 020/456-111, fax 020/456-100, www.hotel-aquarius .net, stjepanka@hotel-aquarius.net). **Hotel Perla,** right on the main drag, has 25 modern rooms (tel. 020/438-244, fax 020/438-245, www.perla-dubrovnik.com, info@perla-dubrovnik.com). **Hotel Dubrovnik,** two doors up from the Perla, has 25 simpler rooms (tel. 020/435-030, fax 020/435-999, www.hoteldubrovnik .hr, info@hoteldubrovnik.com).

Eating in Dubrovnik

Dubrovnik disappoints diners with high prices, surly service, and mediocre quality. With the constant influx of deep-pocketed tourists corrupting greedy restaurateurs, places here tend to go down-

hill faster than a game of marbles on the *Titanic*. Promising new restaurants open all the time, but most quickly fade, and what's great one year can be miserable the next. Therefore, lower your expectations, take my suggestions with a grain of salt, and ask around locally for what's good this month. Don't bother looking for a "local" favorite anywhere near the Old Town—people who live here eat out at restaurants in the 'burbs. The good news is that it's atmospheric. Anywhere you dine, breezy outdoor seating is a no-brainer, and scrawny, adorable kittens beg for table scraps. In general, seafood restaurants are good only at seafood; if you want pasta, go to a pasta place.

In the Old Town

Nishta ("Nothing"), featuring a short menu of delicious vegetarian fusion cuisine with Asian flair, offers a welcome change of pace from the Dalmatian seafood-pasta-pizza rut. Busy Swiss owner/ chef Gildas cooks, while his wife Ruža cheerfully serves a steady stream of return diners. This tiny place—which, in my experience, is just about the only reliably good eatery in town—has just a few indoor and outdoor tables. Even if you're not a vegetarian, it's worth a visit; reserve the day ahead in peak season (60-85-kn main courses, May-Oct Mon-Sat 11:30-22:00, Nov-April generally open Mon-Sat for lunch only, closed Sun year-round, on the restaurant-clogged Prijeko street—near the Pile Gate end of the street, tel. 020/322-088).

Dalmatino offers some of the best traditional Dalmatian cooking in the city—and doesn't charge a premium. South African-Croatian owner Robert prides himself on cooking each dish to order; while this may take a few minutes longer, you can taste the results. While there's no seating on a street or square, you'll find cozy tables tucked along the alley leading to the spacious, classy-but-not-stuffy dining room (45-110-kn pastas, 65-125-kn main dishes, daily 11:00-23:00, Miha Pracata 6, tel. 020/323-070).

Konoba Kamenice, a no-frills fish restaurant, is a local institution offering inexpensive, fresh, and good meals on a charming market square, as central as can be in the Old Town. On the limited menu, the seafood dishes are excellent (try their octopus salad, even if you don't think you like octopus), while the few non-seafood dishes are uninspired. Some of the waitstaff are notorious for their playfully brusque service, but loyal patrons happily put up with it. Arrive early, or you'll have to wait (35-70-kn main courses, daily 8:00-23:00, until 22:00 off-season, Gundulićeva poljana 8, tel. 020/323-682).

Lokanda Peskarija enjoys an enticing setting, with a sea of tables facing the Old Port. Servings are hearty and come in a pot, "home-style." The 70-kn seafood risotto easily feeds two, and sharing is no problem. The menu's tiny—with only seafood options, and not much in the way of vegetables. Locals complain that the quality has taken a nosedive (crank-'em-out food and disinterested service) ever since the restaurant's following has grown and its idyllic dining area has been expanded to the hilt. But for reasonably priced seafood dishes on the water, this remains an acceptable option (60-85-kn main courses, daily 12:00-24:00, very limited indoor seating fills up fast, plenty of outdoor tables—which can also fill up, tel. 020/324-750, no reservations taken in summer).

Lady Pi-Pi, named for a comical, anatomically correct, and slightly off-putting statue out front, sits high above town just inside the wall. The food, prepared on an open grill, is just an excuse to sit out on their terrace, with several tables overlooking the rooftops of Dubrovnik (65-70-kn pastas, 65-110-kn main dishes, daily May-Sept 9:00-24:00, closed Oct-April, Peline b.b., tel. 020/321-288).

Pizza: Dubrovnik seems to have a pizzeria on every corner. Little separates the various options—just look for a menu and outdoor seating option that appeals to you. I've eaten well at **Oliva Pizzeria,** just behind St. Blaise's Church (40-65-kn pizzas, Lučarica 5, daily 10:00-24:00, tel. 020/324-594). Around the side is a handy take-out window for a bite on the go (though **Tutto Bene,** a few blocks down on od Puča, has better take-away slices). Close to the Old Town, but just far away to be frequented mostly by locals, **Tabasco Pizzeria** is tucked at the corner of the parking lot beneath the cable-car station. Unpretentious and affordable, this is the place to come if the pizza is more important than the setting—though the outdoor terrace does have views of the Old Town walls...over a sea of parked cars (40-50-kn pizzas, 70-80-kn "jumbo" pizzas, daily 9:00-23:00, Hvarska 48A, tel. 020/429-595).

Pasta: **Spaghetteria Toni** is popular with natives and tourists. While nothing fancy, it offers good pastas at reasonable prices. Choose between the cozy 10-table interior or the long alley filled with outdoor tables (45-80-kn pastas, 45-65-kn salads, daily in summer 11:00-23:00, closed Sun in winter, closed Jan, Nikole Božidarevića 14, tel. 020/323-134).

Bosnian Cuisine: For a break from Croatian fare, consider the grilled meats and other tasty Bosnian dishes at the misnamed **Taj Mahal.** Though the service can be lacking, the menu offers an enticing taste of the Turkish-flavored land to the east. Choose between the tight interior, which feels like a Bosnian tea house, or tables out on the alley (40-55-kn salads, 50-120-kn main courses, daily 10:00-24:00, Nikole Gučetića 2, tel. 020/323-221).

DUBROVNIK

Sandwiches: **Buffet Škola** is a rare bit of pre-glitz Dubrovnik just a few steps off the Stradun, serving take-away or sit-down sandwiches on homemade bread. Squeeze into the hole-in-the-wall interior, or sit at one of the outdoor tables (25-30 kn, 60-80-kn plates, daily 8:00-22:00 or 23:00, Antuninska 1, tel. 020/321-096).

Pub Grub: **The Gaffe Irish Pub** offers a break from traditional Dalmatian food, with a simple menu of British Isles-style pub food, including burgers and some international flavors (Thai curry, tandoori, and so on). It isn't exactly high cuisine...but at least it's a break from seafood risotto (40-52-kn light meals, 50-90-kn big meals, open long hours daily, Miha Pracata 4, mobile 098-196-2149).

Ice Cream: Dubrovnik has lots of great *sladoled*, but locals swear by the stuff at **Dolce Vita** (daily 9:00-24:00, a half-block off the Stradun at Nalješkovićeva 1A, tel. 020/321-666).

Other Desserts: Two good dessert shops in Dubrovnik have been getting raves from locals and visitors. If you have a sweet tooth, drop by one or both to survey their display cases (12-20-kn cakes). They're within a few short blocks of each other: **Sugar and Spice** (pink-and-stone hole-in-the-wall, "global desserts with a Dalmatian twist," Mon-Sat 9:00-22:00, Sun 11:00-19:00, Sv. Josipa 5, mobile 091-361-9550) and **Pupica** (also has good coffee drinks, long hours daily, Cvijete Zuzorić b.b., mobile 099-216-545).

The Old Town's "Restaurant Row," Prijeko Street: The street called Prijeko, a block toward the mainland from the Stradun promenade, is lined with outdoor, tourist-oriented eateries—each one with a huckster out front trying to lure in diners. (Many of them aggressively try to snare passersby down on the Stradun, as well.) Don't be sucked into this vortex of bad food at outlandish prices. The only place worth seeking out here is Nishta (described earlier); the rest are virtually guaranteed to disappoint. Still, it can be fun to take a stroll along here—the atmosphere is lively, and the sales pitches are entertainingly desperate.

Just Outside the Old Town, with a View

Orhan Restaurant, overlooking the tranquil cove at the Pile neighborhood outside the Old Town, feels just beyond the tourist crush. It features disinterested service and unremarkable food, but great views on a large terrace (reserve a seat here in advance). Watch the people walk the Old Town walls across the cove. This is a handy spot for a scenic breakfast (75-100-kn pastas, 80-180-kn main courses, daily 8:00-23:00, cash only, Od Tabakarije 1, tel. 020/414-183).

Komarda serves up forgettable food on a memorably romantic terrace, with views of Dubrovnik's walls and Old Port. Tables are scattered around a tranquil garden just above the sea and a concrete beach. As there's no point eating here unless you have a good view, consider dropping by early in the day to pick out and reserve the table of your choice for dinner (50-80-kn pastas, 75-135-kn main courses, 60-kn lunch special, daily 7:00-2:00 in the morning, reservations essential in summer, mobile 098-428-239). To find it, exit the Old Town through the Ploče Gate (east). After walking through the final fortification, you'll reach a block of travel agencies. Once you pass these, look for the stairs down to Komarda, on the right.

Picnic Tips

Dubrovnik's lack of great restaurant options makes it a perfect place to picnic. You can shop for fresh fruits and veggies at the open-air produce market (each morning near the cathedral, on the square called Gundulićeva Poljana). Supplement your picnic with grub from the cheap **Konzum grocery store** (one location on the market square near the produce-vendors: Mon-Sat 7:00-21:00, Sun 7:00-13:00; another near the bus stop just outside Pile Gate: Mon-Sat 7:00-21:00, Sun 8:00-13:00). Good picnic spots include the shaded benches overlooking the Old Port; the Porporela breakwater (beyond the Old Port and fort—comes with a swimming area, sunny no-shade benches, and views of Lokrum Island); and the green, welcoming park in what was the moat just under the Pile Gate entry to the Old Town.

Breakfast

If you're sleeping in a *soba*, you'll likely be on your own for breakfast. Fortunately, you have plenty of cafés and pastry shops to choose from, and your host probably has a favorite she can recommend. In the Old Town, **Dubrava Bistro**—which locals call "Snack Bar"—has great views and fine outdoor seating at the most colorful end of the Stradun. While the ham resembles Spam and the continental breakfast is paltry, you can't beat the real estate. Locals who hang out here—catching up with their friends as they stroll by—call this their low-tech version of "Facebook" (basic 38-46-kn egg dishes, 24-kn caffè lattes; you'll pay 25 percent less if you sit inside—but then there's no point eating here; daily 8:00-24:00, Placa 6, tel. 020/321-229). For better food in a less atmospheric setting, **The Gaffe Irish Pub** has a good menu of breakfast options (30-42 kn, served daily 9:00-11:30, Miha Pracata 4, mobile 098-196-2149). In the Pile neighborhood, I like **Restaurant Orhan,** right on the cove (described earlier; 50 kn for omelet or continental breakfast, served daily 8:00-11:00). Some of the other restaurants listed in this section (including **Konoba Kamenice**) also serve breakfast. Not many places serve before 9:00 or 10:00; if you'll be departing early, stock up on groceries the night before.

On Lapad Bay

If you want a break from the Old Town, consider venturing to Lapad Bay. The ambience is pleasant and Lapad is worth an evening stroll. This area's main drag, **Šetalište Kralja Zvonimira,** is an amazingly laid-back pedestrian lane where bars have hammocks, Internet terminals are scattered through a forested park, and a folksy Croatian family ambience holds its own against the better-funded force of international tourism. Stroll from near Hotel Zagreb to the bay, marked by Hotel Kompas. From Hotel Kompas, a romantic walk—softly lit at night—leads past some splurge restaurants along the bay through the woods, with plenty of private little stone coves for lingering.

Dubrovnik Connections

Note that the boats listed here leave from Dubrovnik's Port Gruž, a bus ride away from the Old Town (described earlier, under "Arrival in Dubrovnik—By Car Ferry or Catamaran"). Be aware that eventual redevelopment of the port area will likely move the Jadrolinija ferries and *Nona Ana* catamaran departure point out to the far end of the port, under the big bridge. If I've listed a range of prices, the specific fare depends on the season.

From Dubrovnik by Big Jadrolinija Car Ferry: From June to September only, the big boats leave Dubrovnik twice weekly in the morning and go to **Sobra** on Mljet Island (1.25 hours, plus a 1.25-hour bus ride to the national park, 75-90 kn), **Korčula** (4.5 hours, 90-110 kn), **Stari Grad** on Hvar Island (8.75 hours, 110-130 kn), **Split** (11 hours, 110-130 kn), and **Rijeka** (21 hours including overnight from Split to Rijeka, 215-255 kn). These ferries do not run October through May, and the price range depends on the season. However, boat schedules are subject to change—confirm your plans at a local TI, or see www.jadrolinija.hr.

From Dubrovnik by Speedy *Nona Ana* Catamaran: This handy service connects Dubrovnik to popular islands to the north (Mljet, Korčula, and Lastovo). This schedule is subject to change from year to year, so carefully confirm the details before planning your trip. In the summer (June-Sept), the boat departs Dubrovnik each morning and heads for **Sobra** (1.5 hours, 40 kn) and **Polače** (1.75 hours, 54 kn) on Mljet Island. In the peak months of July and August, it sometimes continues on to **Korčula** (4/week, 2.75 hours, 58 kn) and **Lastovo Island** (2/week, 4 hours, 68 kn). In the winter (Oct-May), the boat goes each afternoon at 14:30 to Sobra and Polače on Mljet, but does not go all the way to Korčula or Lastovo. The catamaran leaves from Dubrovnik's Port Gruž (buy tickets at the kiosk next to the boat, ticket window opens 1 hour before departure; in peak season, it's smart to show up about an hour ahead to be sure you get on the boat). Confirm schedules at the Dubrovnik TI, or check www.gv-line.hr.

By Bus to: Split (almost hourly, generally at the top of each hour, less off-season, 3.5-5 hours, 100 kn), **Korčula** (summer: 2/day at 9:00 and 15:00; off-season: Mon-Sat 1/day at 15:00, Sun 2/day at 15:00 and 18:00; 3.5 hours, 90 kn; also consider the shuttle-bus service described next), **Rijeka** (5/day, 12.5-13 hours, 410-510 kn), **Zagreb** (7/day including some overnight options, 10 hours, 200-220 kn), **Kotor** in Montenegro (2/day, 2.5 hours, 90-110 kn), **Mostar** (5/day in summer, 3/day in winter, 4-5 hours, 80-115 kn), **Sarajevo** (2/day at 8:00 and 15:15, 5-6.5 hours, 245-255 kn; also a night bus at 21:00; only 1/day in winter), **Pula** and **Rovinj** (nightly, 15 hours to Pula, 16 hours to Rovinj). As usual, schedules are subject to change—confirm locally before making the trip to the bus station. For bus information, call 060-305-070 (a pricey toll line, but worth it).

By Shuttle Bus to Korčula: Korčula-based Korkyra Info Travel Agency runs a handy door-to-door shuttle service from your Dubrovnik accommodations to Korčula (departs at various times—call to ask and to reserve, may stop briefly in Ston if you want, by request only Nov-Feb, 2 hours, 150 kn one-way, mobile 091-571-4355, www.korkyra.info, info@korkyra.info).

By Plane: To quickly connect remote Dubrovnik with the rest of your trip, consider a cheap flight. For information on Dubrovnik's airport, see "Arrival in Dubrovnik—By Plane," earlier.

Can I Get to Greece from Dubrovnik? Not easily. Your best bet is to fly (though there are no direct flights, aside from the occasional charter flight from Dubrovnik to Athens—you'll generally have to transfer elsewhere in Europe). Even though Croatia and Greece are nearly neighbors, no direct boats connect them, and the overland connection is extremely long and rugged.

What About Italy? Flying is the easiest option, though there are only a few direct flights (on Croatia Airlines to Rome, Venice, or Milan; or on easyJet to Rome or Milan). You can take a direct night boat from Dubrovnik to Bari, or head to Split for more boat connections. The overland connection is overly long (figure 5 hours to Split, then 5 hours to Zagreb, then 7 hours to Venice).

NEAR DUBROVNIK

Excursions from Dubrovnik's Old Port • Cavtat • Trsteno Arboretum • Pelješac Peninsula • Mljet National Park

The more time you spend here, the clearer it becomes: Dubrovnik isn't just a town, it's an entire region. Stretching up and down the glimmering Dalmatian Coast from Dubrovnik are a variety of worthwhile getaways. Just offshore from the city's Old Town—and accessible via scenic boat trip from its historic port—are enticing islands and villages, where time stands still for lazy vacationers: the playground islet of Lokrum and the sight-studded archipelago of the Elaphite Islands. The serene resort town of Cavtat, just south of Dubrovnik, has some of the best art treasures of this part of Dalmatia (including a gorgeous mausoleum designed by Ivan Meštrović). To the north is a lush arboretum called Trsteno, with a playful fountain, a 600-year-old aqueduct, a villa, a chapel...and, of course, plants galore. Poking into the Adriatic is the vineyard-covered Pelješac Peninsula, anchored by the mighty little town of Ston. And out at sea is the sparsely populated island called Mljet, a third of which is carefully protected as one of Croatia's most appealing national parks, where you can hike, bike, boat, and swim to your heart's content. Best of all, there's no better place to "come home to" than Dubrovnik—after a busy day exploring the coastline, strolling the Stradun to unwind is particularly sweet.

Planning Your Time

Give yourself at least a full day and two nights to experience Dubrovnik itself. But if you can spare the time, set up in Dubrovnik for several nights and use your extra days for some of these excursions. (This also gives you the luxury of keeping an eye on the weather reports and saving the most weather-depen-

Dubrovnik Day Trips at a Glance

The international excursions to Bosnia-Herzegovina and Montenegro—which are worth considering for overnight stops—are covered in their own chapters.

In Bosnia-Herzegovina

▲▲▲Mostar The side-trip with the highest degree of cultural hairiness—but, for many, also the most rewarding—lies to the east, in Bosnia-Herzegovina. With its iconic Old Bridge, intriguing glimpse of European Muslim lifestyles, and still-vivid examples of war damage, Mostar is unforgettable. Though not for everyone, this trip is a  must for adventurous travelers interested in Islam or in recent history. Allow a full day or more (best reached by bus or car).

Međugorje Devout Catholics may want to consider a trip to this pilgrimage site in Bosnia-Herzegovina, with a holy hill that some believe is visited regularly by an apparition of the Virgin Mary. Allow a full day or more (best reached by car or bus).

In Montenegro

▲▲The Bay of Kotor For rugged coastal scenery that arguably rivals anything in Croatia, head south of the border to Montenegro. The Bay of Kotor is a dramatic, fjord-like inlet crowned by the historic town of Kotor, with twisty Old World lanes, one of Europe's best town walls, and oodles of atmosphere. Allow a full day or more (best reached by car or bus).

The Montenegrin Interior A visit to Montenegro's scruffy but historic former capital, Cetinje, comes with a twisty drive up a mountain road and across a desolate, forgotten-feeling plateau. Allow a full day or more (best reached by car).

Budva Riviera Montenegro's best stretch of sandy beaches isn't worth a special trip, but it's a fun excuse for a drive if you've got extra time to kill. The highlight is the famous resort peninsula of Sveti Stefan. Allow a full day or more (best reached by car).

On the Mainland near Dubrovnik

▲**Cavtat** A charming resort/beach town, unassuming Cavtat holds a pair of wonderful and very local art experiences: an elaborate mausoleum designed by the sculptor Ivan Meštrović, and the house and museum of Cavtat-born modern painter Vlaho  Bukovac. Allow a few hours (best reached by boat or bus).

▲**Pelješac Peninsula** This long, narrow spit of land—between the main coastal road and Korčula Island—is a favorite of wine-lovers, who can joyride through its vineyards and sample its product. Allow a half-day to a full day (best reached by car).

Trsteno Arboretum Plant-lovers will enjoy this surprisingly engaging botanical garden just outside Dubrovnik, punctuated by a classical-style fountain and aqueduct. Allow a half-day (best reached by bus or car).

Ston A small town with giant fortifications, Ston (on the Pelješac Peninsula) is worth a short stop to scramble up its extensive walls. Allow an hour (best reached by car or bus).

Off the Coast of Dubrovnik

▲**Mljet National Park** While this largely undeveloped island is time-consuming to reach from Dubrovnik, Mljet offers an opportunity to romp on an island without all those tacky tourist towns. This is for serious nature-lovers eager to get away from civilization. Allow a full day (best reached by boat).

Lokrum Island The most convenient excursion from Dubrovnik, this little island—just a short hop offshore from the Old Port—is a good chance to get away from (some of) the tourists. Allow a few hours (best reached by boat).

Elaphite Islands This inviting archipelago offers a variety of island experiences without straying too far from Dubrovnik. With more time, Korčula (for a small town) or Mljet (for a back-to-nature experience) is better, but the "Elafiti" (as they're known) are more convenient. Allow a half-day to a full day (best reached by boat).

dent activities for the sunniest days.) Use a map to strategically line up these attractions—for example, you can easily do Trsteno, Ston, and the Pelješac Peninsula on a drive between Dubrovnik and Korčula, while Cavtat pairs nicely with a trip to the airport or Montenegro.

I've listed these day trips in order of ease from Dubrovnik—the farther down the list, the more difficult to reach. Choose the trips that sound best to you, and ask locals and other travelers for their impressions...or for new leads.

Getting There

Lokrum, Cavtat, and the Elaphite Islands are easy to reach by **excursion boat** from Dubrovnik's Old Port; Cavtat also works by bus. The other destinations are farther afield, best reached by **boat** (Mljet) or by **car** or **bus** (Montenegro, Mostar, Trsteno, Pelješac Peninsula). I've listed public transportation options for each, but consider renting a car for the day—or even splurging for your own private driver.

Alternatively, the big Atlas Travel Agency in Dubrovnik offers **guided excursions** (by bus and/or boat) to nearby des-

tinations. Popular itineraries include everything mentioned in this chapter, plus Korčula and others (figure €30-100/person, depending on the itinerary; book tickets at Atlas in Dubrovnik or at other travel agencies; Atlas tel. 020/442-574, www.atlas-croatia .com). While these excursions can be a convenient way to see otherwise difficult-to-reach destinations, the experience is generally disappointing. I've been on two of these trips, and have gotten reports about several others. The consensus is that the buses are packed, the guides are uninspired (reading from a dull script—often in multiple languages), and quality time at the destinations is short. If you have no other way to reach a place you're dying to visit, guided excursions can be worth considering. But explore your other options first—consider renting a car for the day or hiring your own driver (expensive, but less so if you can split the cost with other travelers).

Excursions run by **other companies** can be smaller, more personalized, and more satisfying than Atlas' big-bus tours. Unfortunately, since this scene is constantly evolving, it's difficult to recommend one company in particular. Look around for flyers and ask locals for their best tips—but be aware that many smaller agencies simply sell seats on the big Atlas trips.

Excursions from Dubrovnik's Old Port

At Dubrovnik's salty Old Port, local captains set up tiny booths to hawk touristy boat trips. It's fun to chat with them, page through their sun-faded photo albums, and see if they can sell you on a short cruise. The basic option is a 50-minute "panorama cruise" out into the water and back again (75 kn, departures every hour). Among your vessel choices is the **Sv. Ivan,** a cargo boat dating from 1878. Or consider visiting one of the following destinations.

In addition to the islands noted below, you can also take a boat from the Old Port to **Cavtat** (described later).

Lokrum Island
This island, just offshore from the Old Town, provides a handy escape from the city. Lokrum features a monastery-turned-Habsburg-palace, a small botanical garden, an old military fort, hiking trails, a café, some rocky beaches, and a little lake called the "Dead Sea" (Mrtvo More) that's suitable for swimming. Since

the 1970s, when Lokrum became the "Island of Love," it's been known for its nude sunbathing. If you'd like to (carefully) subject skin that's never seen the sun to those burning rays, follow the *FKK* signs from the boat dock for about five minutes to the slabs of waterfront rock, where naturists feel right at home. Boats run

regularly from Dubrovnik's Old Port (50 kn round-trip, 10 kn for a map, runs April-Sept, 2/hour, 9:00-17:00, mid-June-Aug until 19:00, none Oct-March).

Elaphite Islands (Elafiti)

This archipelago, just north of Dubrovnik, is popular among day-trippers because you can hit three different islands in a single day. The main island, **Lopud,** has most of the attractions: a lively little town, boat and bike rental, and some rare sandy beaches. The other two islands—**Koločep** and **Šipan**—are less developed and (for some) a bit boring. Along the way, you'll discover fishing ports, shady forests, and forgotten escape mansions of old Dubrovnik aristocracy. The easiest way to cruise the Elafiti is to buy an excursion at Dubrovnik's Old Port, which includes a "fish picnic" cooked up by the captain as you cruise (about 250 kn with lunch, 180 kn without, several boats depart daily around 10:30-11:00, return around 15:45-19:30; so they can buy enough food, companies prefer you to reserve and pay a 50-kn deposit the day before). You generally spend about three hours on Lopud and about an hour each on Koločep and Šipan, with about 2.5 hours on the boat. To get to the Elaphite Islands without a tour (on a cheap ferry), you'll sail from Dubrovnik's less convenient Port Gruž. Note that if you're going to Korčula or Hvar, this trip is redundant—skip it unless you've got time to kill, need a break from Dubrovnik's crowds, and want a lazy day cruising Dalmatia.

Cavtat

This sleepy little resort town—just 12 miles to the south, near the Montenegrin border—offers a milder alternative to bustling Dubrovnik. With its strategic location sheltered inside a nearly 360-degree bay, this settlement was thriving long before there was a Dubrovnik. The Greeks called it Epidaurus, while the Romans called it Epidaurum—but these days, it's Cavtat (TSAV-taht). The town is best known as a handy spot to find a room when Dubrovnik's booked up, and a fun excuse to take a cruise from Dubrovnik's Old Port. Even those suffering from beach-resort fatigue will enjoy a side-trip to Cavtat, if they appreciate local art. The restaurant- and people-lined promenade is inviting, but the town's best features are its two gems of Croatian art: a breathtaking hilltop mausoleum by the great Croatian sculptor Ivan Meštrović, and the former home-turned-museum of the Cavtat-born, early 20th-century painter Vlaho Bukovac.

Getting to Cavtat

Boats to Cavtat leave about hourly from Dubrovnik's Old Port (80 kn round-trip, 50 kn one-way, about 45 minutes each way, hourly return boats from Cavtat). The boat deposits you right along Cavtat's main seafront promenade. Note that a round-trip ticket is cheaper, but you'll have to return with the same company (rather than on whichever boat is leaving next).

You can also reach Cavtat by public **bus** #10, which leaves from Dubrovnik's main bus station and also stops at the "cable car" bus stop above the Old Town (1-2/hour, 30-40 minutes, 17 kn). The bus brings you to Cavtat's parking lot (described next). For variety, consider going to Cavtat by boat (buy a one-way ticket), then returning by bus.

Drivers find Cavtat an easy detour when heading to points south, including Montenegro or the airport; the town is well-signed off the main road. The big parking lot is at the back of Cavtat's peninsula, just around the corner from the main part of town and seafront promenade: Just walk past the TI, hook right at the busy street, and head for the waterfront.

Orientation to Cavtat

Cavtat is set within an idyllic, horseshoe-shaped harbor hemmed in by a pair of peninsulas. Tucked around the back side of the peninsula is the parking lot, left-luggage office *(garderoba)*, and **TI** (July-Aug daily 8:00-21:00; Sept and June daily 8:00-20:00; May and Oct Mon-Sat 8:00-19:00, Sun 8:00-14:00; Nov-April

Mon-Fri 8:00-15:00, closed Sat-Sun; Zidine 6, tel. 020/479-025, www.tzcavtat-konavle.hr). Cavtat is basically a one-street town, but that street is a fine pedestrian promenade running along the harbor, with a few narrow lanes winding steeply up into the hill. Capping the hill above town is a cemetery with the Meštrović mausoleum.

Sights in Cavtat

Waterfront Wander—Strolling along Cavtat's waterfront, you'll be immersed in a wrap-around bay and surrounded by Europeans vacationing well. At the near end of the promenade, notice the big water polo court roped off in the bay; Cavtat and Dubrovnik provide the core for the Croatian national water-polo team. Across the street is **St. Nicholas Church,** with a humble, dull interior (though hanging high in the altar area are  Bukovac paintings of the four evangelists). Next door is the skippable **Baltazar Bogišić Collection,** a museum with a library and other items once belonging to a wealthy lawyer. About halfway along the drag, one of the narrow lanes leading up the hill (appropriately named Bukovčeva) takes you to the fine **Vlaho Bukovac House** (described next). At the end of the main waterfront area is the **Church of Our Lady of the Snows,** commemorating a freak (and seemingly miraculous) mid-summer snowstorm in ancient Rome, believed to have been a sign sent by the Virgin Mary. Inside, above the altar, is a Vlaho Bukovac painting (from 1909) of Mary and the Baby Jesus watching over Cavtat. Climbing the steep steps up to the right of the church leads you up to Ivan Meštrović's **Račić Mausoleum** (described later). With more time, consider continuing your walk around the peninsula to its pointy tip for distant views of Dubrovnik's Old Town. This is one of the favorite spots in this area for watching the sunset. (If you continue all the way around the point, in about 20 minutes you'll wind up back at the parking lot at the start of town.)

▲**Vlaho Bukovac House (Kuća Bukovac)**—One of the joys of traveling is getting the opportunity to learn about locally beloved artists who are little known outside their homelands. Cavtat proudly introduces you to native son Vlaho Bukovac (1855-1922), who grew up in this very house and went on to become the most important Croatian painter of the modern period. Bukovac moved to New York City with his uncle at age 11, beginning a life of great adventure. After a brief career as a sailor (traveling to Peru and San Francisco), he trained as an artist in Paris, then in Zagreb. For his last 20 years, Bukovac spent his summers in Prague and his winters here in Cavtat. Touring the collection (with good English explanations), you'll get to know Bukovac's life and his works. Bukovac's paintings are mostly realistic (in accordance with his formal Salon training in Paris),

but shimmer with a hint of Post-Impressionism; his later works echo the slinky Art Nouveau Slavic pride of the Czech painter Alfons Mucha, who was Bukovac's contemporary. The ground

floor displays photos of his early life; upstairs you'll find old furniture, early sketches, and portraits of Bukovac and his family (the painting of his children's disembodied heads hanging on the wall is macabre but strangely tender). The top floor houses one big atelier room filled with can-

vases from various periods, allowing you to survey his impressive artistic development with a sweep of the head. Throughout the house are murals painted by Bukovac in his early days, offering a glimpse of a burgeoning artist who would go on to make Cavtat very proud.

Cost and Hours: 20 kn, good 40-kn guidebook; May-Oct Tue-Sat 9:00-13:00 & 16:00-20:00, Sun 16:00-20:00, closed Mon; Nov-April Tue-Sat 9:00-13:00 & 14:00-17:00, Sun 14:00-17:00, closed Mon; Bukovčeva 5, tel. 020/478-646, www.kuca-bukovac.hr.

▲▲**Račić Family Mausoleum (Mauzolej Obitelji Račić)**— This harmonious masterwork of Croatia's greatest artist is the gem of Cavtat, and worth ▲▲▲ to fans of Ivan Meštrović's powerful sculptures.

Cost and Hours: 10 kn, Mon-Sat 10:00-17:00, closed Sun and mid-Oct-mid-April. If she's not too busy, helpful Nena will show you around.

Getting There: Capping the hill above town, it's a steep 10-minute walk from the Cavtat waterfront. From the Church of Our Lady of Snows at the far end of the waterfront, climb up the stairs (following *mauzolej* signs).

Touring the Mausoleum: Over the course of one tragic year, all four members of the wealthy Račić family—father, mother, son, daughter—died of the Spanish flu. From 1920-1922, in accordance with their will, Ivan Meštrović was commissioned to craft their final resting place. He used the opportunity to create a cohesive meditation on Christian faith and death, made entirely of brilliant white stone from the island of Brač. As you enter, take a moment to appreciate how the interior ponders birth, life, and death. The four inner walls of the octagonal hall hold the tombs of the departed; above each tomb, an angel lovingly carries their soul up to heaven—spiriting them into a cupola studded with angel heads. The floor has symbols for the four evangelists: Matthew (angel), Mark (lion), Luke (bull), and John (eagle). The chapel to the left holds a crucifix; to the right, an altar to St. Rok (the patron saint of illness, to whom the chapel is dedicated—the dog licking the wound in his leg is his symbol). Straight ahead is an altar with Mary holding the Baby Jesus above a relief of the Lamb of God, and below that, Jesus' body being taken down from the cross. Flanking this altar, notice the bases of the twisting candelabras: alternating angels look down to honor the dead. The chapel rewards those who linger over the details, such as the bronze doors, with four saints, Glagolitic inscriptions, and the 12 Apostles. The saints chosen for this door preach both ecumenism and Yugoslav unity: Cyril and Method (the Byzantine missionaries who first brought Christianity to this region), along with a Catholic bishop (Bishop Gregory of Nin) and an Orthodox saint (St. Sava). Taken together, the mausoleum is an astonishing display of talent, especially considering it was Meštrović's first architectural work.

Nearby: The mausoleum sits in the middle of a tranquil cemetery that's still used for the funerals of Cavtat residents (a plot costs €20,000). As you exit the mausoleum, head straight out and a bit to the right to find two communal graves for the poor—with smaller markers lined up along a large plinth. Also in this cemetery is the grave of the artist Vlaho Bukovac.

Near Cavtat

A village near Cavtat, **Čilipi,** hosts a Sunday-morning folk festival through the summer (Easter-Oct, starting at 9:00). There's a special Mass at the church, an open-air market, and—starting at 11:15—a costumed folk-dancing show (tel. 020/771-007, www .cilipifolklor.hr).

Trsteno Arboretum

Take a stroll through the shaded, relaxing botanical garden in Trsteno (worth ▲), just up the coast from Dubrovnik. Non-gardeners may find it a bit dull, but Trsteno is a horticultural-

ist's heaven. Spread over 63 acres on a bluff overlooking the sea, this arboretum features hundreds of different Mediterranean, Asian, and American plants (each one labeled in six languages, including English). The whole complex is laced with easy footpaths and sprinkled with fun attractions—a column-studded Renaissance Garden, a desolate villa, a little chapel, an old mill and olive-oil press, and a seaview pavilion.

As you wander, the world melts away and you're alone with the sounds of nature: wind, water, birds, and frogs. The garden's centerpiece is the whimsical 18th-century Neptune Fountain, featuring the god of the sea flanked by water-spouting nymphs and fishes, and holding court over a goldfish-stocked, lily-padded pond. Circling around behind the fountain, you'll discover that it's fed by an impressive 230-foot-long aqueduct that was built in the 15th-century.

Cost and Hours: 35 kn, daily May-Oct 8:00-19:00, Nov-April 8:00-16:00, tel. 020/751-019.

Nearby: On the waterfront below the arboretum, next to the little village harbor, you'll see the shell of a once-grand 18th-century palace, which was damaged during the siege of Dubrovnik and is now abandoned. It's still owned by the government, but investors are lining up for a chance to buy this prime real estate—possibly the most desirable ruin in Croatia.

Getting There: Trsteno works best with a car, particularly if you're taking your time driving to Dubrovnik from the north (the main coastal road goes through the town of Trsteno, right past the well-marked arboretum). You also have two bus options from Dubrovnik (around 20 kn, 20-30 minutes). Any long-distance northbound bus can drop you in Trsteno—ask about the next bus at the main station. Alternatively, the slower local buses #12 and #15 also reach Trsteno. Coming back from Trsteno to Dubrovnik is trickier: Wait at the bus stop with the glass canopy by the park entrance and wave down any Dubrovnik-bound bus that passes (at least hourly).

Pelješac Peninsula

North of Trsteno, the skinny, 55-mile-long Pelješac (PEHL-yeh-shahts) Peninsula—practically an honorary island—splits off from the Croatian coastline as if about to drift away to Italy. (The far tip of Pelješac comes within a stone's throw of Korčula island.) This sparsely populated peninsula, famous for its rugged terrain—and the grapes that thrive here—is worth a detour for wine-lovers. But its heavily fortified town of Ston, just a short side-trip from the main coastal road, merits a stretch-your-legs visit for anyone. Notice that if you're connecting from Korčula to anywhere else in Croatia by car, you'll probably be taking the ferry to the Pelješac Peninsula anyway; consider slowing down to sample a few wines, to scramble up the walls at Ston, or to have a meal at Mali Ston.

Getting There: Buses between Dubrovnik and Korčula traverse the Pelješac Peninsula, but drivers have the option of stopping where they like (such as at Ston or a winery). Some public buses also stop at Ston.

Ston

The town of Ston, at the base of the peninsula, is the gateway to Pelješac. This "Great Wall of Croatia" town is famous for the impressive wall that climbs up the mountain behind it (about a half-mile encloses the town itself, while another three miles clamber up the hillsides). The unassuming town was heavily fortified (starting in 1333) for two reasons: to defend its strategic location, where mountains and bays create  a bottleneck along the road from Dubrovnik to Pelješac, near the Republic of Dubrovnik's northern boundary; and to protect its impressive salt pans, which still produce salt. Filling a low-lying plain that sprawls in front of Ston's doorstep, these pans provided

A Bridge Too Far?

If you're driving along the coast between Split and Dubrovnik, you may be surprised when you have to stop and show your passport to enter another country—Bosnia-Herzegovina, around the resort town of Neum. How is it that Bosnia wound up with its very own five-and-a-half-mile stretch of the Dalmatian Coast? During the heyday of the Republic of Dubrovnik, the city's leaders granted this land to the Ottoman Empire to provide a buffer between Dubrovnik's holdings and the Republic of Venice, to the north. (They knew the Venetians would never enter the territory of the Ottomans—their feared enemy—in order to invade Dubrovnik.) Later, as the borders of Europe were being redrawn in modern times, Bosnia retained possession of this strip of land as a sort of inheritance from their former rulers.

For years, coastal Bosnians and their Croatian neighbors have coexisted, albeit tensely at times. Prices for hotel rooms, groceries, and other staples are slightly cheaper in Neum, whose rest stops lure tourist buses with low prices and generous kickbacks for bus drivers. Visitors are inconvenienced by having to go through a passport checkpoint as they enter Bosnia and again, just a few minutes later, as they exit Bosnia. From a practical standpoint, this is rarely an issue. But on busy days, there can be lines, and it's always smart to have your passport and rental car's "green card" (proof of insurance) ready.

Croatians are irritated with the red tape, and—even more—by the way Neum merchants undersell the Croatian alternatives nearby. As Croatia extends its expressway southward, the most logical approach would be a route through Bosnia to Dubrovnik. But some Croatian politicians have been looking for a way to avoid Neum altogether. One solution is to build a 1.5-mile-long bridge from just north of Neum to the Pelješac Peninsula, then re-join the coastal road back in Croatia, just south of Neum—effectively bypassing Bosnian territory. Environmentalists worry about the impact the bridge will have on the ecosystem around Mali Ston. But, because of the proposed bridge's popularity with a certain segment of the voting population, work actually began on this project prior to a recent election (notice that one mountaintop on Pelješac has already been cleared). After the election—and with the global economic crisis—plans were put on hold. It remains to be seen whether this very expensive project will ever come to fruition...and if so, whether the bridge will be completed before Croatia and Bosnia both join the EU and open their borders anyway.

Dubrovnik with much of its wealth, back in the days when salt was worth more than its weight in gold. The pans would be flooded with saltwater, then sealed and left to evaporate—leaving the salt easy to harvest.

Today, the sleepy town—with more than its share of outdoor cafés and restaurants—is notable only for the chance to scramble up its massive **fortifications** (park your car in the big lot, then cross the street into town and look right; the entrance to the walls is in the big tower). These walls have been undergoing an extensive restoration, and the long, skinny strip running over the ridge to the town of Mali Ston (described

next) is already complete. For a short wall experience, you can just do a circle around the stout lower walls (about 20-30 minutes); for a more serious hike, you can climb all the way up and over to Mali Ston (figure 45-60 minutes). Be warned that the walls—with all that glistening limestone reflecting heat—are much hotter than ground level, and there's virtually no shade (30 kn to enter walls regardless of how far you walk, daily May-Sept 8:00-19:00, April and Oct 8:00-18:00, Nov-March generally 9:00-16:00).

Other than the walls, there's not much to do in Ston. The town's deserted feel is a result of a devastating 1996 earthquake, from which Ston is still rebuilding. But there are several inviting cafés for a lazy drink. If you want a meal, skip Ston's mediocre offerings and head over to Mali Ston instead.

Eating near Ston, in Mali Ston: From Ston, the walls scamper over a ridge to its little sister, the bayside village of Mali Ston ("Small Ston"). Surrounded by a similar, but smaller, fortified wall, Mali Ston is known for its many mussel and oyster farms, and for its good restaurants. A local favorite is **Kapetanova Kuća,** a memorable restaurant with a fine location on Mali Ston's waterfront. Celebrity chef Lidija Kralj prides herself on her unpretentious but delicious food, made with fresh produce from the restaurant's own garden. For dessert, her bizarre macaroni cake is tastier than it sounds (10-kn cover charge, 75-100-kn pastas, 100-130-kn seafood and meat dishes, daily 9:00-23:00, tel. 020/754-264).

Pelješac Wine Country

Farther along, the sparsely developed Pelješac Peninsula is blanketed with vineyards. Wine is a big draw here, and several vintners open their doors for passing visitors to sample their products. While it's a bit distant from Dubrovnik (about a two-hour drive to the heart of the wine-producing area), it's a worthwhile pilgrimage for wine-lovers and an easy stop-off for those driving from Korčula.

Tours of Pelješac: To really do the peninsula justice, consider hiring a guide to take you for a spin around Pelješac. **Sasha Lušić,** who runs the D'Vino Wine Bar in Dubrovnik, is a gregarious Aussie-Croat guide. He prides himself on taking you to a wide variety of vintners, who represent the best of what's happening here. Sasha's tours can go late into the evening (also offers cheaper half-day tours to the Molinat area closer to Dubrovnik, www .dvino.net, sasha@dvino.net). Other Dubrovnik-based drivers also do good wine tours (which also include several other worthwhile, scenic stops), including **Petar Vlašić.**

◑ Self-Guided Driving Tour: I've arranged this tour in the order you'll come from the tip of Pelješac (Orebić, just across the channel from Korčula). If you're doing it from Dubrovnik, begin by driving all the way to the village of Potomje (you can skip the section between there and Orebić) and visit the wineries on your way back (since it's a long, skinny peninsula, you'll have to backtrack anyway). I've included a detour to some of Croatia's finest (and largely undiscovered) vineyards, and saved the best wines for last.

If you're crossing from Korčula Island, you'll begin the tour in **Orebić.** It's basically one main road from here back to Ston (where you'll meet up with the main coastal road to Dubrovnik or Split), so you can't really get lost—though we will make an off-the-beaten-path vineyard detour.

Follow the main road (toward *Ston*) up, up, up to a dramatic **viewpoint** (there's a pullout on the right with benches) looking back toward Korčula. The jagged cliffs to your left are the Pelješac Peninsula (where we're about to drive), and the island straight ahead (left of Korčula) is Mljet National Park. On a clear day, you can almost see to Italy. This also gives you a good view of the two best wine-growing regions of Pelješac: Below you and to the right, you can see some vineyards in the **Postup** region; to the left (not quite visible from here) are the vineyards of **Dingač.** Both areas are steeply angled, so they catch a maximum amount of sun, which creates very sweet grapes that produce high-alcohol, very dark (actually called "black" in Croatian) wine with strong legs (or, as Croatians call them, "tears"). The rugged, rocky limestone provides natural irrigation (since water can flow freely through it), and the high winds here keep off bugs and other pests. It all adds up to extremely healthy vines; because disease is rare, pesticides are not needed.

Continuing along the road, you'll crest the hill and drop down into a **plateau** surrounded by cliffs. The vines you'll see in this so-called "continental" area are the same kind of grapes as in Postup and Dingač, but they receive less sun and are less sweet. These *plavac mali* ("little blue") grapes are a distant relative of California Zinfandel and Italian *primitivo*. Notice that many of the vines appear to be almost wild; these are older vineyards, which aren't irrigated, so they must let the vines grow this way to help them survive the hot summer months. This method maximizes yield but reduces quality. Newer vineyards are irrigated and use guide wires, and generally look more manicured.

Soon you'll arrive in the village of **Potomje,** which is at the center of this important wine-growing area. Several wineries cluster here, including some that are open for tastings and tours. Two are particularly accessible to visitors and—while a bit touristy (with big bus tours passing through occasionally)—offer a helpful introduction to Pelješac wines: Madirazza and Matuško. Both are staffed by friendly

English-speakers who are eager to introduce you to their wines; while the tastings are free, they're hoping you'll buy a bottle or two. Both are open long hours daily (around 8:00-20:00, close earlier in shoulder season, generally closed Nov-March—but call ahead and they may be able to open for you, cash only).

The reds are the real draw here; I'd skip the whites. The wines, which are quite fruity, come in various types. In general, bottles marked with the type of grape *(plavac mali)* are lower-quality, from the vines here in the valley. The ones marked with the specific region (Dingač and Postup) come from the sunny slopes and are of better quality, more full bodied, and more expensive; they go well with red meat and dark chocolate. Both Madirazza and Matuško also have various brandies to try (including *travarica,* an herb-infused brandy).

First, near the far end of town, look for the big, pink building of the **Madirazza** winery. Notice the roses that line the vineyards—like a canary in a coal mine, these are more quickly affected by disease than the vines, offering an early-warning system in the event of an unwanted infestation. Madirazza's fairly acidic wines cost 30-90 kn per bottle (mobile 099-700-5146, www.dingac.hr).

Across the main road from Madirazza's parking lot is a smaller road (marked with a *Matuško* sign) leading to the **Matuško** winery. With smoother wines than Madirazza's, this place also has a sprawling network of atmospheric cellars where tour groups sip wines between aging barrels (20-110-kn bottles, most 20-60 kn, reserve bottles for 150-700 kn, free tastings upstairs, good place for a WC stop, tel. 020/742-399, www.matusko-vina.hr). **Miličić,** also in Potomje, is a well-regarded winery, but its hours are less predictable than Madirazza and Matuško.

Very near the Matuško parking lot, look for the **tunnel** through the mountain marked *Dingač Winery,* with the picture of a donkey. Before this tunnel was dug, beasts of burden trod surefootedly up and over this mountain to carry the grapes from Dingač, on the far side, to this village. The donkey remains a symbol of this wine-growing region. In the 1970s, this tunnel was built to make everyone's lives easier. Take advantage of it by driving through the mountain and into another world.

Popping out at the sea, you're in the heart of the **Dingač** vineyards. Turn left (toward *Borak*) and drive on the one-lane road

above all those vines, with a green and jagged waterline that looks almost Celtic. Croatia's best reds are lovingly raised right here, bathed in ample sunshine and struggling against a very rocky soil. At the fork, continue down to the right, toward *Borak;* at the next fork, when the Borak road

turns sharply to the right, keep going straight onto the smaller road.

As you enter an area of trees, look across the harbor to see a building perched on a cliff over the water—that's our next stop.

Turn right to pass through the village of Trstanik and drive along its little waterfront. At the far end of town, on the way up the hill, turn into the parking lot for the **Grgić** winery. Perhaps the best-known and best-regarded Croatian vintner, Mike Grgić's facility here is less appealing than the others

we've visited, and you have to pay for the tasting (20 kn)...but the quality of the wine compensates. Keeping things simple, Grgić does a white wine (*pošip,* with grapes grown on Korčula but produced here, 135 kn per bottle) and a red wine (210 kn per bottle); breaking with convention, he names his red simply *plavac mali* partly to help promote this largely unknown and underappreciated grape (grown here in Trstanik and in Dingač). He also sells wines from his California winery, Grgich Hills, at or below their California prices (230-440 kn). While Grgić's staff doesn't speak much English, they enjoy sharing the wines (Mon-Fri 10:00-17:00, sometimes also Sat-Sun—call ahead, tel. 020/748-090).

Exiting the winery, turn right (uphill) and twist up to the main road, where you'll turn right, toward Ston. (Another good winery, **Roso,** is to the left, back toward Potomje in the village of Kuna, but its opening times are unpredictable.) From here, you'll continue straight along all the way to Ston. You may be tempted by the *vino* signs in **Janjina,** but these are geared mainly for Croatians buying table wine in bulk—100 liters at a time. After Drače, the road takes you along the **Bay of Ston,** which is famous for its shell-fish production. Here where the Neretva River (which runs under Mostar's Old Bridge) empties into the sea, conditions are perfect for cultivating mussels, oysters, and clams. You can already see the mainland on the far side of the bay. The road climbs up once more, passing a viewpoint café overlooking the dock for the ferry to the national park on Mljet Island, before continuing into the walled town of Ston.

Leaving Ston, turn right (toward Dubrovnik) once you hit the main road; from here, it's about an hour back into town. En route, watch out for the speed traps at the towns of Doli and Orešac.

Mljet National Park

Carefully protected against modern development, the island hideaway of Mljet National Park offers a unique back-to-nature escape. With ample opportunities for hiking, swimming, biking, and boating—and without a nightclub, tacky T-shirt, or concrete "beach" pad in sight—Mljet (muhl-YAYT) is a potential highlight for active, outdoorsy travelers.

Though Mljet Island is one of Dalmatia's largest, it has fewer than 1,500 residents. Nearly three-quarters of the island is covered in forest, leaving it remarkably untamed. Aside from its beautiful national park, Mljet has inspired some of the most memorable tales of the Croatian coast—the poet Homer, his protagonist Ulysses, and the Apostle Paul all spent time here...or so the locals love to boast.

Many Croatians swoon over Mljet. Take it with a grain of salt. They appreciate it primarily for its relative lack of people. One local told me, "Mljet is basically Hvar or Korčula with no towns." For foreign visitors, the park, while enjoyable, is a bit overrated. Still, if a peaceful, uncrowded island sounds like your kind of scene, make the trip.

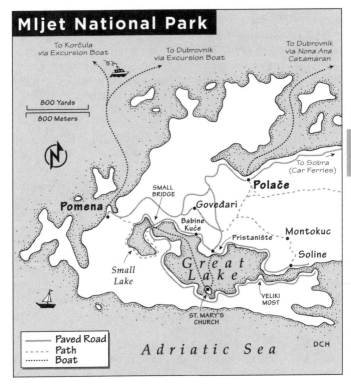

Planning Your Time

Thanks to a handy catamaran connection, Mljet works perfectly as a full-day side-trip from Dubrovnik (only possible in summer). But because of inconvenient boat schedules to other destinations, it's challenging to splice it into a one-way itinerary (say, between Korčula and Dubrovnik). So if you want to visit Mljet, either do it as a day trip on your own from Dubrovnik, or buy a package day-trip excursion from Korčula, Hvar, or Split. For details, see "Mljet Connections," at the end of this chapter.

No matter how you arrive, one day is plenty for Mljet. I've suggested a day-trip plan under "Sights on Mljet."

Be warned that everything's very seasonal and weather-dependent, so visiting outside of peak season (June-Sept) may come with some frustration.

Orientation to Mljet

The island of Mljet is long (23 miles) and skinny (less than two miles wide). The national park occupies the western third of the island. You're likely to reach Mljet via one of three port towns.

Polače (POH-lah-cheh) and **Pomena** (POH-meh-nah) are handy entry points into the national park, while **Sobra** (SOH-brah) is much less convenient (a 1.25-hour bus trip across the island from the park). The *Nona Ana* catamaran from Dubrovnik puts in at Polače and Sobra; most excursions use Pomena; and the car ferries (the big Jadrolinija Korčula-Dubrovnik car ferry, plus smaller ferries to the mainland) use Sobra.

Polače and Pomena flank the heart of the national park, a pair of saltwater "lakes" called simply **Great Lake** (Veliko Jezero) and **Small Lake** (Malo Jezero). The two bodies of water meet at a cute little bridge, appropriately named **Small Bridge** (Mali Most), where you can rent kayaks and bikes and catch a boat out to the little **island** in the Great Lake. A 15-minute walk around the Great Lake from the Small Bridge brings you to **Pristanište** (meaning, roughly, "transit hub"), where you can also catch a boat to the island or a shuttle bus to Polače. The nearby cliff-climbing town of **Govedari** is home to many of the people who work at the park, but is not interesting to tourists.

Everything's well-signed, and there are enough landmarks that it's difficult to get really lost. Even so, I bought the detailed park map (at the entry kiosk) and was glad I had it.

Tourist Information

The **TI** is in Polače, just across from where the *Nona Ana* catamaran from Dubrovnik docks (mid-June-Aug daily 8:00-20:00; early June and Sept daily 8:00-13:00 & 17:00-20:00; Oct-May Mon-Fri 8:00-13:00, closed Sat-Sun; tel. 020/744-186). The island's lone hotel, the **Hotel Odisej** in Pomena, acts as a second tourist information point. The hotel is a hub of services for visitors (whether you stay there or not): bike, scooter, car, and boat rentals; scuba diving lessons; walking tours around the island; cruises to some of the island's caves; and even help finding private accommodations. For more on the hotel, see "Sleeping and Eating on Mljet," later.

The general-information website for the island (which covers the towns, Hotel Odisej, *sobe* and apartments, and more) is www.mljet.hr; for information on the national park, visit www.np-mljet.hr.

Arrival in Mljet

At Polače: Arriving on the *Nona Ana* catamaran from Dubrovnik, exit the boat to the right, walk a few steps, and look for the TI on your left. A few minutes' walk up the coast (near the Roman ruins) is a kiosk where you can buy your park entry ticket and catch a minibus to the Pristanište transit hub at the Great Lake (runs hourly, scheduled to coincide with boat arrival). From Pristanište, you can take a boat out to the island in the Great Lake (about hourly), or walk around the lake toward the Small Bridge, Small Lake, and on to Pomena.

At Pomena: If you arrive at Pomena, you're most likely on a package excursion, in which case your park entry ticket is included and you'll probably stick with your guide for a while. But in case you're on your own, exit the boat to the left (passing Hotel Odisej) and buy your park entry ticket at the kiosk. A few steps up the road beyond the kiosk, you'll see a shortcut to the right that takes you up and down some steps on your way to the Small Lake; once at the lake, bear left and continue to the Small Bridge, where you can catch the boat to the island in the Great Lake or rent a bike or kayak.

Note that there's no official bus between Polače and Pomena, but Hotel Odisej operates a shuttle to coincide with the Dubrovnik catamaran. Several informal minibus-taxis can also take you for a fee.

At Sobra: If you come on a car ferry, you're in for a long haul over to Polače and Pomena—about a 1.25-hour bus trip on twisty roads. Avoid arriving via Sobra unless you're desperate.

Sights on Mljet

▲Mljet National Park

All of the following attractions are inside the park.

Cost and Hours: The steep 90-kn entry fee includes the shuttle bus from Polače to the Great Lake and a boat ride to the lake's island. The park is open daily May-mid-Oct 7:00-19:00, shorter hours in shoulder season, closed Nov-Feb; park information tel. 020/744-041.

Day-Trip Plan: If you're doing the trip on your own from Dubrovnik, try this itinerary: From Polače, take the minibus to Pristanište, where you can catch the boat to the island in the Great Lake. Take the boat back to Mali Most (Small Bridge), where you can rent a bike for a ride along the shore of the Great Lake. If you're heating up, take a dip in the Small Lake at the beach near the Small Bridge. When you're ready for a bit of civilization, walk into Pomena and relax by the seaside, then take the hotel's shuttle bus or a minibus-taxi back to Polače to catch the catamaran back home to Dubrovnik. With more energy, skip Pomena and hike up to Montokuc (you can hike down to Polače on the other side).

The Lakes—The "Great Lake" and "Small Lake" are technically saltwater bays—fed by the sea and affected by ocean currents (as you'll clearly see if you're at the little channel by the Small Bridge at the right time of day). Scientists love these lakes, which contain various shellfish species unique to Mljet.

The Tales of Mljet

For a mostly undeveloped island, Mljet has had a surprisingly busy history. Home to Illyrians, Greeks, Romans, Slavs, Venetians, Habsburgs, Yugoslavs, and now Croatians, the island has hosted some interesting visitors (or supposed visitors) that it loves to brag about.

Around the eighth century B.C., the Greek epic poet Homer possibly spent time here. He was so inspired by Mljet that he used it as the setting for one of the adventures of his hero Ulysses (a.k.a. Odysseus). This is the island where Ulysses fell in love with a beautiful nymph named Calypso and shacked up with her in a cave for seven years. Today there's a much-vaunted "Ulysses' Cave" (Odisejeva Spilja), a 40-minute hike below the island's main town, Babino Polje (at the far end of the island—skip it unless you're a Ulysses groupie).

Flash forward nearly a millennium, when a real-life traveler found his way to Mljet. According to the Bible (Acts 28), the Apostle Paul was shipwrecked on an island called "Melita"—likely this one—for three months. While on the island, Paul was bitten by a deadly snake, which he threw into a fire. The natives were amazed that he wasn't affected by the poison, and he proceeded to cure their ailments. This event was long believed to have happened on the similarly named isle of Malta, in the Mediterranean Sea. But more recently, many historians began to believe that Paul was on Mljet. The most convincing argument: Malta never had poisonous snakes. Incidentally, Mljet no longer does, either—the Habsburgs imported an army of Indian mongooses to rid the island of problematic serpents. Because of this historical footnote, people from Mljet are nicknamed "mongooses" by other Croatians.

The heroics continue with today's "mongooses." There have been more than 100 fires on the island in the last 20 years (most caused by lightning, some by careless visitors), but only three have spread and caused significant destruction. That's because the people of Mljet—well aware of the fragility of the island that provides their income—are also a crack volunteer firefighting force, ready to spring into action and save their island at the first wisp of smoke.

The Island—The main activity in the park is taking a boat out to the Great Lake's little island-in-an-island (boats depart about hourly from the Small Bridge and from Pristanište). The tiny island's main landmark is St. Mary's Church (Sv. Marija) and the attached monastery, left behind by Benedictine monks who lived on Mljet starting in the 12th century. Though the monastery complex has been modified over the ages, fragments of the original Romanesque structure still survive. You can hike the easy trail up to the top of the island, passing remains of fortifications and old chapels, and look for the island's only permanent residents: a handful of goats, donkeys, and chickens. You'll have about an hour on the island, but it only takes half that to see everything—then relax with an overpriced drink at the restaurant by the boat dock.

Biking—The Great Lake is surrounded by a paved, mostly level road that's good for an hour or two of pedaling (unfortunately, you can't go all the way around because the path is broken by the channel connecting the lakes to the sea). The unpaved path around the Small Lake is rough and rocky, making biking there more difficult. The handiest place to rent a bike for a quick ride around the Great Lake is right at the lake itself, by the Small Bridge. Other bike rental points are scattered around the island, including in both Polače and Pomena. But those towns are separated from the lakes—and from each other—by steep hills, making cycling from either town to the lakes a headache for casual bikers.

Swimming—Options are everywhere, most temptingly at the Great Lake and Small Lake. In fact, even though it's fed by seawater, the Small Lake is always about seven degrees Fahrenheit warmer than the sea. The beach by the Small Bridge is particularly handy (but there are no showers or WCs).

Boating—You can rent kayaks at the Small Bridge. Motorized boats—except for the occasional local resident's dinghy—aren't allowed on the island's lakes.

Hiking to Montokuc—The most rewarding hike takes you up to the national park's highest point, Montokuc. At 830 feet above sea level, this is a serious hike up a steep hill—skip it unless you're in good shape, and be sure to bring water (allow at least one hour round-trip at a steady pace). The trail runs between Polače, at the north end of the island, and the village of Soline, beyond the far end of the Great Lake (past the old, broken bridge called Veliki Most). If you're doing this or any other hike, the park map is essential (sold at park entry kiosks and other merchants).

Sleeping and Eating on Mljet

(€1 = about $1.40, country code: 385, area code: 020)
$$$ Hotel Odisej, the only hotel on the island, has more charm than most renovated communist hotels. Sitting right on the waterfront, with 157 rooms, it's a predictably comfortable home base (July-Aug: non-view Sb-€80-90, Sb with sea view and balcony-€95-110, non-view Db-€100-120, Db with sea view or balcony-€120-145, Db with sea view and balcony-€140-160; cheaper in shoulder season, no extra charge for 1- or 2-night stays, closed mid-Oct-mid-April, air-con, elevator, tel. 020/362-111, fax 020/744-042, www.hotelodisej.hr, info@hotelodisej.hr).

**$-$$ Sobe *and Apartments:* ** Mljet has a wide range of private accommodations, with a few in each town or village. *Sobe* run about €15-20 per person in peak season, or €10-15 off-season; for apartments, figure €40-60 for two people in peak season, €25-40 off-season (20 percent more for 1- or 2-night stays). If you arrive without a room, the TI in Polače or Hotel Odisej in Pomena can help you find something. If you're looking in advance, check out the island website, www.mljet.hr. I'd choose a place in the population centers of Polače or Pomena (for their easy access to the park) or in the cute Great Lake-front village of Babine Kuće (near the Small Bridge). To really get away from it all, little end-of-the-road Soline (near the channel connecting the Great Lake to the sea) is rustic and remote, and has several options.

For **eating,** many good restaurants are scattered around the island. There isn't one that's particularly worth seeking out—just eat when it fits your itinerary (or bring a picnic).

Mljet Connections

To Dubrovnik and Korčula by Catamaran: The speedy, made-for-day-trippers catamaran called *Nona Ana* runs daily in each direction between Dubrovnik and Mljet. In the summer (June-Sept), it goes every morning from **Dubrovnik** to **Sobra,** then on to **Polače** (the best stop for the national park, 1.75 hours, 54 kn). In the peak months of July and August, it sometimes continues to **Korčula** town (1 hour beyond Polače, 4/week) and **Lastovo Island** (2.25 hours beyond Polače, 2/week). In the afternoon, it returns to Dubrovnik via the same route, bringing tired but happy side-trippers back to the city. It's less handy in the winter (Oct-May), when it departs Dubrovnik in the afternoon and goes only as far as Sobra and Polače. Confirm the schedule at www.gv-line.hr, and double-check your plans with the Dubrovnik TI. To be sure you get a ticket in peak season, show up early (at least an hour before the boat leaves).

Even though this boat works perfectly in summer for day-tripping from Dubrovnik to Mljet National Park, it doesn't work as well for connecting to Korčula, because it just goes there on some mornings and is handy only if you're heading north after spending the night on Mljet.

Between Mljet and Other Destinations: All other destinations (including Hvar, Split, and day-tripping from Korčula) are more conveniently connected to Mljet by **excursion** than by public transit. The approximately €50 price tag for an all-day excursion seems high, but remember that it includes the 90-kn (€12) park admission fee and saves you the hassle of getting to the island on your own. Otherwise, you can reach Mljet only by the **car ferry** that stops at Sobra (2-3/week in peak season going between Dubrovnik and Korčula, plus other connections from the mainland).

There's no good, straightforward way to visit Mljet in a single day en route between destinations (say, on the way from Dubrovnik to Korčula). But it might work if you're lucky, flexible, and adventurous. If the excursion boats aren't full—and they rarely are—you can buy a last-minute, one-way ticket for a fraction of the full price. So, for example, you can take the morning catamaran from Dubrovnik to Mljet, enjoy the park, then continue on to Korčula in the evening on one of the day-trip boats. (It works vice versa, too: Pay for a morning excursion from Korčula to Mljet, then continue to Dubrovnik on the public catamaran.) Call the staff at Hotel Odisej—who know which excursions are coming to town—the night before to see if they have any ideas. The downside: You can't arrange this in advance, and there's always a chance the boat will be full—and you'll be stranded on Mljet for the night.

MONTENEGRO
Crna Gora

MONTENEGRO

*The Bay of Kotor • Kotor • The Montenegrin Interior •
The Budva Riviera*

If Dubrovnik is the grand finale of a Croatian vacation, then Montenegro is the encore. One of Europe's youngest nations awaits you just south of the border, with dramatic scenery, a refreshing rough-around-the-edges appeal, and the excitement of a new independence. If you're looking for the "next Croatia," this is it.

And yet, crossing the border, you know you've left sleek, prettified-for-tourists Croatia for a place that's gritty, raw, and a bit exotic. While Croatia's showpiece Dalmatian Coast avoided the drab, boxy dullness of the Yugoslav era, less affluent Montenegro wasn't so lucky. Between the dramatic cliffs and time-passed villages, you'll drive past grimy, broken-down apartment blocks and some truly unfortunate concrete architecture. Montenegro is also a noticeably poorer country than its northern neighbor...with all that entails.

Historically, Montenegro has been even more of a crossroads of cultures than the rest of the Balkans. In some ways, there are two Montenegros: the remote, rugged, rustic mountaintop kingdom that feels culturally close to Serbia; and this chapter's focus, the staggeringly strategic, sun-drenched coastline that has attracted a steady stream of rulers over the millennia. At one point or another, just about every group you can imagine—from the usual suspects (Venetians, Austrians) to oddball one-offs (Bulgarian kingdoms, Napoleon's Ljubljana-based Illyrian Provinces, Russian czars)—has planted its flag here. In spite of their schizophrenic lineage, or maybe because of it, Montenegrins have forged a unique cultural identity that defies many of the preconceived notions of the Balkans. Are they like Serbs or Croats? Do they use the Cyrillic or the Roman alphabet? Do they worship the Roman Catholic God or the Eastern Orthodox one? Yes, all of the above.

Since gaining independence in 2006, the Montenegrin coast has become a powerful magnet for a very specific breed of traveler: millionaires from Russia (and, to a lesser extent, Saudi Arabia), who have chosen to turn this impressionable, fledgling country—with its gorgeous coastline—into their very own Riviera. The Tivat airport is jammed with charter flights from Moscow, signs along the coast advertise Russian-language radio stations, and an extravagant luxury yacht marina is being built near Tivat (Porto Montenegro, www.portomontenegro.com). And so Montenegro finds itself in an awkward position: trying to cultivate an image as a high-roller luxury paradise, while struggling to upgrade what is—in places—a nearly Third World infrastructure. Glittering new €500-a-night boutique hotels are built, then suffer power and water outages. It sometimes feels as if Montenegro is skipping right past an important middle step in its tourist development (that of an on-the-rise, moderately priced destination). I guess what I'm saying is...lower your expectations, and don't expect a fancy facade and high prices to come with predictable quality.

Still, nothing can mar the natural beauty of Montenegro's mountains, bays, and forests. For a look at the untamed Adriatic, a

spin on the winding road around Montenegro's steep and secluded Bay of Kotor is a must. The area's main town, also called Kotor, has been protected from centuries of would-be invaders by its position at the deepest point of the fjord—and by its imposing town wall, which scrambles in a zig-zag line up the mountain behind it. Wander the enjoyably seedy streets of Kotor, drop into some Orthodox churches, and sip a coffee at an al fresco café.

With more time, romantic historians can corkscrew up into the mountains to visit the remote original capital of the country at Cetinje, beach bums will head for the Budva Riviera, and celebrity-seekers can daydream about past glories at the striking hotel-peninsula of Sveti Stefan.

Getting to Montenegro

This chapter is designed for day-tripping to Montenegro from Dubrovnik; all of the sights are within about a three-hour drive of Dubrovnik, and within about an hour of each other.

By Car: Driving is easily the best option, giving you maximum flexibility for sightseeing—but be aware of possible border delays (see "Helpful Hints," later). I've narrated a handy self-guided

Montenegro Almanac

Official Name: After being part of "Yugoslavia," then "Serbia and Montenegro," it's now the Republic of Montenegro (Republika Crna Gora)—which means "Black Mountain" in the native language. It might have gotten its name from sailors who saw darkly forested cliffs as they approached, or it may have been named for a mythical mountain in the country's interior.

Snapshot History: Long overshadowed by its Croatian and Serbian neighbors, Montenegro finally achieved independence on June 3, 2006, in a landmark vote to secede from Serbia—its influential and sometimes overbearing "big brother."

Population: Montenegro is home to 662,000 people. Of these, the vast majority are Eastern Orthodox Christians (45 percent Montenegrins, 29 percent Serbs), with minority groups of Muslims (including Bosniaks and Albanians, about 13 percent total) and Catholics (1 percent).

Area: 5,415 square miles (slightly smaller than Connecticut).

Red Tape: Americans and Canadians need only a passport (no visa required) to enter Montenegro. Drivers must pay a €10 "eco-tax" at the border.

Geography: Montenegro is characterized by a rugged, rocky terrain that rises straight up from the Adriatic and almost immediately becomes a steep mountain range. The country has 182 miles of coastline, about a third of which constitutes the Bay of Kotor. The only real city is the dreary capital in the interior, Podgorica (144,000 people). Each of Yugoslavia's six republics had a town called Titograd, and Podgorica was Montenegro's.

Economy: Upon declaring independence in 2006, Montenegro's economy was weak. But the privatization of its economy

---

driving tour of the Bay of Kotor, and another for the most accessible slice of the Montenegrin interior. Even if you don't have a rental car during your Dubrovnik visit, consider renting one just for the day to visit Montenegro. Perhaps most satisfying—but expensive—is to hire your own Dubrovnik-based driver to bring you here. While this is pricey (€250 for the day), you can try to team up with other travelers to split the cost.

By Bus: Bus service between Dubrovnik and Montenegro is workable but infrequent (2/day each way between Dubrovnik and Kotor town, 2.5 hours). Unfortunately, the bus schedules don't line up conveniently for a day trip—you can take a morning bus from Dubrovnik to Kotor (departing Dubrovnik around 10:30), then take an early-afternoon bus back to Dubrovnik (departing Kotor at 14:45)—leaving you very little time in the town itself. And, of course, if you ride the bus, you can't stop to explore (including its dominant industry, aluminum) and the aggressive development of its tourist trade (such as soliciting foreign investment—mostly Russian—to build new luxury hotels) have turned things around. In fact, in 2008, Montenegro had the most foreign investment, per capita, of any country in Europe. Its unemployment rate has dropped from the high-20s to a somewhat more respectable 15 percent. But it's still a poor place: Montenegro's per capita GDP is just $10,100—a fraction of Croatia's or Slovenia's.

Currency: Though it's not a member of the European Union, Montenegro uses the euro as its currency: €1 = about $1.40.

Language and Alphabet: The official language is Montenegrin, which is nearly identical to Serbian but predominantly uses "our" Roman alphabet (rather than Cyrillic). Still, you'll see plenty of Cyrillic here—targeting the country's large Serb minority as well as Russian tourists and investors.

Telephones: Montenegro's country code is 382. When calling from another country, first dial the international access code (00 from Europe, 011 from the US), then 382, then the area code (minus the initial zero), then the number. Note that Montenegro recently changed its area codes. If you see the former code for the Bay of Kotor area, 082, you'll have to replace it with the new one: 032.

Flag: It's a red field surrounded by a gold fringe. In the middle is the national seal: a golden, two-headed Byzantine eagle topped with a single crown, holding a scepter in one hand and a ball in the other (symbolizing the balance between church and state). The eagle's body is covered by a shield depicting a lion with one paw raised (representing the resurrected Christ).

the sights along the way. As the schedule is always in flux, it's important to confirm times carefully at the Dubrovnik TI or bus station.

It's also possible to take a bus directly from Montenegro to **Mostar** in Bosnia-Herzegovina. The daily bus (run by Globtour in Mostar) departs Budva at 14:15 and Kotor at 15:00, arriving in Mostar at 20:00. The return bus from Mostar departs at 7:00, and arrives at Kotor at 12:30 and Budva at 13:30.

By Excursion: As a last resort, consider taking a package excursion that follows basically the same route covered in this chapter (sold by various travel agencies in Dubrovnik).

Planning Your Time

Assuming you have your own car, for a straightforward one-day plan, drive to Kotor and back (figure about eight hours, including driving time and sightseeing stops). To extend your time, you can add as much Montenegro as you like. Get an early start (to avoid lines at the border, I'd leave Dubrovnik at 7:30 in the morning). It takes about two hours to drive from Dubrovnik to Kotor (add about 1.5 hours if you stop in Perast for the boat trip out to the island). Kotor is worth two or three hours. From Kotor, you can return directly to Dubrovnik (about 1.5 hours if you use the ferry shortcut); or drive another hour up to Cetinje in the Montenegrin interior, or a half-hour to the Budva Riviera (from either place, figure about 2.5-3 hours back to Dubrovnik). To cram everything into one extremely long day, you can do Dubrovnik-Kotor-Cetinje-Budva Riviera-Dubrovnik. If you're taking the bayside road home (not the ferry shortcut) and don't mind getting to Dubrovnik late, consider stopping for dinner at the recommended Konoba Ćatovića Mlini or Stari Mlini restaurants.

Helpful Hints

Border Delays: Crossing the Croatian-Montenegrin border at **Debeli Brijeg** is relatively straightforward—though you will need to stop, show your passport (and potentially your rental car's proof of insurance, called a "green card"), and pay a one-time "eco-tax" of €10. While I've gotten across this border within about 15 or 20 minutes on each visit, on busy days it's possible you'll be delayed. You'll most likely encounter long waits (of an hour or more) on Saturdays and Sundays in August, and to a lesser degree in July and early September. Locals suggest trying to reach the border by 8:00 (leaving Dubrovnik around 7:30 or 7:45) to beat the tour buses. Getting an early start also gives you even more time to enjoy Montenegro once across the border.

In a pinch, there's a second crossing, called **Konfin,** that rarely has a line, although the road leading there may be torn up from an aborted construction project. If you don't mind driving along a stretch of unfinished gravel, it could save you some time: To reach this road coming from Dubrovnik, branch off to the right soon after Gruda and before the main border (following signs for *Pločice*). At the fork, continue straight following signs toward *Vitaljina* and *Molunat,* then go through the villages of Đurinići, Višnjići, and Vitaljina. At the next fork, head left toward *Park Prevlaka* (an old Austro-Hungarian and Yugoslav army fortress that has recently been converted into a park). Along this stretch, you may be driving along some very rough, unfinished roads, so proceed carefully. At the turnoff for the fort (look for it out on a peninsula to the right), take the left turn, following signs for *granični prijelaz Konfin* to reach the border. After entering Montenegro, you'll curve along the small bay into Igalo, where you can pick up the self-guided driving tour described later.

Local Guide: While many Dubrovnik-based drivers/guides can bring you to Montenegro, if you really want the Montenegrin perspective, consider hiring a local guide here. I spent a great day learning about this area from **Stefan Đukanović,** a young, energetic, knowledgeable guide who speaks good English and has an infectious enthusiasm for his homeland. Hiring Stefan is a great value. The catch is that he can't come and get you in Dubrovnik, so it works best if you drive yourself to Montenegro and pick him up when you get there. Stefan is also an excellent choice if you're arriving in Kotor by cruise ship (€60/half-day, €80/day, mobile 069-297-221 or 069-369-994, djukan@t-com.me).

Cruise Passengers: Kotor is becoming an increasingly popular destination for cruises. If you arrive on a cruise ship, you'll likely dock along the pier directly in front of Kotor's Old Town—so your sightseeing options couldn't be easier: Simply walk across the street and you're in the heart of town. To see farther-flung sights in Montenegro, you may want to hire a local guide or driver (consider Stefan Đukanović, recommended above).

The Bay of Kotor

With dramatic cliffs rising out of the glimmering Adriatic, ancient towns packed with history and thrilling vistas, an undeveloped ruggedness unlike anything in Croatia, and a twisty road to tie it all together, the Bay of Kotor represents the best of Montenegro. To top it off, it's easy to reach by car from Dubrovnik.

Self-Guided Driving Tour

▲▲Bay of Kotor Day Trip (from Dubrovnik)

The Bay of Kotor (Boka Kotorska—literally the "Mouth of Kotor"; sometimes translated as "Boka Bay" in English) is Montenegro's most enjoyable and convenient attraction for those based in Dubrovnik. This self-guided driving tour narrates the drive from the Croatian border to the town of Kotor, in the Bay of Kotor's deepest corner.

The Montenegrin border is about 30 to 45 minutes south of Dubrovnik (don't forget your passport). Simply follow the main coastal road south, past Cavtat and the airport. You'll be passing through the Croatian region called **Konavle** (literally "canal,"

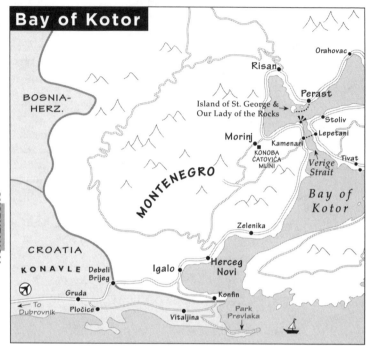

recalling how the Romans built aqueducts through this area to supply their settlement at today's Cavtat. Historically part of the Republic of Dubrovnik, this farming region was badly damaged during the recent war, when the Yugoslav People's Army invaded from the south, forcing villagers to flee to safety in Dubrovnik.

Approaching the **border,** if there's a long back-up, consider turning off to take the much less-traveled road to the secondary border at Konfin (see "Helpful Hints," earlier). Regardless of where you enter Montenegro, you'll pay a one-time "eco-tax" of €10 at the border. (Your rental car might already have a toll sticker for this tax—ask when you pick up your car.) If you don't have your rental car's proof of insurance (called a "green card"), you may be asked to pay another fee as well.

From the border, you can make it to Kotor in about an hour without stopping, but with all the diversions en route you should plan for much more time. Coming back, you can trim a good half-hour off the drive by crossing the fjord at its narrowest point, using the Lepetani-Kamenari ferry. Navigating on this tour is really simple: It's basically the same road, with no turn-offs, from Dubrovnik to Kotor.

• *From the Croatian border, you'll approach the coast at the town called...*

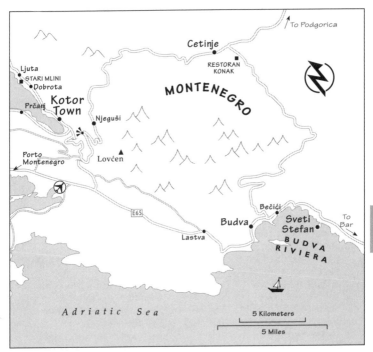

Igalo

Driving through Igalo, keep an eye out (on the right) for a big concrete hotel called **Institut Dr. Simo Milošević** (no relation to war-criminal Slobodan). This internationally regarded spa, especially popular among Scandinavians, offers treatment for arthritis and nerve disorders. Capable of hosting more than 1,000 patients at once, this complex boasts that it's one of the world's premier treatment facilities for these conditions. Yugoslav President-for-Life Tito had a villa nearby and took treatments here.

• *A couple of miles beyond Igalo, you enter the biggest city you'll see today...*

Herceg Novi

The drab economic and industrial capital of the Bay of Kotor, Herceg Novi (with 25,000 people) is hardly the prettiest introduction to this otherwise striking landscape. Herceg Novi flourished during the Habsburg boom of the late 19th century, when a railroad line connected it to Dubrovnik, Sarajevo, and Vienna. Back then, Austrians vacationed here—but more recent development has been decidedly less elegant than the Habsburgs'. While there is a walled Old Town core to Herceg Novi, it's not worth stopping to see.

MONTENEGRO

The History of Kotor

With evidence of prehistoric settlements dating back to 2500 B.C., the Bay of Kotor has been a prized location for millennia. Its unique bottleneck shape makes the Bay of Kotor the single best natural harbor between Greece and Venice. Predictably, this scenic and strategic strip has attracted more than its share of overlords across the centuries—so many, in fact, that it's difficult to keep track.

One of the earliest known civilizations in Kotor (third century B.C.) was that of the Illyrians, whose Queen Teuta held court here until her lands were conquered by the Romans. Later, when the Roman Empire split (fourth century A.D.), Montenegro straddled the cultural fault line between West (Roman Catholic) and East (Orthodox Christian). As Rome crumbled in the sixth and seventh centuries, the Slavs moved in. Initially rejecting Roman culture, many later converted to Christianity (some Orthodox, some Catholic).

By the 10th century, Montenegro's Slavs had organized into a sovereign state, affiliated with but partially independent from the Byzantine (Eastern Roman) Empire. Thanks to its protected location, medieval Kotor became a major city of the salt trade.

The Bay of Kotor further flourished in the 14th century, under the Serbian emperor Dušan the Mighty. Notorious for his aggressive law enforcement—chopping off the hand of a thief, slicing off the nose of a liar—Dušan made the Bay of Kotor a particularly safe place to do business. One of his strategies was making the nobility responsible for safe passage. If a visiting merchant was robbed, the nobleman who controlled that land would be ruthlessly punished. Soon 2,000-horse caravans could pass without a worry along this fjord. During storms, ships would routinely

Passing through the Old Town, keep an eye out on the right for Herceg Novi's stout 15th-century **fortress,** which was built by the Ottomans—who controlled this area, but never made it deeper into the bay.

Also in Herceg Novi, keep an eye out for **banana trees.** Locals pride themselves on their particularly mild climate, kept warm year-round thanks to the mitigating effects of the water from the adjacent fjord. Supposedly, "it never drops below 50 degrees Fahrenheit." While these banana trees are just decorative (the fruit they produce is too small to eat), they're a local symbol. So is the mimosa flower, which blooms all winter long, and is the inspiration for the town's annual Mimosa Festival—held each February, when much of Europe (including most of Montenegro) is under a blanket of snow.

Other than its banana trees and mimosas, Herceg Novi is basically a mess. (Don't worry—the drive gets better.) Why so much seek protection in this secluded bay.

But the Serbian Empire went into steep decline after Dušan. As the Ottomans threatened to invade in the 15th century, Kotor's traders turned to Venice for help. The Venetian Republic would control this bay for the next 450 years, and it was never taken by enemies. In fact, Montenegro managed to evade Ottoman rule entirely...unlike its neighbors Albania, Kosovo, Serbia, and Bosnia-Herzegovina. (Meanwhile, neighboring Croats enjoy pointing out that, while the Bay of Kotor was nominally part of Venice, much of the territory was privately owned by a Croat family.)

In the late 19th century, when Venice fell to Napoleon, the Bay of Kotor came briefly under the control of France, then Russia, then Austria. Feudal traditions fell by the wayside, industry arrived, and the area's old-fashioned economy went into a sharp decline. As trading wealth dried up, the Bay of Kotor entered a period of architectural stagnation. But thanks to this dark spell in Montenegrin history, today's visitors can enjoy some wonderfully preserved time-warp towns.

When Montenegro became part of Yugoslavia following World War I, the Serbs (who felt a cultural affinity with the Montenegrins that wasn't always reciprocated) laid claim to the Montenegrin coast as their own little patch of seafront. Serbs flooded into Montenegro, altering the demographics and making it, in effect, an outpost of the Republic of Serbia. This helped Montenegro avoid the initial violence of the breakup of Yugoslavia, but put them in an awkward position when it came time for them to request secession a few years later. For the rest of the story, see the "Montenegro: Birth of a Nation" sidebar, later.

MONTENEGRO

ugliness compared to Croatia? For one thing, Tito viewed Croatia's Dalmatian Coast as a gold mine of hard Western currency—so he was inclined to keep it Old World-charming. And Croatia remained in the cultural and political orbit of Zagreb, which was motivated to take good care of its historic towns. But Belgrade, which exerted more influence on Montenegro, didn't offer it the same degree of TLC. And because Montenegro has traditionally been poorer than Croatia, its officials are more susceptible to bribery and corruption. ("Would a few thousand dinar convince you to ignore my new hotel's code violations?") From an architectural point of view, it's a sad irony that gorgeous Dubrovnik was devastated by bombs and the gritty cities of Montenegro survived the war essentially unscathed. To this day, locals aren't crazy about the Serbs who flock here in summer for as-cheap-as-possible beach holidays. Instead, Montenegrins are encouraging the construction of top-end resort hotels to lure high rollers from around the world (such as James Bond, who played poker in the 2006 movie version of *Casino Royale* in "Montenegro"—though it was actually filmed in the Czech Republic). But even this new development is poorly regulated, threatening to turn Montenegro into a charmless, concrete Costa del Sol-style vacation zone. Enjoy the Bay of Kotor's pristine areas (which we'll enter soon) while you still can.

• *As you go through Herceg Novi, follow signs for Kotor. Leaving town, you'll pass through* **Zelenika,** *once the end of the line for the Habsburg rail line from Vienna, which first brought tourism to this area.*

After a few more dreary towns, you'll emerge into a more rustic setting. This fjordside road is lined with fishing villages, some now developed as resorts (including a few with severe communist-era touches). You'll pass through the town of **Kamenari,** *which has a handy ferry that you could use to shave time off your return trip to Dubrovnik (described at the end of this drive). Two minutes after leaving Kamenari (just after the* Kostanjica *sign), watch for a convenient gravel pull-out on the right (likely packed with tour buses, by the small white lighthouse). Pull over to check out the narrowest point of the fjord, the...*

Verige Strait

This tight bottleneck at the mouth of the bay is the secret to the Bay of Kotor's success: Any would-be invaders had to pass through here to reach the port towns inside the bay. It's narrow enough to carefully monitor (not even a quarter-mile wide), but deep enough to allow even today's large megaships through (more than 130 feet deep). Because this extremely narrow strait is relatively easy to defend, whoever controlled the inside of the fjord was allowed to thrive virtually unchecked.

Centuries before Christ, even before the flourishing of Roman culture, the Bay of Kotor was home to the Illyrians—the mysterious ancestors of today's Albanians. In the third century B.C., Illyrian Queen Teuta spanned this strait with an ingenious ship-wrecking mechanism to more effectively collect taxes. To this day, many sunken ships litter the bottom of this bay. (Teuta was a little too clever for her own good—her shrewdness and success attracted the attention of the on-the-rise Romans, who seized most of her holdings.)

In later times, chains were stretched across the bay here to control the entrance (the name "Verige" comes from a Slavic word for "chain"). Later still, the Venetians came up with an even more elaborate plan: Place cannons on either side of the strait, with a clear shot at any entering ships. Looking across the wide part of the bay, notice the town of Perast (by the two islands). Perast—where we'll be stopping soon—was also equipped with cannons that could easily reach across the bay. Thanks to this extensive defense network, Ottomans or any other potential invaders were unlikely to penetrate the bay, either by sea or by land.

Montenegro is currently drafting plans to build a bridge across the strait (effectively replacing the ferry connection we just passed)—though concerns about both securing funding and preserving the unique ecosystem of the bay have delayed progress. Stay tuned.

• *Continue driving around the fjord. You'll pass through the village of...*

Morinj

This town is known for two starkly different reasons: First, it's the home of a recommended restaurant with fine food in a gorgeous setting (Konoba Ćatovića Mlini). And second, it was the site of a concentration camp for Croat prisoners captured during the 1991-1992 siege of Dubrovnik. Some 300 civilians from in and near Dubrovnik were forcibly brought here, where they lived in horrifying conditions. After the war, six of the guards from this camp were convicted of war crimes.

• *After going through Morinj and some other small villages, you'll pass through the larger resort town of...*

Risan

Back in Greek times, when the Bay of Kotor was known as *"Sinus Rhizonicus,"* Risan was the leading town of the bay. Later, during the Illyrian Queen Teuta's brief three-year reign, Risan was her capital. Today the town is still home to the scant remains of Teuta's castle (on the hilltop just before town), but it's mostly notable for its giant communist eyesore hotel—named, appropriately enough, Hotel Teuta.

• *Continue on to Perast. As you approach the town, take the right fork (marked with brown sign) directly down into Perast; or you can first take the left fork to pass above town for sweeping views over the bay, then backtrack down into the town center.*

Perast

This second-most appealing town on the fjord (after Kotor) is considered the "Pearl of Venetian Baroque." It's worth taking some time to wander and explore its buildings and enjoy its relaxed small-town feel (minus the bustle

of bigger Kotor). During the summer, you're required to park near the entrance of town (€0.50), and then walk or ride the free shuttle bus into the town center; at other times, you'll be allowed to drive along the waterfront road and park for free in front of the church.

Montenegro: Birth of a Nation

Montenegro, like Croatia and Slovenia, was one of the six republics that constituted the former Yugoslavia. When these republics began splitting away in the early 1990s, Montenegro—always allied closely with Serbia, and small enough to slip under the radar—decided to remain in the union. When the dust had settled, four of the six Yugoslav republics had seceded (Croatia, Slovenia, Bosnia-Herzegovina, and Macedonia), while only two remained united as "Yugoslavia": Serbia and Montenegro.

At first, Montenegrin Prime Minister Milo Đukanović was on friendly terms with Serbia's Slobodan Milošević. But in the late 1990s, as Milošević's political stock plummeted, Montenegro began to inch away from Serbia. Eager to keep its access to the coast (and the many Serbs who lived there), Serbia made concessions that allowed Montenegro to gradually assert its independence. In 1996, Montenegro boldly adopted the German mark as its official currency to avoid the inflating Yugoslav dinar.

By 2003, the country of Yugoslavia was no more, and the loose union was renamed "Serbia and Montenegro." Thus began a three-year transition period that allowed Montenegro to test the waters of real independence. During this time, Serbia and Montenegro were united only in defense—legislation, taxation, currency, and most governmental functions were separate. And it was agreed that after three years, Montenegro would be allowed to hold a referendum for full independence.

That fateful vote took place on May 21, 2006. In general, ethnic Montenegrins tended to favor independence, while ethnic Serbs wanted to stay united with Serbia. To secede, Montenegro needed 55 percent of the vote. By the slimmest of margins—half a percent, or just 2,300 votes—the pro-independence faction won. On June 3, 2006, Montenegro officially declared independence. (To save face, two days later, Serbia also "declared independence" from Montenegro.)

Today's Montenegrins are excited to have their own little country and enthusiastic about eventually joining the European Union. Serbia's greatest concern was that in losing Montenegro, it would also lose its lone outlet to the sea—both for shipping and for holiday-making. The Serbs also feared that Montenegrin independence might inspire similar actions in the Serbian province of Kosovo (which did, in fact, declare independence from Serbia less than two years later).

But for many people in both countries, independence is an epilogue rather than a climax. Shortly after the referendum, I asked a Montenegrin when the countries would officially separate. He chuckled and said, "Three years ago."

Remember that Perast, with its cannons aimed at the Verige Strait across the bay, was an essential link in the Bay of Kotor's fortifications. In exchange for this important duty, Venice rewarded Perast with privileged tax-free status, and the town became extremely wealthy. Ornate mansions proliferated here during its 17th- and 18th-century heyday. But after Venice fell to Napoleon, and the Bay of Kotor's economy changed, Perast's singular defensive role disappeared. With no industry, no hinterland, and no natural resources, Perast stagnated—leaving it a virtual open-air museum of Venetian architecture.

Go to the tallest steeple in town, overlooking a long and narrow harborfront square. Perast is centered on its too-big (and incomplete) church, **St. Nicholas**—dedicated to the patron saint of fishermen. It was originally designed to extend out into the sea (the old church, still standing, was to be torn down). But Napoleon's troops came marching in before the builders got that far, so the plans were scuttled—and this massive partial-church was instead simply grafted on to the existing, modest church.

Go inside (free, €1 to enter treasury, sporadic hours, generally open April-Nov daily 9:00-18:00, July-Aug until 19:00, closed dur-

ing Mass, closed Dec-March except by request—ask locals around the church if someone can let you in). Beyond the small sanctuary, you'll find a treasury with relics and icons. Look for the priceless crucifix from the school of the 18th-century Venetian artist Giovanni Battista Tiepolo (#1, in the display case in the center of the room), with Jesus on one side, and Mary and the saints on the other. Beyond the treasury is what was to be the main apse (altar area) of the unfinished massive church (notice it's at a right angle to the actual, in-use altar of the existing smaller church). The rough, unadorned brick walls make it clear that they didn't get very far. Check out the model of the ambitious but never-built church. The Baroque main altar is by Bernini's student Francesco Cabianca, who lived in this area and was always trying to earn money to pay off his gambling debts. The small room at the end displays old vestments.

If you have the time and energy, pay €1 to climb the **church tower** for the view.

Perast's only other "sight" is its **Town Museum,** which fills a grand old hall with paintings, furniture, navy uniforms, pistols, portraits of VIPs (very important Perastians), medals, traditional musical instruments, and other historic bric-a-brac. It's pretty dull

MONTENEGRO

but has nice sea views (€2.50; May-Oct Mon-Sat 9:00-18:00, Sun 9:00-14:00; Nov-April Mon-Sat 9:00-13:00 or 14:00, closed Sun; along the water near the start of town, in the ornate building with the arcade and balcony).

Eating in Perast: For an enjoyable drink or meal, consider the **Conte** restaurant, filling a pier on the bay in the middle of town (€8-12 pastas, €11-20 main dishes). On the far side of the square is another, well-shaded pier restaurant, **Admiral** (€8-10 pastas, €11-20 main dishes). Both are open daily and attached to recommended hotels.

• *Before leaving Perast, take a close look at the two islands just offshore (and consider paying a visit).*

St. George (Sv. Đorđe) and Our Lady of the Rocks (Gospa od Škrpjela)

These twin islands—one natural, the other man-made—come with a fascinating story.

The **Island of St. George** (the smaller, rocky island with trees and a monastery—closed to tourists), named for the protector of Christianity, was part of the fortification of the Bay of Kotor. This natural island had a small underwater reef nearby. According to legend, two fishermen noticed a strange light emanating from this reef in

the early-morning fog. Rowing out to the island, they discovered an icon of Our Lady. They attempted to bring it ashore, but it kept washing back out again to the same spot. Taking this celestial hint, local seamen returning home from a journey began dropping rocks into the bay in this same place. The tradition caught on, more and more villagers dropped in rocks of their own, and eventually more than a hundred old ships and other vessels were filled with stones and intentionally sunk in this spot. And so, over two centuries, an entire island was formed in the middle of the bay.

Flash forward to today's **Our Lady of the Rocks** (the flat island with the dome-topped Catholic church). In the 17th century, locals built this Baroque church on this holy site and filled it with symbols of thanks for answered prayers. Step inside (free entry) to explore the collection: silver votive plaques—many of them with images of ships in storms or battles—given by appreciative sailors who survived; 1,700 silver and gold votive plaques from other grateful worshippers; 68 canvases by local Baroque painter Tripo Kokolja; and a huge collection of dried wedding bouquets given by those who had nothing else to offer (the church is a popular place for weddings).

The adjacent **museum** is an entertaining mishmash of items, and the entry price includes a fun little tour by Davorka, Nešo, or Nataša (€1, June-Oct daily 9:00-19:00, April-May and Nov opens sporadically with boat arrival, closed Dec-March). You'll see a wide range of ancient arti-facts, 65 paintings of ships com-missioned by local sailors (notice that most have a saintly image of Mary and the Baby Jesus hover-ing nearby), and other gifts given through the ages. Upstairs, near the gift shop counter, look for the amazing embroidery made by a local woman who toiled over it

for more than 25 years. She used her own hair for the hair of the angels—which you can see fade from brown to gray as she aged (beginning at around 3 o'clock and going clockwise, you'll see the subtle change in color).

Getting There: Boats to Our Lady of the Rocks leave from in front of St. Nicholas' Church in Perast—look for the guys milling around the harborfront with boats ready to go (€5/person round-trip, but show them this book to pay €4/person, or €3/person for a group of 4 or more).

• *When you're ready to move on, continue driving around the fjord. After the large town of Orahovac, you'll see part of the bay roped off for a mussel farm; these farms do best when located where mountain rivers spill into the bay. And a hundred or so yards later, you cross a bridge spanning the don't-blink-or-you'll-miss-it...*

Ljuta River

According to locals, this is the "shortest river in the world"—notice that the source (bubbling up from under the cliff) is just to the left of the bridge, and it meets the sea just to the right. Short as it is, it's hardly a trickle—in fact, its name means "Angry River" for its fierce flow during heavy rains. The river actually courses under-ground for several miles before emerging here. Like the Karst area south of Ljubljana, this is a karstic landscape—limestone that's honeycombed with underground rivers, caves, and canyons. Many other waterfalls and streams feed the Bay of Kotor with snowmelt from the surrounding mountains. Because of this steady natural flushing, locals brag that the bay's water is particularly clear and clean.

• *Immediately after the bridge, look for the turnoff (on the right) to the recommended Restoran Stari Mlini—a tranquil spot for a meal or drink. Continuing along the fjord, as you pass through the town of Dobrota, look across the bay to the village of...*

Prčanj

This town is famous as the former home of many centuries' worth of wealthy sea captains. When the Bay of Kotor was part of the Austrian Empire, Emperor Franz Josef came to Prčanj. Upon being greeted by some 50 uniformed ship captains, he marveled that such a collection of seafarers had been imported for his visit... not realizing that every one of them lived nearby.

• *Keep on driving. When you see the giant moat with the town wall, and the smaller wall twisting up the hill above, you'll know you've arrived in* **Kotor** *(see facing page).*

Before leaving Kotor, make a decision about where you want to go next. You have three basic options: Budva Riviera; Montenegrin interior; or back to Croatia (see instructions for the third option in the next section).

Continuing past Kotor's Old Town, you'll follow the edge of the fjord. At the far end of town (and the fjord), you'll come to a roundabout. Bearing left at the roundabout takes you toward the handy tunnel to the **Budva Riviera**—*or, along this same road, if you turn right after the cemetery and just before the tunnel, you'll take the extremely twisty road up, up, up into the* **Montenegrin interior** *(Njeguši and Cetinje).*

Once you're finished in Montenegro, it'll be time to head...

Back to Croatia: Lepetani-Kamenari Ferry Shortcut

When you're ready to return to Dubrovnik, you can go back the way you came. Or, for a quicker route, consider the ferry that cuts across the narrow part of the fjord (between the towns of Lepetani and Kamenari). On the Kotor side of the bay, the boat departs from the town of Lepetani.

From Kotor, you have two options to reach the ferry: The easiest option is to leave Kotor, bear left at the roundabout at the far end of town, and take the tunnel toward Budva. Once through the tunnel, follow signs into Tivat, and continue straight through Tivat on the main road to reach Lepetani, which is a few miles beyond the end of town. Or, for a more challenging but more scenic route, you can simply turn right at the roundabout and continue driving on the waterfront road clockwise around the bay (through Prčanj and Stoliv) until you land in Lepetani. But be warned that this road is extremely narrow (one lane with an Adriatic shoulder) and can be exhausting if oncoming traffic is heavy.

No matter how you approach, remember that "ferry" is *trajekt* (it's also signed for *Herceg Novi*—the big city across the bay). The boat goes continuously (in slow times, you may have to wait briefly for enough cars to show up), and the crossing takes just four minutes (it takes longer to load and unload all the cars than it does to cross). A small car and its passengers pay €4 each way.

Kotor

Butted up against a steep cliff, cradled by a calm sea, naturally sheltered by its deep-in-the-fjord position, and watched over by an imposing network of fortifications, the town of Kotor is as impressive as it is well-protected. Though it's enjoyed a long and illustrious history, today's Kotor is a time-capsule retreat for travelers seeking a truly unspoiled Adriatic town.

There's been a settlement in this location at least since the time of Christ. The ancient town of Catarum—named for the Roman word for "contracted" or "strangled," as the sea is at this point in the gnarled fjord—was first mentioned in the first century A.D. Like the rest of the region, Kotor's next two millennia were layered with history as it came under control of a series of foreign powers: Illyrians, Romans, Serbs, Venetians, Russians, Napoleonic soldiers, Austrians, Tito's Yugoslavia...and now, finally, Montenegrins. Each group left its mark, and Kotor has its share of both Catholic and Orthodox churches (sometimes both at once), plus monuments and reminders of plenty of past colonizers and conquerors.

Through all those centuries, Kotor avoided destruction by warfare. But it was damaged by earthquakes—including the same 1667 quake that leveled Dubrovnik (known here as the "Great Shaking"), as well as a devastating 1979 earthquake from which the city is still cleaning up. While only 3,000 people live within the Old Town walls, greater Kotor has a population of about 12,000.

With an extremely inviting Old Town that seems custom-built for aimless strolling, Kotor is an idyllic place to while away a few hours. Though it's sometimes called a "little Dubrovnik," Kotor is more low-key, less ambitious, less historic, flatter, and much smaller than its more famous neighbor. And yet, with its own special spice that's exciting to sample, Kotor is a hard place to tear yourself away from.

Orientation to Kotor

Kotor (or Cattaro in Italian) has a compact Old Town shaped like a triangle. The two sides facing the bay are heavily fortified by a thick wall, and the third side huddles under the cliff face. A meandering defensive wall climbs the mountainside directly behind and above town.

The Old Town's mazelike street plan is confusing, but it's so small and atmospheric that getting lost is more fun than frustrating. The natives virtually ignore addresses, including the names of streets and squares. Most Old Town addresses are represented

MONTENEGRO

simply as "Stari Grad," then a number (useless if you're trying to navigate by streets). To make matters worse, a single square can have several names—so one map labels it Trg od Katedrale (Cathedral Square), while another calls it Pjaca Sv. Tripuna (Piazza of St. Tryphon). My advice: Don't fret about street or square names. Simply navigate with a map and by asking locals for directions. Thanks to the very manageable size of the Old Town, this is easier than it sounds.

Tourist Information

The TI is in a kiosk just outside the Old Town's main entrance gate (daily May-Oct 8:00-20:00, Nov-April 8:00-17:00, tel. 032/325-950, www.tokotor.com). Pick up the free map and browse the collection of guidebooks and brochures. They can help you find a room for no fee.

Arrival in Kotor

By Car: Approaching town, you'll first see Kotor's substantial wall, which overlooks a canal. You can park in one of two pay lots: "Parking Riva," immediately across from the main gate (more expensive but convenient, to the right just after crossing the bridge by the wall); or "Parking Benovo," in the lot across the canal (on the left just before the bridge by the wall—you'll be sent back here if the first lot is full). Either is a quick walk from the Old Town entrance. Be sure you've parked legally; some of my readers report having been towed and fined for parking in what they thought were legal spaces. When in doubt about a parking spot, either don't park there or ask the TI if it's OK.

By Bus: The bus station is about a half-mile south of the Old Town. Arriving here, simply exit to the right and walk straight up the road—you'll run into the embankment and town wall in 10 minutes.

Sights in Kotor

Because of its tangled alleys and irregular street plan, Kotor feels bigger than it is. But after 10 minutes of wandering, you'll discover you're going in circles and realize it's actually very compact. (In fact, aimless wandering is Kotor's single best activity.) How such a cute town manages to be so delightfully lazy and traffic-free without being overrun by tourists, I'll never know (though the recent arrival of cruise ships is threatening Kotor's until-now-untrampled appeal).

As you ramble, keep an eye out for these key attractions. I've listed them roughly in the order of a counterclockwise route through town, beginning outside the main entrance gate.

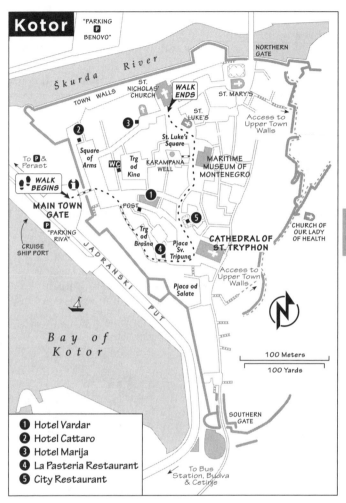

Kotor

"PARKING P BENOVO"

Škurda River

TOWN WALLS

ST. NICHOLAS' CHURCH

WALK ENDS

ST. MARY'S

NORTHERN GATE

ST. LUKE'S

Access to Upper Town Walls

St. Luke's Square

❷

❸

To P & Perast

Square of Arms

WC

Trg od Kina

KARAMPANA WELL

MARITIME MUSEUM OF MONTENEGRO

WALK BEGINS

❶

MAIN TOWN GATE

POST

❶

❺

CHURCH OF OUR LADY OF HEALTH

P "PARKING RIVA"

CRUISE SHIP PORT

JADRANSKI PUT

Trg od Brašna

❹

Pjaca Sv. Tripuna

CATHEDRAL OF ST. TRYPHON

Access to Upper Town Walls

Pjaca od Salate

N

B a y o f K o t o r

100 Meters

100 Yards

SOUTHERN GATE

To Bus Station, Budva & Cetinje

MONTENEGRO

❶ Hotel Vardar
❷ Hotel Cattaro
❸ Hotel Marija
❹ La Pasteria Restaurant
❺ City Restaurant

▲**Main Town Gate (Glavna Gradska Vrata)**—The wide-open **square** fronting the bay and waterfront marina now welcomes visitors. But for centuries, its purpose was exactly the opposite. As the primary point of entry into this heavily fortified town, it was the last line of defense. Before the embankment was built, the water came directly to this door, and there was only room for one ship to tie up at a time. If a ship got this far (through the gauntlet we saw back at the Verige Strait), it was carefully examined here again (and taxes were levied) before its passengers could disembark. This double-checkpoint was designed to foil pirates who might fly the flag of a friend to get through the strait, only to launch a surprise attack once here. By the way, pirates' primary booty wasn't silver or gold, but men—kidnapped for ransom, or, if ransom wasn't paid, as slaves to row on ships.

Check out the pinkish **gate** itself. The oldest parts of this gate date from 1555. It once featured a Venetian lion, then the double-

headed eagle of the Habsburg Empire. But today, most of the symbolism touts Tito's communism (notice the stars and the old Yugoslav national seal at the top). The big date (November 21, 1944) commemorates when this area was liberated from the Nazis by Tito's homegrown Partisan Army. The Tito quote *(tuđe nećemo svoje nedamo)* means, roughly, "Don't take what's ours, and we won't take what's yours"—a typically provocative statement in these troubled Balkans.

• *Notice the* **TI** *in the kiosk just to the left of the gate. Then go through the gate into town. You'll emerge into the...*

Square of Arms (Trg od Oržja)—Do a quick spin-tour of the square, which is ringed with artifacts of the city's complex his-

tory. Looking to the left, you'll see a long building lined with cafés, ATMs (which dispense euros), and (behind the umbrellas) a small casino. The building was once the palace of the rector, who ruled Kotor on behalf of Venice; princes could watch the action from their long balcony overlooking the square, which served as

the town's living room. Later, the palace became the Kotor Town Hall. Beyond that, two buildings poke out into the square (on either side of the lane leading out of the square). The one on the right is the Venetian arsenal, the square's namesake. The one on the left is the "French Theater," named for its purpose during the time this area was under Napoleon's control. Directly across from the gate you just came through, you'll see the town's Bell Tower, one of Kotor's symbols. The odd triangular structure at its base was once the town pillory. Wrongdoers would be chained to this with their transgression printed on a placard hanging from their neck, open to public ridicule of the rudest kind imaginable. In the little recessed square just right of that, you'll spot the recommended, copper-roofed Hotel Vardar.

• *Walk down the long part of the square directly ahead of where you entered (toward Hotel Vardar). About 20 yards in front of the hotel, take the broad lane angling off to the right (paved with red-and-white-*

striped tiles), which leads past mansions of Kotor's medieval big shots. Turn left down the little lane next to the Montenegro Airlines office. Soon you'll hit Pjaca Sv. Tripuna (a.k.a. Trg od Katedrale), home to the...

▲**Cathedral of St. Tryphon (Katedrala Sv. Tripuna)**—Even though most Kotorians are Orthodox, Kotor's most significant church is Catholic. According to legend, in A.D. 809, Venetian merchants were sailing up the coast from Nicea (in today's Turkey) with the relics of St. Tryphon—a third-century martyr and today's patron saint of gardeners. A storm hit as they approached the Bay of Kotor, so they took shelter here. Every time they tried to leave, the weather worsened...so they finally got the message that St. Tryphon's remains should remain in Kotor.

Take in the cathedral's **exterior.** The earliest, Romanesque parts of this church, dating from the mid-12th century, are made of limestone from the Croatian island of Korčula. But the church has been rebuilt after four different earthquakes—most extensively after the 1667 quake, when it achieved its current Renaissance-Baroque blend. That earthquake, which also contributed to Dubrovnik's current appea

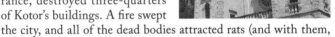

rance, destroyed three-quarters of Kotor's buildings. A fire swept the city, and all of the dead bodies attracted rats (and with them, the plague)—a particularly dark chapter in Kotor's history.

Why are the two **towers** different? There are plenty of legends, but the most likely is that restorers working after 1667 simply ran out of money before they finished the second one. Notice the Church of Our Lady of Health way up on the hill above this church—built in thanks to God by survivors of the plague (it also serves as part of the town fortifications—described later).

Cost and Hours: €2.50, daily June-Sept 9:00-19:00, April-May and Oct 9:00-18:00, Nov-March 9:00-15:00, Mass on Sun at 10:00.

Touring the Cathedral: Within the cathedral, the **nave** of the church is marginally interesting: stout columns; surviving Byzantine-style frescoes under the arches—all that's left of paintings that once covered the church; and a fine 15th-century silver-and-gold altar covered by a delicate canopy.

But the best part is the **reliquary** upstairs. Find the stairs at the rear and walk up to the chapel. Behind the Baroque altar (by Bernini's student Francesco Cabianca, whose work we saw in

Perast) and the screen are 48 different relics. In the center is St. Tryphon—his bones in a silver casket and his head in the golden chalice to the right. In the small room up the stairs, examine the fascinating icon of the Madonna and Child from the 15th century. The painting (like the icons in the adjacent room) exemplifies this town's position as a bridge between Western and Eastern Christianity: The faces, more lifelike, are Western-style (Catholic) Gothic; the stiff, elongated bodies are more Eastern (Orthodox) and Byzantine-style. From here, take a slow walk around the upper gallery of the church to see its displays of paintings, vestments, and other ecclesiastical items.

• *Exit the church. Notice the recommended La Pasteria restaurant immediately across from the cathedral, with Italian- and Serb-style fare and scenic al fresco tables. On the right, the trees mark another recommended eatery, City Restaurant.*

When you're ready to continue, face the cathedral facade and exit the square to your left (at the back-left corner of the square, down the street near City Restaurant). In a block, you'll wind up on a little square that's home to the...

MONTENEGRO

Maritime Museum of Montenegro (Pomorski Muzej Crne Gore)

—Like so many Adriatic towns, Kotor's livelihood is tied to the sea. This humble museum explores that important heritage. As you climb the stairway, notice the evocative maps and etchings of old Kotor. Portraits of salty swashbucklers, traditional costumes, and 98 coats of arms representing aristocratic families who have lived here (ringing the main room upstairs) are all reminders of the richness of Kotor's history. You'll see a display of rifles and swords (some with fun ornamental decorations illustrating the art of killing) and lots of model ships. The museum is housed in the Gregorina Palace, one of dozens of aristocratic mansions that dot the Old Town—yet another reminder of the historically high concentration of wealth and power in this little settlement.

Cost and Hours: €4, includes English audioguide; July-Aug Mon-Fri 8:00-23:00, Sat-Sun 10:00-16:00; mid-April-June and Sept-mid-Oct Mon-Fri 8:00-18:00, Sat-Sun 9:00-13:00; mid-Oct-mid-April Mon-Fri 9:00-17:00, Sat-Sun 9:00-12:00; on Trg Grgurina, tel. 032/304-720, www.museummaritimum.com.

• *Facing the museum, go around the left side. After 10 yards, you'll pass a well on your left called the...*

Karampana

—This well served as Kotor's only public faucet until the early 20th century (swing the pendulum to get things flowing). As such, it was also the top place in town for gossip, like the office water cooler. It's said that if your name is mentioned here, you know you've arrived. Today, though the chatter is no longer raging on this square, the town's gossip magazine is called *Karampana*.

• *Continue straight past the well into the next square...*

▲▲**St. Luke's Square (Trg Svetog Luke)**—There are two Serbian Orthodox churches on this pretty square, each with the typical Orthodox church features: a squat design, narrow windows, and portly domes. Little **St. Luke's Church** (Crkva Sv. Luka), in the middle of the square, dates from the 12th century. Locals debate long and hard as to whether St. Luke's was originally built as a Catholic church or an Orthodox one. (Although it "looks" Orthodox, it was constructed during the rule of Serbian King Vukan Nemanjić, when even Catholic churches were built in the Orthodox style.) Regardless of its origin, during the Venetian era, the church did double duty as a house of worship for both. These days, it's decidedly Orthodox (free, daily May-Oct 10:00-20:00, Nov-April 8:00-13:00 & 17:00-19:00).

The bigger and much newer **St. Nicholas' Church** (Crkva Sv. Nikola), at the far corner of the square, was built in 1909—because of its Neo-Byzantine design, it has similarly spherical domes and slitlike windows (free, same hours as St. Luke's).

Notice how the Orthodox crosses on the steeples of St. Nicholas' Church differ from the cross seen in Roman Catholic churches (known as a Latin cross). In addition to the standard crossbar, Orthodox crosses often also have a second, smaller crossbar near the top (representing the *I.N.R.I.* plaque that was displayed above Jesus' head). Sometimes Orthodox crosses also feature a third, angled crossbar at the bottom. Many believe that rather than being nailed directly to the cross, Jesus' feet were nailed to a crossbar like this one to prolong his suffering. The slanted angle represents Jesus' forgiveness of the thief crucified to his right (the side

that's pointing up)...and suggests where the unrepentant thief on his left ended up.

Stepping into these (or any other Orthodox) churches, you'll immediately notice some key differences from Catholic churches: no pews (worshippers stand through the service as a sign of respect), tall and skinny candles (representing prayers), and a screen of icons, called an iconostasis, in the middle of the sanctuary to separate the material world from the holy world (where the Bible is kept).

Before continuing on, enjoy this square's

lazy ambience. The big building fronting the square is a music school, and the students practicing here fill this already pleasant public space with an appealing soundtrack.

• *If you go down the street to your left as you face St. Nicholas, you'll wind up back at the Square of Arms. But first try getting lost, then found again, in Kotor's delightful maze of streets. The town's final attraction is above your head (to head there directly, face St. Nicholas' Church, turn right, and walk straight for two blocks).*

▲▲**Town Walls (Gradske Zidine)**—Kotor's fortifications begin as stout ramparts along the waterfront, then climb up the sheer cliff face behind town in a dizzying zigzag line. If there's a more elaborate city wall in Europe, I haven't seen it. A proud Kotorian bragged to me, "These fortifications cost more to build than any palace in Europe."

Imagine what it took to create this "Great Wall of Kotor": nearly three miles long, along extremely inaccessible terrain. It was built in fits and starts over a millennium (9th-19th centuries,

though most of it was during the Venetian occupation in the 17th and 18th centuries). Its thickness varies from 6 to 50 feet, and the tallest parts are 65 feet high. Sections higher on the hill—with thinner walls, before the age of gunpowder—are the oldest, while the thick walls along the water are most recent. It was all worth it: The fortified town survived many attacks, including a two-month Ottoman siege in 1657.

If you're in great shape, consider scrambling along the walls and turrets above the Old Town.

Cost and Hours: You'll pay €3 to enter the walls if you visit May-Oct daily 8:00-20:00; otherwise they're free.

Hiking the Walls: If you go all the way up to the top fortress and back again, it'll take around an hour and a half round-trip (depending on how fast you go). This involves climbing 1,355 steps (an elevation gain of more than 700 feet)—don't overestimate your

endurance or underestimate the heat. ("Am-I-*that*-out-of-shape?" tourists routinely find themselves winded and stranded high above town.) Bring plenty of water, along with a hat and sunscreen, and wear sturdy shoes. Most of the way, there's both a ramp and uneven stairs, but the route is in poor repair, with a lot of rough, rocky patches.

It's best to tackle the walls clockwise. (Even if you're not doing the hike, you can visually trace this route.) Find the entrance at the back-left corner of town (near St. Mary's Church, through the alley with the two arches over it, including one with a Venetian lion). Pay the entry fee and begin hiking up. On the way up, notice the sign explaining that the fortress reconstruction was funded by the United States (Nov 2004)—if you're a US taxpayer, consider this hike your tax dollars at work.

First climb as high as the **Church of Our Lady of Health** (Crkva Gospe od Zdravlj). This is the halfway mark—about 20 minutes from the base at a good pace. While some believe this church has miraculous healing powers, most everyone agrees it offers some of the best views down over Kotor.

From this church, you can either cut back down toward the Old Town, or—if you're not exhausted yet—keep hiking up to the tippy-top **Fortress of St. John** (figure another 25-30 minutes from the church, if you're in decent shape). Built on the remains of fortifications from the Illyrians (you can scan the third-century B.C. remains just beyond the fort), this was the headquarters for the entire wall network below it. There's not much to see here, but it is fun to play "king of the castle" exploring the ruined shell—and the views, with 360 degrees of Montenegrin cliffs, are spectacular.

Then head back down, enjoying your reward: a downhill walk with head-on views of the Bay of Kotor. On the way down, watch

your step on the slippery-even-when-dry marble stairs, highly polished by the feet of centuries of visitors. At the round terrace below the church, you can head to the right (back the way you came); or, for a different path, head left following *powder magazine* signs, then down (right) at the fork. The ticket-seller warned me that he's often seen people wipe out on the very last step on their way down—so exhausted after the demanding hike that they let their guard down.

Sleeping in Kotor

Kotor's hotels are a poor value, and they feel very "Balkan" (a mix of colorful, tacky, and chaotic). You'll sleep cheaper in Dubrovnik, but Kotor might seduce you into spending the night. My recommendations are all inside the Old Town. Be warned that

Sleep Code

(€1 = about $1.40, country code: 382, area code: 032)
S = Single, **D** = Double/Twin, **T** = Triple, **Q** = Quad, **b** = bathroom. Unless otherwise noted, credit cards are accepted and breakfast is included, but the modest tourist tax (about €1 per person, per night) is not. Everyone listed here speaks English.

Rates: If I list two rates for an accommodation, the second rate applies off-season (generally Oct-May); if I list three rates, separated by slashes, the first is for peak season (July-Aug), the second is for shoulder season (May-June and Sept), and the third is for off-season (Oct-April). The dates for seasonal rates vary by hotel, and prices can change without notice; verify the hotel's current rates online or by email. For other updates, see www.ricksteves.com/update.

To help you sort easily through these listings, I've divided the accommodations into two categories based on the price for a double room with bath during high season:

$$ Higher Priced—Most rooms €100 or more.
$ Lower Priced—Most rooms less than €100.

loud nightclubs can bother light sleepers, especially in summer. Most of the town's cheaper *sobe* are outside the city walls (ask for details at TI).

$$ Hotel Vardar has 24 rooms with mod bathrooms smack dab in the middle of the Old Town. This classic old copper-roofed hotel was recently renovated from top to bottom, leaving it stylish but not gaudy. While convenient, the dead-central location can come with some noise, especially on weekends—request a quieter room (Sb-€125/€115/€95, Db-€185/€155/€125; 20 percent less Fri-Sat nights for two people, pricier and larger apartments have views on the square, air-con, elevator, free Wi-Fi in lobby, free cable Internet, Stari Grad 476, tel. 032/325-084, www.hotelvardar .com, info@hotelvardar.com).

$$ Hotel Cattaro offers 20 newish, Balkan-plush rooms— with dark wood and bold old-meets-new decor—above a casino right on the Square of Arms (Sb-€89/€69, Db-€119/€99, cheaper rates are for Nov-April, pricier suites, some noise from square, air-con, elevator, free Wi-Fi, tel. 032/311-000, fax 032/311-080, www .cattarohotel.com, cattarohotel@t-com.me).

$ Hotel Marija, a somewhat ramshackle throwback on an Old Town square, offers 17 rooms and wood-paneled halls. Rooms overlooking the square come with noise and the windows are thin, so request a quieter room in the back. Communicating with the staff can be challenging but is workable (Sb-€65/€50, Db-€90/€70,

Tb-€103/€90, Qb-€130/€110, air-con, free Wi-Fi, on Trg od Kina, Stari Grad 449, tel. 032/325-062, hotel.marija.kotor@t -com.me).

Near Kotor, in Perast

If you're overnighting in Montenegro, tiny Perast is sleepier than Kotor—which is both good (quiet after dark) and bad (quiet after dark). These two hotels flank the main square along the waterfront road, right in the heart of town. Both have restaurant piers with fine seating right on the water.

$$ Conte Hotel has 10 apartments, each one with a sea view (small studio-€100/€80/€70, big studio-€120/€90/€80, more for larger apartments, air-con, free Wi-Fi, Obala Kapetana Marka Martinovića bb, tel. 032/373-687, www.hotel-conte.com, hotel conte@yahoo.com).

$$ Admiral Hotel has eight rooms in an old officer's mansion (Db-€60-120/€50-100, lower rates are for Sept-Oct and May-June, closed Nov-April, price depends on size—highest are for rooms with seaview balcony, air-con, free Wi-Fi, Obala Kapetana Marka Martinovića 82, tel. 032/373-556, mobile 069-209-052, www.admiralperast.com, hoteladmiral@t-com.me).

Eating in Kotor

There's no shortage of dining options in Kotor's Old Town; even locals suggest simply wandering the streets and squares, following your nose, and choosing the ambience you like best. Truly great cuisine is rare here—I'd just settle for something scenic and functional. I've eaten well at **La Pasteria,** which has good pizzas and pastas, and breezy outdoor tables facing St. Tryphon's Cathedral (€6-9 pizzas and pastas, €11-15 main courses, daily 8:00-1:00 in the morning, Pjaca Sv. Tripuna/Trg od Katedrale, tel. 032/322-269). Nearby, **City Restaurant** lacks cathedral views but offers a fine, shady perch—its well-varnished picnic tables are set within the little forest in the Old Town, and more tables fill a small square out front (€6-10 pizzas, pastas, and salads; €7-17 main courses; daily 8:00-1:00 in the morning; mobile 069-049-653).

Near Kotor

Consider these two very scenic options, situated along the bayside road.

In Ljuta

Restoran Stari Mlini has a cozy interior and wonderful outdoor seating scattered around a spring-fed stream near an old, namesake water mill. Surrounded by trickling water, you'll dine on local cuisine—you can even choose your own trout from the pond (€12-18 pastas, €13-22 main dishes, long hours daily, tel. 032/333-555).

Near the Verige Strait, in Morinj

Konoba Ćatovića Mlini is a memorable restaurant worth going out of your way to reach. Hiding in a sparse forest off the main fjordside road, this oasis is situated amidst a series of ponds, streams, waterfalls, and bubbling springs. The traditionally clad waiters are stiffly formal, and the cuisine is good and surprisingly affordable. Choose between several different stony seating options, indoors and out. Family-run for 200 years, this place is a local institution, yet it feels like a well-kept secret (despite the crowds in summer). Reservations are essential (€8-14 pastas, €10-24 fish dishes, extensive wine list—Vranac is a popular local dry red, daily 11:00-23:00, tel. 032/373-030). The best plan might be to dine here on your way back to Dubrovnik from Kotor.

Getting There: At the town of Morinj, watch for burgundy *Konoba Ćatovića Mlini* signs and fish-shaped signs leading away from the water. You'll make several turns, but the signs will lead you right to the restaurant.

Kotor Connections

From Kotor by Bus to: Herceg Novi (2/hour, 1 hour), **Budva** (1-4/hour, 40 minutes), **Cetinje** (2-3/hour, 1 hour), **Dubrovnik** (daily at 8:30 and 14:45, also sporadic connections on other days, 2.5 hours), **Mostar** via Trebinje (1/day in the afternoon, 5.5 hours), **Zagreb** (daily at 14:45). Bus info: tel. 032/325-809, www.autobuskastanica kotor.me.

The Montenegrin Interior

Although Montenegro is trying to cultivate a glitzy beach-break cachet, for most of its history it has been thought of as a rugged mountain kingdom. While the coast—the focus of most of this chapter—was traditionally Venetian or Austrian, the real heart of Montenegro beat behind the sheer wall of mountains rising up from that seafront. Romantics, caught up in outdated Balkan fantasies, still think of this inland area as the "real" Montenegro.

While the Bay of Kotor is the most accessible and appealing

part of the country, if you have more time, consider a joyride up into the mountains. For a quick look at this area, the easiest loop takes you to the historic capital of Cetinje—a dull little town in its own right, but a fine excuse for a mountain drive. You could do this whole loop in about two and half hours without stopping (about an hour from Kotor to Cetinje, then another hour to Budva, then a half-hour back to Kotor), but if you want to stretch your legs in Njeguši or Cetinje, allow more time.

Self-Guided Driving Tour

The Road into the Mountains

The road to Cetinje twists you up the mountain face that stretches high above Kotor—it's an incredibly scenic, white-knuckle drive.

From Kotor, leave town toward Budva (bearing left at the roundabout). At the edge of Kotor, after the cemetery but before the big tunnel, take a right (marked for *Cetinje*) and begin your ascent. Cresting the first hill, go left to get to Cetinje (also marked for *Njeguši*). You'll wind up and up (past a small Roma encampment) on 25 numbered switchbacks. The road is a souvenir from the Habsburg era (1884). While Venetian rule brought sea trade, Austrian rule brought fortresses and infrastructure. After switchback #13, you'll pass an old customs house marking the former border between the Austro-Hungarian Empire and the Kingdom of Montenegro—a reminder that the coastline was not historically an integral part of Montenegrin cultural identity. As you near the top, look across the canyon to the left to spot the impossibly rough little donkey path that once was Cetinje's connection with the coast...like a tenuous umbilical cord tethering the mountainous interior to the outside world.

As you crest the hill, the vegetation changes—you're high above the Adriatic, with commanding views of Kotor and its bay (and great photo-op pull-outs; the best is just after switchback #25). Continuing inland, you find yourself in another world: poor, insular, and more Eastern (you'll see more Cyrillic lettering). Country farmhouses sell smoked ham, mountain cheese, and *medovina* (honey brandy). Before long, you reach a broad plain and the hamlet of...

Njeguši

The humble-seeming village of Njeguši (NYEH-goo-shee) is actually well-known among Montenegrins, with two very important claims to fame. This was the hometown of the House of Petrović-Njegoš, the dynasty that ruled Montenegro for much of its history (1696-1918). The family's favorite son was Petar II Petrović-Njegoš (1813-1851). Aside from ruling the country,

Petar II is remembered most fondly as a great poet and playwright—sort of the Montenegrin Shakespeare.

Njeguši is also famous for producing its own special type of air-dried ham, called *Njeguški pršut.* Locals explain that, because this meadow overlooks the sea on one side, and the mountains on the other, the wind changes direction 10 times each day, alternating between dry mountain breeze and salty sea air—perfect for seasoning and drying ham hocks. For good measure, the *pršut* is also smoked with beech wood. The blocky, white buildings lining the road that look like giant Monopoly houses are actually smokehouses, jammed with five layers of hanging ham hocks—thousands of euros' worth—silently aging. (More industry than you realize hides out in sleepy villages.) A couple of traditional restaurants at the heart of the village are happy to serve passing tourists a lunch of this local specialty.

From Njeguši to Cetinje

Continuing through Njeguši toward Cetinje, you'll twist up into more mountains—soon arriving in an even more rugged and inhospitable landscape than you passed on the road that brought you here from the coast. Eyeing this desolate scenery, you can understand why the visiting Lord Byron said of this place, "Am I in paradise or on the moon?" Along the mountain road that drops you down into Cetinje, each rock has the phone number of a vulture-esque road repair service *(auto slep)* spray-painted onto it. Low-profile plaques mark the site of Tito-era ambush assassinations.

Keep an eye out (on the horizon to the right) for the pointy peak of the mountain called **Lovćen,** which is capped by an elaborate mausoleum, designed by the great Croatian sculptor Ivan Meštrović, and devoted to King Petar II Petrović-Njegoš. With more time, you could actually drive up to the top of this mountain for sweeping views across Montenegro.

When you get into Cetinje, take a right when you hit a fork and find a place to park. To find your way into the old center, ask "guh-DEH yeh TSEHN-tar?"

Cetinje

Cetinje (TSEH-teen-yeh)—the historic capital of Montenegro—is a fine but fallen-on-hard-times little burg that sits cradled in a desolate valley surrounded by mighty peaks. Run-down as Cetinje is, it's still more pleasant than the current, drab capital, Podgorica.

Observing Cetinje from afar, it seems made to order as the historic capital of a remote and rustic people. It was the home of the Montenegrin king since the 15th century, but has always been pretty humble. In fact, it's said that when the Ottomans conquered it and moved in ready to rampage, they realized there wasn't much to pillage and plunder—so they just destroyed the town and moved on. The town was destroyed several other times, as well—and each time, the local people rebuilt it.

This "Old Royal Capital," once the leading city in the realm, is today a victim of Tito's quirky economic program for Yugoslavia. It used to provide shoes and refrigerators for the country, but when Yugoslavia disintegrated, so did the viability of Cetinje's economy. As you explore the two-story town today, it seems there's little more than a scruffy dollop of tourism to keep its 17,000 people housed and fed. Many of its younger generation have left for employment along the coast in the tourism industry.

Stroll the main street (Njegoševa) past kids on bikes, old-timers with hard memories, and young adults with metabolisms as low as the town's. At the end of this drag is the main square (Balšića Pazar), surrounded by low-key sights with sporadic opening hours: the **Ethnographic Museum** (traditional costumes and folk life), **Historical Museum** (tracing the story of Montenegro), **Njegoš Museum** (dedicated to the beloved poet-king Petar II Petrović-Njegoš), and **National Museum,** which honors King Nikola I, who ruled from 1860 until 1918. While his residence is as poor and humble a royal palace as you'll see in Europe, Nikola I thought big. He married off five of his daughters into the various royal families of Europe.

A short walk from the palace is the birthplace of the town, **Cetinje Monastery.** It's dedicated to St. Peter of Cetinje, a leg-

endary local priest who carried a cross in one hand and a sword in the other, established the first set of laws among Montenegrins, and inspired his people to defend Christianity against the Muslims. The monastery also holds the supposed right hand of St. John the Baptist. You are free to wander respectfully through the courtyard and church of this spiritual capital of Serbian Orthodox Montenegro.

From Cetinje Back to the Coast

To avoid backtracking down the same twisty road you came up, consider heading more directly back toward the coast from Cetinje. Just follow signs for *Budva.* A few miles outside of Cetinje along this road, look for the good **Restoran Konak,** which serves up tasty traditional dishes with indoor and outdoor seating (open long hours daily, tel. 041/761-011).

Continuing along this road, you'll pop out high above the

Budva Riviera. Looking out to sea, you'll spot the distinctive peninsula of Sveti Stefan off to the left, and the town of Budva to the right. If you have even more time, linger along the coast to visit these sights (described next). Otherwise, head right to return to Kotor or Dubrovnik.

The Budva Riviera

Montenegrins boast, "Croatia's got islands, but we've got beaches!" Long swaths of coarse-sand and fine-pebble beaches surround the resort town of Budva, just south of Kotor. This 15-mile stretch of coast, called the "Budva Riviera," is unappealingly built up, with endless strings of cheap resort hotels (and quite a few new five-star ones)—making it pale in comparison to the jagged saltiness of the Bay of Kotor or the romantic tidiness of Dalmatia. This region has recently become a mecca for super-wealthy Russians, staking their claim to this patch of Adriatic seafront. But the area isn't without its charm. Aside from the pleasant Old Town of the region's unofficial capital, Budva, you'll discover a near-mythical haunt of the rich and famous: the highly exclusive resort peninsula of Sveti Stefan (not possible to visit, but alluring from afar). For me, more time in Kotor or an earlier return to Dubrovnik would be more satisfying than the trek to the Budva Riviera. But beach-lovers who have plenty of time and a spirit of adventure will find this area merits a look.

Getting to the Budva Riviera

Budva is about a 30-minute drive south of **Kotor.** The easiest approach is to continue past Kotor along the fjord, left at the roundabout, then through the tunnel (following *Budva* signs; exiting the tunnel, notice the sign in Cyrillic letters for Russki Radio 107.3—catering to the Russian jet-setters). For a more scenic route, take a right before the tunnel for the upper road to Budva that twists over the mountain (described earlier, under "The Montenegrin Interior"). After winding up several switchbacks (with giddy views back over the Bay of Kotor) and cresting the hill, go right (again following *Budva* signs). You'll coast down into a valley, through the town of Lastva, then back over another mild hill that deposits you above the beaches of Budva.

First you'll reach the town of **Budva** (turn right at traffic light, following brown *Stari Grad* signs to the Old Town; parking is well-marked in modern complex next to Old Town). Continuing around the bay, you'll pass the busy, modern resort cluster of Bečići before reaching **Sveti Stefan.**

Sights on the Budva Riviera

Between the strings of resort hotels are two towns that deserve a quick visit.

Budva

The Budva Riviera's best Old Town has charming Old World lanes crammed with souvenir shops and holiday-making Serbs and

Russians. While far less appealing than Kotor (and Dalmatian towns such as Korčula, Hvar, and Trogir), Budva at least offers a taste of romance between the resort sprawl.

Budva's ancient history (dating back at least to the fifth century B.C.) is arguably more illustrious than Kotor's. It began as an "emporium" (market and trading center) for Greek seamen, and extremely valuable jewelry uncovered here indicates that some pretty important people spent time in Budva. And yet, Budva isn't about history; it's about today. As in many Mexican vacation areas, the Old Town is just one more part of the resort experience—it's basically treated as a backdrop for outdoor dining and nightclubs.

A 10-minute stroll tells you all you need to know about Budva. The layout is simple and intuitive—a peninsula (flanked by beaches) with a big Venetian-style bell tower. From the parking lot, a pedestrian-only, tree-and-café-lined boulevard runs away from the Old Town. But to see the historic core of town, go instead through the Old Town walls and wander up the main drag, Njegoševa; just before the small square, on the right, is the **TI** (July-Sept daily 9:00-21:00, shorter hours off-season, at #28, tel. 033/452-750, www.budva.travel).

Out at the tip of town, you'll pop out into a small café-lined square with a **Catholic church** (on the left, with an unusually modern 1970s mosaic behind the altar depicting St. John preaching on the Montenegrin coast) facing the Orthodox **Holy Trinity Church,** with gorgeous and colorful Orthodox decorations inside. Beyond that is a huge **citadel** that's imposing on the outside but dull on the inside; it's not worth paying the €2 to tour its museum of model ships, antiquarium (old library), restaurant, and less-than-thrilling sea views (daily May-Sept 9:00-24:00, April and Oct-Nov 9:00-20:00, Dec-March 9:00-17:00).

MONTENEGRO

Sveti Stefan

Like a mirage hovering just offshore, the famously exclusive luxury hotel that makes up the resort peninsula of Sveti Stefan beckons curious travelers to come, see, snap a photo…and then wish they'd spent more time elsewhere. While scenic, there's not much to actually experience at Sveti Stefan (unless you've got a thousand bucks to rent a room); while it's a great photo op, it disappoints many who make the trip. But for those caught up in Robin Leach-ian memories of this hotel's glory days, it's worth a pilgrimage.

Once an actual, living town (connected to the mainland only by a narrow, natural causeway), Sveti Stefan was virtually abandoned after World War II. The Yugoslav government developed it into a giant resort hotel in the 1950s. As old homes were converted to hotel rooms, the novelty of the place—and its sterling location, surrounded by pebbly beaches and lush scenery—began to attract some seriously wealthy guests.

During this resort's heyday in the 1960s and 1970s, it ranked with Cannes or St-Tropez as *the* place to see or be seen on Europe's

beaches. You could rent a room, a house, an entire block of houses, or even the entire peninsula. Anonymity was vigilantly protected, as the nicest "rooms" had their own private pools (away from public scrutiny), lockable gates, and security guards. Lured by Sveti Stefan's promise of privacy, celebrities, rock stars, royalty, and dignitaries famously engaged in bidding wars to decide who'd be granted access to the best suites: Whoever put the most money in a sealed envelope and slipped it to the manager, won. (According to local legend, Sly Stallone's money talked.) Guests were pampered—indulged no matter how outrageous their requests. Sophia Loren, Kirk Douglas, Doris Day, and Claudia Schiffer are just a few of the big names who basked on Sveti Stefan's beaches.

By the late 2000s, Sveti Stefan had experienced a dramatic decline. Warfare in nearby places (such as Dubrovnik and Kosovo) kept visitors away, its cachet faded, and the resort grew a bit rough around the edges. Then the Indian company Aman Resorts swept in with ambitious plans to restore the island to its former status as one of the world's most exclusive, crème-de-la-crème resorts (cheapest Db-€700, www.amansvetistefan.com). These days, no-neck thugs guard the causeway, letting only guests (no exceptions) cross over into the fantasy world of Sveti Stefan. If you're desperate to check it out, you can reserve a meal at the restaurant (€25 per person minimum, but count on paying far more). If you want to relax on the beaches flanking the causeway, most areas charge €30-50 per person for the day, but there are a few free areas—ask the guard for details.

Even if you can't enter the peninsula, let your imagination run as you gaze upon it. Strolling through the dead town, peeking through gates, visitors hope to spot a withered old celebrity who forgot to go home. "Rooms" come with varying degrees of privacy (each more expensive than the last): no fence, small fence, big fence. At the far end is the biggest and most famous "suite," where guests have an entire corner of the peninsula to themselves. At the top of the peninsula is a big Russian Orthodox church and a smaller Serbian Orthodox church—though both are little more than hotel decorations today.

Across the water from Sveti Stefan, on its own little cove, is one of Tito's former vacation villas (Villa Miločer, also part of the Aman resort).

Getting to Sveti Stefan: Sveti Stefan is just three miles (5 km) beyond Budva. Coming around the bay from Budva (following signs toward *Bar*), you'll pass above the peninsula on the main road, watching for the well-marked pull-out on the right that offers classic views. After snapping your photos, if you want to get closer, continue down and turn off to the right, following signs to *Hotel Sveti Stefan*; you can park in the pay lot (€1/hour) and walk along the beach as far as the causeway.

From Sveti Stefan to Dubrovnik: Figure 1.5 hours to the Croatian border (if you go via Tivat—rather than Kotor—and use the shortcut ferry across the Bay of Kotor), then another 45 minutes to Dubrovnik.

BOSNIA-HERZEGOVINA
Bosna i Hercegovina

BOSNIA-HERZEGOVINA

 The mid-1990s weren't kind to Bosnia-Herzegovina: War. Destruction. Genocide. But apart from the tragic way it separated from Yugoslavia, the country has long been—and remains—a remarkable place, with ruggedly beautiful terrain, a unique mix of cultures and faiths, kind and welcoming people who pride themselves on their hospitality, and some of the most captivating sightseeing in southeastern Europe.

Little Bosnia-Herzegovina is a country with three faiths, three languages, and two alphabets. While the rest of Yugoslavia has splintered into countries dominated by one ethnicity, Bosnia remains an uneasy mix of scattered communities, with large contingents of all three major Yugoslav groups: Muslim Bosniaks, Eastern Orthodox Serbs, and Catholic Croats. These same three factions fought each other in that brutal war just two decades ago, and today they're struggling to reconcile, work together, and put the country back on track.

A visit here offers a fascinating opportunity to sample the cultures of these three major faiths within a relatively small area. In the same day, you can inhale incense in a mystical-feeling Serbian Orthodox church, hear the subtle clicking of rosary beads in a Roman Catholic church, and listen to the Muslim call to prayer echo across a skyline of prickly minarets. Few places in Europe—or the world—cram so much diversity into such a small space.

About half of the people in Bosnia are "Bosniaks"—that is, Muslims. Travel in Bosnia offers an illuminating and unique glimpse of a culture that's both devoutly Muslim and fully European. Here, just a short drive from the touristy Dalmatian Coast, you can step into a mosque and learn about Islam directly from a Muslim. The country also holds one of the most important pilgrimage sites of the Roman Catholic world: Međugorje, where six residents have reported seeing visions of the Virgin Mary.

More than any other country in this book, Bosnia rearranges your mental furniture. While repairs are ongoing, you'll still be confronted by vivid and thought-provoking scars of the 1990s war, especially outside of the tourist zones. Poignant roadside memori-

Bosnia-Herzegovnia Political Regions

☐ Republika Srpska

☐ Muslim-Croat Federation

als to fallen soldiers, burned-out husks of buildings, unmistakable starburst patterns in the pavement, and bullet holes in walls

are a constant reminder that the country is still recovering—physically and psychologically. Driving through the countryside, you'll pass between Muslim, Croat, and Serb towns—each one decorated with its own provocative sectarian symbols. In an age when we watch news coverage of conflicts abroad with the same detachment we accord Hollywood blockbusters, Bosnia teaches an essential lesson about how real—and destructive—war and interethnic strife truly are.

Bosnia-Herzegovina Almanac

Official Name: Bosna i Hercegovina (abbreviated "BiH"); the *i* means "and"—Bosnia and Herzegovina (the country's two regions). For simplicity, I generally call it "Bosnia" in this book. "Bosna" (literally "running water") is the name of a major river here, while the tongue-twisting name "Herzegovina" (hert-seh-GOH-vee-nah) comes from the German word for "dukedom" (*Herzog* means "duke").

Snapshot History: Bosnia-Herzegovina's early history is similar to the rest of the region: Illyrians, Romans, and Slavs (oh, my!). In the late 15th century, Turkish rulers from the Ottoman Empire began a 400-year domination of the country. Many of the Ottomans' subjects converted to Islam, and their descendants remain Muslims today. Bosnia-Herzegovina became part of the Austro-Hungarian Empire in 1878, then Yugoslavia after World War I, until it declared independence in the spring of 1992. The bloody war that ensued came to an end in 1995. (For details, see the Understanding Yugoslavia chapter.)

Population: About 4.6 million. (There were about 100,000 identified casualties of the recent war, but many estimates of total casualties are double that number.) Someone who lives in Bosnia-Herzegovina, regardless of ethnicity, is called a "Bosnian." A southern Slav who practices Islam is called a "Bosniak." Today, about half of all Bosnians are Bosniaks (Muslims), a little more than a third are Orthodox Serbs, and about 15 percent are Catholic Croats.

Area: 19,741 square miles (about the size of West Virginia). In both size and population, Bosnia is comparable to Croatia.

Geography: Bosnia and Herzegovina are two distinct regions that share the same mountainous country. Bosnia constitutes the majority of the country (in the north, with a continental climate), while Herzegovina is the southern tip (about a fifth of the total area, with a hotter Mediterranean climate). The nation's capital, Sarajevo, has an estimated 310,000 people; Mostar is

In this book I focus on a few key destinations, including several fascinating, user-friendly places within easy reach of the Dalmatian Coast: the Turkish-flavored city of Mostar (with its restored Old Bridge—one of Europe's most inspiring sights), some nearby attractions offering a more complete view of Herzegovina (Blagaj, Počitelj, and Stolac), and the Catholic shrine at Međugorje. A longer trip from Dalmatia—but well worth the trek—is the Bosnian capital of Sarajevo, with a spectacular mountain-valley setting, a multilayered history, powerful wartime stories, and a resilient populace of proud Sarajevans eager to show you their fine city.

Bosnia is highly recommended as a detour—both geographi-

Herzegovina's biggest city (with approximately 130,000 people) and unofficial capital.

Red Tape: To enter Bosnia-Herzegovina, Americans and Canadians need only a passport (no visa required).

Economy: The country's economy has struggled since the war—the per capita GDP is just $6,600, and the official unemployment rate is around 43 percent.

Currency: The official currency is the Convertible Mark (Konvertibilna Marka, abbreviated KM locally, BAM internationally). The official exchange rate is $1 = about 1.40 KM. But merchants are usually willing to take euros, and (in Mostar) they'll often accept Croatian kunas, roughly converting prices with a simple formula:

2 KM = €1 = 8 kn (= about $1.40)

Telephones: Bosnia-Herzegovina's country code is 387. If calling from another country, first dial the international access code (00 in Europe, 011 in the US), then 387, then the area code (minus the initial zero), then the number.

Flag: The flag of Bosnia-Herzegovina is a blue field with a yellow triangle along the top edge. The three points of the triangle represent Bosnia-Herzegovina's three peoples (Bosniaks, Croats, Serbs), and the triangle itself resembles the physical shape of the country. A row of white stars underscores the longest side of the triangle. These stars—and the yellow-and-blue color scheme—echo the flag of the European Union (a nod to the EU's efforts to bring peace to the region). While this compromise flag sounds like a nice idea, almost no Bosnian embraces it as his or her own; each group has its own unofficial but highly prized symbols and flags (such as the fleur-de-lis for the Bosniaks, the red-and-white checkerboard shield for the Croats, and the cross with the four C's for the Serbs)—many of which offend the other groups.

cal and cultural—from the Croatian and Slovenian mainstream. Inquisitive visitors come away from a visit to Bosnia with a more nuanced understanding of the former Yugoslavia. Practically speaking, Bosnia offers lower prices and a warmer welcome than you'll find on the Croatian coast.

Nervous travelers might be tempted to give Bosnia-Herzegovina a miss. The country can be unsettling, because of its in-your-face war damage and exotic mélange of cultures that seems un-European. But to me, for exactly these reasons, Bosnia ranks alongside Croatia and Slovenia as a rewarding destination. Overcome your jitters and dive in.

Bosnian History

With its mountainous landscape, remote from the more mainline areas of the western Balkans, Bosnia's evolution has followed a unique course. Even now, the people of Bosnia struggle with being outsiders—afloat on an oddball cultural island flanked by the Roman Catholic West (Croatia) and the Orthodox East (Serbia), borrowing elements from both but not fully belonging to either.

After periods of rule by the Illyrians (ancestors of today's Albanians) and the Romans, Bosnia fostered its own thriving Slavic culture during the Middle Ages. This was the time of the Bogomil culture: A homegrown branch of Christianity that was neither Catholic nor Orthodox—and was viewed with suspicion by both faiths. The Bogomil (literally "dear to God") faith was simple, ascetic, and somewhat mystic, combining elements of Slavic, Illyrian, and Celtic traditions. The Bogomils—who comprised a majority of the population of medieval Bosnia—had a thriving civilization. Vivid artifacts of the Bogomil kingdom are still around, such as their engraved burial grave markers, called *stećaks* (some of the best-preserved are in Stolac, near Mostar).

When the Ottomans (from what's now called Turkey) took over this land in the 15th century, they tolerated different faiths... but offered economic and political incentives to those who converted to Islam. In negotiating their religious freedoms with the sultans, Bosnia's Roman Catholics (who identified as Croats) and Eastern Orthodox (who identified as Serbs) both had the support of larger church hierarchies outside of Bosnia. But the Bogomils had no bargaining power, and were more likely to swap one monotheistic faith for another—creating the Muslim South Slav ethnicity that would come to be known as "Bosniak."

Under the Ottomans, Bosnia flourished. The Ottoman sultans invested in infrastructure (primarily bridges—including Mostar's Old Bridge—and fountains) and architecture, including many mosques, hammams (baths), caravanserais (inns), madrassas (theological schools), and so on. Bosnian Muslims rose through the ranks of the empire, becoming military generals, religious leaders, beloved poets, and even grand viziers (top-level advisors to the sultans).

After four centuries of rule, the Ottoman Empire entered a steep decline. Unable to continue to rule over its vast holdings, in 1878 the sultan passed control of Bosnia-Herzegovina to its Habsburg rival, the Austro-Hungarian Empire (which already controlled neighboring Croatia and Slovenia). The Habsburgs quickly moved to modernize Bosnia, erecting buildings and investing in infrastructure. But just 40 years later, that empire, too, would topple—losing a war that began when its heir, the Archduke Franz Ferdinand, was assassinated in Sarajevo.

Following World War I, Bosnia was swept up in the movement to create a union of the South Slavs. The original incarnation of Yugoslavia, called "the Kingdom of the Serbs, Croats, and Slovenes," ignored the Bosniaks both in name and in political influence—they were merely along for the ride.

During World War II, Bosnia was part of the so-called "Independent State of Croatia" (run by the Nazis' puppet Ustaše government). Some of the most dramatic WWII battles between the Yugoslav Partisans and the Nazis took place here in Bosnia. The postwar communist state of Yugoslavia was born in the Bosnian town of Jajce on November 29, 1943, when Partisan generals met to outline the future of a hoped-for post-Nazi state. But in the new incarnation of Yugoslavia, many Bosniaks still felt like second-class citizens. Local Muslims recall that Yugoslav government-issued textbooks reinforced negative stereotypes. For example, they might say "Sasha [a typically Serb name] is working," but "Mujo [a typically Muslim name] is a bad boy."

Even after the outbreak of violence between breakaway republics Slovenia and Croatia and Serb-dominated Yugoslavia in 1991, things stayed strangely calm in Bosnia. When the Bosnian conflict finally erupted in 1992, it was war of the most brutal kind. The early to mid-1990s saw the worst human, architectural, and cultural devastation in Bosnian history. Sarajevo, Srebrenica, and Mostar became synonymous with sectarian strife, horrific sieges, and shocking genocide.

The Dayton Peace Accords that ended the conflict here in 1995 gerrymandered the nation into three separate regions: the Federation of Bosnia and Herzegovina (FBiH, shared by Bosniaks and Croats, roughly in the western and central parts of the country), the Republika Srpska (RS, dominated by Serbs, generally to the north and east), and the Brčko District (BD, a tiny corner of the country, with a mix of the ethnicities). For the most part, each of the three native ethnic groups stay in "their" part of this divided country, but tourists can move freely between them.

On your visit, tune into the many ways that the Bosniaks, Croats, and Serbs of Bosnia work hard to coexist. To satisfy the country's various factions, the currency uses both the Roman and the Cyrillic alphabets, and bills have different figureheads and symbols (some bills feature Bosniaks, others Serbs). Until

Fundamentalist Islam in Bosnia?

Islam is a hot topic in today's Europe, where many citizens are blaming Muslim immigrants for their society's woes. And even though Bosnia's Muslims are indigenous, they're not immune to the criticism—especially from their Serb and Croat rivals. While Bosniaks have a long history as a peace-loving people, critics allege that elements of the population are experimenting with some alarming fundamentalist Islamic ideologies.

These allegations do have some basis in fact. During the war and genocide of the 1990s, many Bosniaks felt abandoned by their western allies in Europe and the US, who were too timid to step in and "take sides" to end the violence. In his people's darkest hour, desperate Bosnian President Alija Izetbegović recruited assistance from the only group willing to offer help: Muslim fundamentalists from the Middle East and North Africa. Several hundred mujahideen (Islamic jihadists) came to Bosnia to train Bosniak soldiers, and participated in bloody massacres of Serbs and Croats. They brought with them the dangerous ideas of Wahhabism—an ultraconservative movement bent on "purifying" Islam, often through violent means. According to reports, Izetbegović was even in contact with Osama bin Laden. In some cases, the mujahideen offered donations to widows of *šehid*s (Bosniak martyrs).

While waning, these groups' influence persists. Muslim countries have helped to fund the postwar reconstruction of Bosnia, especially the building and rebuilding of mosques and madrassas. Just as the end of atheistic, communist Yugoslav rule kick-started a passion for Catholicism in Croatia and the Orthodox faith in Serbia, many Muslims in Bosnia are today actively pursuing their faith. You may even see women wearing traditional Muslim headscarves—a rare sight before the war, when most Bosniaks dressed just like their Serb and Croat neighbors.

Meanwhile, some of the fundamentalist Muslims who came to fight in the war are still here (although they were supposed to leave the country under the Dayton Peace Accords). Mujahideen who fought were initially rewarded with Bosnian citizenship (these passports were revoked in 2007). Some of them married local women, however, and are pursuing a Wahhabist agenda in Bosnia. Small pockets of Wahhabists live in remote areas high in the mountains, separate from mainstream Bosnian society—indeed, the typical Bosniak on the street is as wary of them as you might be. The violent element of Bosnian Wahhabists are just one more example of a terrorist "cell" in a country that doesn't want them. The majority of practicing Muslims in Bosnia explicitly denounce the Wahhabists. As in any country, Bosnia has its share of fanatics—but they make up a tiny fringe in this predominantly peaceful nation.

very recently, the alphabet used on road signs changed with the territory: Roman alphabet in Muslim and Croat areas, Cyrillic alphabet in Serb lands. But now all road signs throughout Bosnia-Herzegovina are required to appear in both alphabets—though that doesn't prevent vandals from spray-painting over the alphabet they don't like. License plates also used different alphabets, but this led to vandalism to cars that crossed into the "other side." Today's license plates use only letters that are common to both alphabets.

Towns with mixed populations are either effectively divided in half, or have buildings clearly marked with symbols indicating the ethnicity of the occupant. Small-town schoolhouses often operate "two schools under one roof," with separate entrances and staggered shifts for the Bosniak and Croat kids...who, virtually from birth, are constantly told they are very different from each other. In some towns, a beautifully restored Orthodox church may sit across from the battered footprint of a long-gone mosque (or vice versa).

Bosnia has a central government, but each population group also has its own autonomous government and sub-agencies, resulting in four different, essentially redundant bureaucracies. The country is also divided into 10 state-like cantons, each of which also has some governmental authority. What's more, these various levels of governments refuse to cooperate—imagine the inefficiency. (For example, nobody knows how many people live in Bosnia, because there's no agreement on how to conduct a national census.) On top of all this, Bosnia is still navigating the complex transition from communism to capitalism, and rebuilding from a devastating war. It's a miracle that things here work as well as they do.

Nearly 20 years later, the delicate compromises that were necessary to end a horrifying war have become almost too complicated to maintain. For Bosnia-Herzegovina to fully recover, all three groups must learn to truly set aside their differences and work together. Pessimists (who are abundant in this region) don't like Bosnia's chances, and Bosnian Serbs still talk loudly about secession (their president, Milorad Dodik, is a separatist who has floated several proposals to hold a referendum for independence). But others see signs of hope, such as the young people from the three faiths now beginning to cautiously intermingle, as their ancestors did for centuries. Will Bosniak, Serb, and Croat youth manage to transcend the fear and anger that tainted their parents' and grandparents' country in the 20th century? Stay tuned.

Bosnian Food

Bosnia-Herzegovina dines on grilled meat, stewed vegetables, soft cheeses, and other foods you may think of as "Turkish" or "Greek."

Balkan Flavors

All of the countries of the Balkan Peninsula—basically from Slovenia to Greece—have several foods in common: The Ottomans from today's Turkey, who controlled much of this territory for centuries, imported some goodies that remained standard fare here long after they left town. Whether you're in Bosnia-Herzegovina, Slovenia, Croatia, Montenegro, Serbia, Kosovo, or Albania, it's worth seeking out some of these local tastes.

A popular, cheap fast food you'll see everywhere is **burek** (BOO-rehk)—phyllo dough filled with meat, cheese, spinach, or apples. The more familiar **baklava** is phyllo dough layered with honey and nuts.

Grilled meats are a staple of Balkan cuisine. You'll most often see **čevapčići** (cheh-VAHP-chee-chee), or simply **čevap** (cheh-VAHP)—minced meat formed into a sausage-link shape, then grilled. **Ražnjići** (RAZH-nyee-chee) is small pieces of steak on a skewer, like a shish kebab. **Pljeskavica** (plehs-kah-VEET-suh) is similar to *čevapčići,* except the meat is in the form of a hamburger-like patty.

While Balkan cuisine favors meat, a nice veggie complement is **đuveđ** (JOO-vedge)—a spicy mix of stewed vegetables, flavored with tomatoes and peppers.

And you just can't eat any of this stuff without the ever-present condiment **ajvar** (EYE-var). Made from red bell pepper and eggplant, *ajvar* is like ketchup with a kick. Many Americans pack a jar of this distinctive sauce to remember the flavors of the Balkans when they get back home. (You may even be able to find it at specialty grocery stores in the US—look for "eggplant/red pepper spread.") Particularly in Bosnia, another side-dish you'll see is the soft, spreadable—and tasty—cheese called **kajmak**. **Lepinje** is a pita-like grilled bread, which is often wrapped around *čevapčići* or *pljeskavica* to make a sandwich.

Ajvar, kajmak, lepinje, and diced raw onions are the perfect complement to a **"mixed grill"** of various meats on a big platter—the quintessence of Balkan cuisine on one plate.

For a rundown of the most common items you'll eat in Bosnia—and throughout the Balkans—see the "Balkan Flavors" sidebar.

Bosnia produces some wine, but it's mostly consumed domestically. Sarajevso Pivo, brewed in the capital, is the favored brand of beer. In Bosnia, "coffee" is *kafa* (not *kava,* as in Croatia and Slovenia).

Bosnian Language

Technically, Bosnia-Herzegovina has three languages—Bosnian, Serbian, and Croatian. But all three are mutually intelligible variants of what was until recently considered a single language: Serbo-Croatian. Bosniaks and Croats use basically the same Roman alphabet we do, while Serbs use the Cyrillic alphabet. You'll see both alphabets on currency, official documents, and road signs, but the Roman alphabet predominates in virtually every destination covered in this book. Many people also speak English.

MOSTAR and NEARBY

Mostar • Blagaj • Počitelj • Stolac • Međugorje

Mostar (MOH-star) encapsulates the best and the worst of Yugoslavia. During the Tito years, its residents enjoyed an idyllic mingling of cultures—Catholic Croats, Orthodox Serbs, and Muslim Bosniaks living together in harmony, their differences spanned by an Old Bridge that epitomized an optimistic vision of a Yugoslavia where ethnicity didn't matter. But then, as the country unraveled in the early 1990s, Mostar was gripped by a gory three-way war among those same peoples...and that famous bridge crumbled into the Neretva River.

Mostar is still rebuilding, and the bullet holes and destroyed buildings are ugly reminders that the last time you saw this place, it was probably on the nightly news. Western visitors may also be struck by the immediacy of the Muslim culture that permeates Mostar—at this crossroads of civilizations, minarets share the horizon with church steeples. During the Ottomans' 400-year control of this region, many Slavic subjects converted to Islam. And, although they retreated in the late 19th century, the Ottomans left behind a rich architectural, cultural, and religious legacy that has forever shaped Mostar. Five times each day, loudspeakers on minarets crackle to life, and the call to prayer warbles through the streets. In many parts of the city, you'd swear you were in Turkey.

If these images intrigue you, read on—Mostar has so much

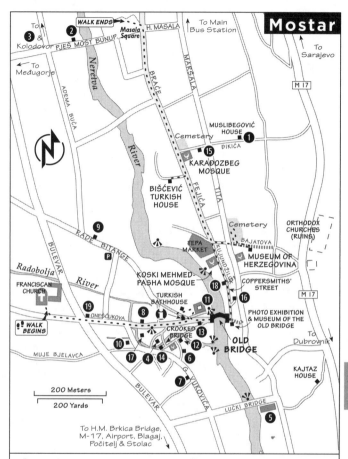

Mostar

WALK ENDS
Masala Square
H. MASALA
To Main Bus Station
To & Kolodvor
PJEŠ MOST BUNUP.
To Sarajevo
To Medugorje
M 17
Neretva
ADEMA BUĆA
BRAĆE
MARŠALA
MUSLIBEGOVIĆ HOUSE ❶
Cemetery
ĐIKIĆA ⓯
River
KARAĐOZBEG MOSQUE
BIŠĆEVIĆ TURKISH HOUSE
FEJIĆA
TITA
Cemetery
ORTHODOX CHURCHES (RUINS)
BAJATOVA
❾ RADE BITANGE
TEPA MARKET
MUSEUM OF HERZEGOVINA
KUJUNDŽILUK
Radobolja
BULEVAR
River
KOSKI MEHMED-PASHA MOSQUE
COPPERSMITHS' STREET
M 17
FRANCISCAN CHURCH
TURKISH BATHHOUSE
⓲
⓰
❿
ⓑ
PHOTO EXHIBITION & MUSEUM OF THE OLD BRIDGE
❿⓳ WALK BEGINS
ONEŠĆUKOVA
❽ ❶
CROOKED BRIDGE
⓭
OLD BRIDGE
To Dubrovnik
❿
⓱ ❹ ⓮
⓬
❻
KAJTAZ HOUSE
MUJE BJELAVCA
G. VUKOVIĆA
❼
BULEVAR
LUČKI BRIDGE
200 Meters
200 Yards
❺
To H.M. Brkica Bridge, M-17, Airport, Blagaj, Počitelj & Stolac

MOSTAR AND NEARBY

❶ Muslibegović House
❷ Hotel Bristol
❸ To Hotel Ero
❹ Hotel Kriva Ćuprija
❺ Hotel Kriva Ćuprija II
❻ Pansion Čardak & Pansion Nur
❼ Villa Anri
❽ Motel Emen
❾ Villa Fortuna
❿ Villa Botticelli
⓫ Bridge-View Eateries
⓬ Restoran Hindin Han
⓭ Šadrvan Restaurant
⓮ Ima Dana Restaurant
⓯ Saray Restaurant
⓰ Ali Baba Nightclub
⓱ Oscar Nightclub
⓲ Fortuna Tours
⓳ Future Synagogue Site

more to offer. Despite the scars of war, its setting is stunning: straddling the banks of the gorgeous Neretva River, with tributaries and waterfalls carving their way through the rocky landscape. The sightseeing—mosques, old Turkish-style houses, and that spine-tingling Old Bridge—is more engaging than much of what you'll find in Croatia or Slovenia. And it's cheap—hotels, food, and museums are less than half the prices you'll pay in Croatia.

In this chapter, I've also included some nearby attractions in Herzegovina that are worth trying to squeeze into your itinerary. Near Mostar is a trio of other mostly Bosniak sights: the river spring and whirling dervish house at Blagaj, the striking fortified hill town of Počitelj, and workaday Stolac, which sits upon some very impressive history. I've also included the top Croat sight in Bosnia-Herzegovina: Međugorje, where Catholic pilgrims flock from around the world to hear tales of a Virgin Mary apparition. All of these places are within a half-hour's drive of Mostar, and all are more or less on the way between Mostar and coastal destinations.

While a visit to Mostar was depressing just a few years ago, the city gets more uplifting all the time: Mostarians are rebuilding at an impressive pace and working hard to make Mostar tourist-friendly. Before long, Mostar will reclaim its status as one of the premier destinations in the former Yugoslavia. Visit now, while it still has its rough-around-the-edges charm—you'll have seen it before it really took off.

Planning Your Time

Because of its cultural hairiness, a detour into Bosnia-Herzegovina feels like a real departure from a Dalmatian vacation. And yet, Mostar is easier to reach from Dubrovnik or Split than many popular Dalmatian islands (it's within a three-hour drive or bus ride from either city).

The vast majority of tourists in Mostar are day-trippers from the coast, which means the Old Town is packed at midday, but empty in the morning and evening. You can get a good feel for Mostar in just a few hours, but a full day gives you time to linger and ponder. My self-guided walk provides a framework for a visit of any duration.

You have three basic options for getting here: take a package tour from Dalmatia; rent a car for a one-day side-trip into Mostar; or (my favorite) spend the night here en route between Croatian destinations. To work a Mostar overnight into your itinerary, consider a round-trip plan that takes you south along the coast, then back north via Bosnia-Herzegovina (for example, Split-Hvar-Korčula-Dubrovnik-Mostar-back to Split).

Getting Around Herzegovina

The destinations I've covered in this chapter aren't as easy to reach as they could be from the Dalmatian Coast, but connections are workable.

By Car: Coming with your own car gives you maximum flexibility, and a number of interesting routes connect Mostar to the coast. If you do plan to drive here, let your car-rental company know in advance, to ensure you have the appropriate paperwork for crossing the border. If you're not up for driving yourself, consider splurging on a **driver** to bring you here. Drivers may suggest several detours en route. Do your homework to know which ones interest you (for example, Međugorje isn't worth the extra time for most visitors), and don't hesitate to say you want to just max out on time in Mostar itself.

By Bus: Especially if you're spending the night in Mostar, bus connections with destinations on the Dalmatian Coast (especially Split and Dubrovnik) are workable—though getting clear and consistent schedule information can be a headache.

By Package Tour: Taking a package excursion from a Dalmatian resort town seems like an efficient way to visit Mostar or Međugorje. Unfortunately, in reality it can be less rewarding than doing it on your own—count on lots and lots of hours on a crowded bus, listening to a lackluster, multilingual tour guide reading from a script, and relatively little time in the destinations themselves. But if you just want a quick one-day look at these places, an excursion could be a necessary evil. These all-day tours are sold from Split, Hvar, Korčula, Dubrovnik, and other Croatian coastal destinations for about €50-60. The best tours focus almost entirely on Mostar (it still won't be enough time); avoid tours that include a pointless boat trip on the Neretva River or time in Međugorje. Those that add a quick visit to the worthwhile town of Počitelj are a better deal. Ask for details at any travel agency in Dalmatia.

Orientation to Mostar

(country code: 387; area code: 036)

Mostar—a mid-sized city with just over 100,000 people—is situated in a basin surrounded by mountains and split down the middle by the emerald-green Neretva River. Bosniaks live mostly on the east side of the river (plus a strip on the west bank) and Croats in the modern sprawl to the west. The populations are beginning to mix again, albeit with tentative baby steps. Virtually all of the sights are in the Bosniak zone, but visitors move freely throughout the city, and most don't even notice the division. The cobbled,

MOSTAR AND NEARBY

Turkish-feeling Old Town (called the "Stari Grad" or—borrowing a Turkish term—the "Stara Čaršija") surrounds the town's center-piece, the Old Bridge.

The skyline is pierced by the minarets of various mosques, but none is as big as the two major Catholic (Croat) symbols in town, both erected since the recent war: the giant white cross on the hilltop (marking the place from where Croat forces shelled the Bosniak side of the river, including the Old Bridge); and the enor-mous (almost 100-foot-tall) bell tower of the Franciscan Church of Sts. Peter and Paul. A monumental Orthodox cathedral once stood on the hillside across the river, but it was destroyed in the war when the Serbs were forced out. Funds are now being col-lected to rebuild it.

A note about safety: Mostar is as safe as any city its size, but it doesn't always *feel* safe. You'll see bombed-out buildings everywhere, even in the core of the city. Some are marked with *Warning! Dangerous Ruin* signs, but for safety's sake, never wan-der into any building that appears damaged or deserted. In terms of petty theft, the Old Town has as many pickpockets as any tourist zone in Europe: Watch your valuables, especially on the Old Bridge.

Tourist Information

The virtually worthless TI shares a building with a tour office, but it does give out a free town map and a few other brochures on Mostar and Herzegovina (sporadic hours, generally open June-Sept daily 9:00-17:00, maybe later in busy times, likely closed Oct-May, just a block from the Old Bridge on Rade Bitange street, tel. 036/580-275, www.bhtourism.ba).

Arrival in Mostar

By Bus or Train: The **main bus station** (where most buses arrive in town) sits next to the giant but mostly deserted **train station,** north of the Old Town on the east side of the river. At the bus station, you'll find ticket windows and a left-luggage counter (2 KM/bag) in the Autoprevoz lobby facing the bus stalls. You can check schedules and buy tickets in this office for most buses *except* the many connections operated by Globtour, whose office is nearby (exit Autoprevoz, turn left, and walk to the end of the bus-station area). Because these two companies don't cooperate, you have to check with both to get the complete schedule. To find your way to the town center, walk through the bus stalls and parking lot and turn left at the big road, which leads you to the Old Town area in about 15 minutes. A taxi into town costs about 10 KM.

If you're arriving by bus it's possible (though unlikely) that you'll arrive at Mostar's makeshift secondary bus station, called "**Kolodvor**," on the west/Croat side of town. From here, it's a dreary 15-minute walk into town: Turn right out of the bus station area, turn left down the busy Dubrovačka street, and head straight to the river to reach the main bus station. From the station, head south along the river into the Old Town.

For details on both stations—and how to get reliable schedule information—see "Mostar Connections," later.

Helpful Hints

Local Cash: Need Convertible Marks? The most convenient ATM in town is to the left of Fortuna Tours' door, right at the top of Coppersmiths' Street (but on a short visit, you can generally skip a trip to the ATM, as most vendors here also accept Croatian kunas and euros).

Travel Agency: The handy **Fortuna Tours** travel agency, right in the heart of the Old Town (at the top of Coppersmiths' Street), sells all the tourist stuff, can book you a local guide, and answers basic questions (open long hours daily, Kujundžiluk 2, tel. 036/551-887, main office tel. 036/552-197, fax 036/551-888, www.fortuna.ba, fortuna_mostar1@bih.net.ba).

Local Guides: Hiring a guide is an excellent investment to help you understand Mostar. I've enjoyed working with **Alma Elezović,** a warm-hearted Bosniak who loves sharing her city and her wartime stories with visitors (€20/person, up to €70/group for 2-3-hour tour, includes entrance to a Turkish house and a mosque, tel. 036/550-514, mobile 061-467-699, aelezovic @gmail.com). If Alma is busy, various companies around town can arrange for a local guide at extremely reasonable prices (2-hour tour—€30/2 people, €40/4 people, includes entrance to mosque and/or Turkish house); try **Fortuna Tours,** listed previously.

If someone approaches you offering to be your guide, ask the price in advance (many charge ridiculously high rates). If they seem cagey or overpriced, decline politely. The official guides are better anyway.

Local Driver: Ermin Elezović, husband of local guide Alma (see above), is a gregarious, English-speaking driver who enjoys taking visitors on day trips from Mostar. You can also hire him for a transfer between Mostar and destinations anywhere in Croatia (prices for a van for up to 6 people: €100 for one-way transfer to Sarajevo, Split, or Dubrovnik, or €150 to add some extra time for sightseeing en route; €200 round-trip from Mostar to Sarajevo, Split, or Dubrovnik; tel. 036/550-514, mobile 061-908-597, elezovicermin@gmail.com).

Sights in Mostar

Mostar's major sights line up along a handy L-shaped axis. I've laced them together as an enjoyable orientation walk: From the Franciscan Church, you'll walk straight until you cross the Old Bridge. Then you'll turn left and walk basically straight (with a couple of detours) to the big square at the far end of town.
• *Begin at the...*

▲Franciscan Church of Sts. Peter and Paul

In a town of competing religious architectural exclamation points, this spire is the tallest. The church, which adjoins a working

Franciscan monastery, was built in 1997, after the fighting subsided (the same year as the big cross on the hill). The tower, which looks at first glance like a minaret on steroids, is actually modeled after typical Croatian/Venetian campanile bell towers. Step inside to see how the vast and coarse concrete shell awaits completion. In the meantime, the cavernous interior is already hosting services. (Sunday Mass here is an inspiration.)
• *The church fronts the busy boulevard called...*

▲Bulevar

"The Boulevard" was once the modern main drag of Mostar. In the early 1990s, this city of Bosniaks, Croats, and Serbs began to fracture under the pressure of politicians' propaganda. In October

1991, Bosnia-Herzegovina—following Croatia's and Slovenia's example, but without the blessing of its large Serb minority—began a process of splitting from Yugoslavia. Soon after, the Serb-dominated Yugoslav People's Army invaded. Mostar's Bosniaks and Croats joined forces to battle the

Serbs and succeeded in claiming the city as their own, forcing out the Serb residents.

But even as they fended off the final, distant bombardments of Serb forces, Mostar's Bosniaks (Muslims) and Croats (Catholics)

began to squabble. Neighbors, friends, and even relatives took up arms against each other. As fighting raged between the Croat and Bosniak forces, this street became the front line—and virtually all of its buildings were destroyed. Then as now, the area to the east of here (toward the river) was held by Bosniaks, while the western part of town was Croat territory.

While many of the buildings along here have been rebuilt, some damage is still evident. Stroll a bit, imagining the hell of a split community at war. Mortar craters in the asphalt leave poignant scars. During those dark war years, the Croats on the hill above laid siege to the Bosniaks on the other side, cutting off electricity, blocking roads, and blaring Croatian rabble-rousing pop music and Tokyo Rose-type propaganda speeches from loudspeakers. Through '93 and '94, when the Bosniaks dared to go out, they sprinted past exposed places, for fear of being picked off by a sniper. Local Bosniaks explain, "Night was time to live" (in black clothes). When people were killed along this street, their corpses were sometimes left here for months, because it wasn't safe to retrieve the bodies. Tens of thousands fled. Scandinavian countries were the first to open their doors, but many Bosnians ended up elsewhere in Europe, the US, and Canada.

The stories are shocking, and it's difficult to see the war impartially. But looking back on this complicated war, I try not to broadly cast one side as the "aggressors" and another as the "victims." Bosniaks were victimized in Mostar, just as Croats were victimized during the siege of Dubrovnik. And, as the remains of a destroyed Orthodox cathedral on the hillside above Mostar (not quite visible from here) attest, Serbs also took their turn as victims. Every conflict has many sides, and it's the civilians who often pay the highest toll—no matter their affiliation.

Cross the boulevard and head down Onešćukova street. A few steps down on the left, the vacant lot with the menorah-ornamented metal fence will someday be the **Mostar Synagogue.** While the town's Jewish population has dwindled to a handful of families since World War II, many Jews courageously served as aid workers and intermediaries when Croats and Bosniaks were killing each other. In recognition of their loving help, the community of Mostar gave them this land for a new synagogue.

• *Continue past the synagogue site, entering the Old Town and following the canyon of the...*

Radobolja River Valley

Cross the creek called Radobolja, which winds over waterfalls and several mills on its way to join the Neretva, and enter the city's cobbled historic core (keeping the small river on your right). As you step upon the smooth, ankle-twisting river stones, you sud-

denly become immersed in the Turkish heritage of Mostar. Around you are several fine examples of Mostar's traditional heavy limestone-shingled roofs. From the arrival of the Ottomans all the way through the end of World War II, Mostar had fewer than 15,000 residents—this compact central zone was pretty much all there was to the city. It wasn't until the Tito years that it became industrialized and grew like crazy. As you explore, survey the atmospheric eateries clinging to the walls of the canyon—and choose one for a meal or drink later in the day (I've noted a couple under "Eating in Mostar," later).

Walk straight ahead until you reach a square viewpoint platform on your right. It's across from a charming little mosque and above the stream (you may have to squeeze between souvenir stands to get there). The mosque is one of 10 in town. Before the recent war, there were 36, and before World War II, there were even more (many of those damaged or destroyed in World War II were never repaired or replaced, since Tito's communist Yugoslavia discouraged religion). But the recent war inspired Muslims to finally rebuild. Each of the town's newly reconstructed mosques was financed by a Muslim nation or organization (this one was a gift from an international association for the protection of Islamic heritage). Some critics (read: Croats) allege that these foreign Muslim influences—which generally interpret their faith more strictly than the extremely progressive and laid-back Bosniaks—are threatening to flood the country with a rising tide of Islamic fundamentalism.

• *Spanning the river below the mosque is the...*

▲Crooked Bridge (Kriva Ćuprija)

This miniature Old Bridge was built nearly a decade before its more famous sibling, supposedly to practice for the real deal. Damaged—but not destroyed—during the war, the bridge was swept away several years later by floods. The bridge you see today is a recent reconstruction.

• *Continue deeper on the same street into the city center. After a few steps, a street to the left (worth a short detour) leads to the **TI**, then a copper-domed hammam (Turkish bathhouse), which was destroyed in World War II and only recently rebuilt. A happening nightlife and restaurant scene tumbles downhill toward the river from here, offering spectacular views of the Old Bridge.*

Back on the main drag, continue along the main shopping zone, past several market stalls, to the focal point of town, the...

▲▲▲Old Bridge (Stari Most)

One of the most evocative sights in the former Yugoslavia, this iconic bridge confidently spanned the Neretva River for more than

four centuries. Mostarians of all faiths love the bridge and speak of "him" as an old friend. Traditionally considered the point where East meets West, the Old Bridge is as symbolic as it is beautiful. Dramatically arched and flanked by two boxy towers, the bridge is stirring—even if you don't know its history.

Before the Old Bridge, the Neretva was spanned only by a rickety suspension bridge, guarded by *mostari* ("watchers of the bridge"), who gave the city its name. Commissioned in 1557 by the Ottoman Sultan Süleyman the Magnificent, and completed just nine years later, the Old Bridge was a technological marvel for its time..."the longest single-span stone arch on the planet." (In other words, it's the granddaddy of the Rialto Bridge in Venice.) Because of its graceful keystone design—and the fact that there are empty spaces inside the structure—it's much lighter than it appears. And yet, nearly 400 years after it was built, the bridge was still sturdy enough to support the weight of the Nazi tanks that rolled in to occupy Mostar. Over the centuries, it became the symbol of the town and region—a metaphor in stone for the way the diverse faiths and cultures here were able to bridge the gaps that divided them.

All of that drastically changed in the early 1990s. Beginning in May of 1993, as the city became engulfed in war, the Old Bridge frequently got caught in the crossfire. Old tires were slung over its sides to absorb some of the impact from nearby artillery and shrapnel. In November of 1993, Croats began shelling the bridge from the top of the mountain (where the cross is now—you can just see its tip peeking over the hill from the top of the bridge). The bridge took several direct hits on November 8; on November 9, another shell caused the venerable Old Bridge to lurch, then tumble in pieces into the river. The mortar inside, which contained pink bauxite, turned the water red as it fell in. Locals said that their old friend was bleeding.

The decision to destroy the bridge was partly strategic—to cut off a Bosniak-controlled strip on the west bank from Bosniak forces on the east. (News footage from the time shows

Bosniak soldiers scurrying back and forth over the bridge.) But there can be no doubt that, like the Yugoslav Army's siege of Dubrovnik, the attack was also partly symbolic: the destruction of a bridge representing the city's Muslim legacy.

After the war, city leaders decided to rebuild the Old Bridge. Chunks of the original bridge were dredged up from the river. But the limestone had been compro- mised by soaking in the water for so long, so it couldn't be used (you can still see these pieces of the old Old Bridge on the riverbank below). Having pledged to rebuild the bridge authentically, restorers cut new stone from the original quarry, and each block was hand- carved. Then they assembled the

stones with the same technology used by the Ottomans 450 years ago: Workers erected wooden scaffolding and fastened the blocks together with iron hooks cast in lead. The project was overseen by UNESCO and cost over $13 million, funded largely by interna- tional donors.

It took longer to rebuild the bridge in the 21st century than it did to build it in the 16th century. But on July 23, 2004, the new Old Bridge was inaugurated with much fanfare and was immediately embraced by both the city and the world as a sign of reconciliation.

Since its restoration, another piece of bridge history has fully returned, as young men once again jump from the bridge 75 feet down into the Neretva (which remains icy cold even in summer). Done both for the sake of tradition and to impress girls, this custom was carried on even during the time when the destroyed bridge was temporarily replaced by a wooden one. Now the tower on the west side of the bridge houses the office of the local "Divers Club," a loosely run organization that carries on this long-standing ritual. On hot summer days, you'll see divers making a ruckus and collecting donations at the top of the bridge. They tease and tease, standing up on the railing and pretending they're about to jump... then getting down and asking for more money. (If he's wearing trunks rather than Speedos, he's not a diver—just a teaser.) Once they collect about €30, one of them will take the plunge.

Before moving on, see how many of the town's 10 mosques you can spot from the top of the bridge (I counted seven minarets).

• If you'd like to see one of the best **views** in town—*looking up at the Old Bridge from the riverbank below*—*backtrack the way you came into the shopping zone, take your first left (at the recommended Šadrvan restaurant—a good place to try the powerful "Bosnian coffee"), then find* *the steps down to the river on the left.*

When you're ready to continue, hike back up to the Old Bridge and cross to the other side. After the bridge on the right are two different exhibits worth a quick visit.

Bookstore near the Old Bridge

This excellent bookstore has a good, free photo exhibition of powerful images of war-torn Mostar, displayed inside a former mosque for soldiers who guarded the bridge. They play a montage of videos and photos of the bridge—before, during, and after the war—that's nearly as good as the similar film shown at the Museum of Herzegovina (described later). The shop also sells an impressively wide range of books about the former Yugoslavia and its troubled breakup.

Cost and Hours: Free, daily 7:00-24:00.

• *Just beyond the bookstore, tucked into the corner on the right, look for the stairs leading up to the...*

Museum of the Old Bridge (Muzej Stari Most)

Located within one of the Old Bridge's towers, this museum features a film and photos about the reconstruction of the bridge, archaeological findings, and a few other paltry exhibits about the history of the town and bridge, all in English. First climb up the stairs just after the bridge and buy your ticket, before hiking the rest of the way up to the top of the tower, where you can enjoy fine views through grubby windows. Then go around below to the archaeological exhibit. The museum offers more detail than most casual visitors need; consider just dropping into the smaller, free photo exhibition described previously, then moving along.

Cost and Hours: 5 KM, Tue-Sun 10:00-18:00, closed Mon, lots of stairs, Bajatova 4, mobile 061-707-307.

• *After the Old Bridge, the street swings left and leads you along...*

▲▲Coppersmiths' Street (Kujundžiluk)

This lively strip, with the flavor of a Turkish bazaar, offers some of the most colorful shopping this side of Istanbul. You'll see Mostar's characteristic bridge depicted in every possible way, along with blue-and-white "evil eyes" (believed in the Turkish culture to keep bad spirits at bay), old Yugoslav Army kitsch, and hammered-copper decorations (continuing the long tradition that gave the street its name). Partway up, the homes

The Muslims of Bosnia

While Muslim immigrants have only recently become a fixture in many European cities, Bosnia-Herzegovina is one place where Muslims have continuously been an integral part of the cultural tapestry for centuries.

During the more than 400 years that Bosnia was part of the Ottoman Empire, the Muslim Turks did not forcibly convert their subjects (unlike some Catholic despots at the time). However, it was advantageous for non-Turks to adopt Islam (for lower taxes and better business opportunities), so many Slavs living here became Muslims. In fact, within 150 years of the start of Ottoman rule, half of the population of Bosnia-Herzegovina was Muslim.

The Ottomans became increasingly intolerant of other faiths as time went on, and uprisings by Catholics and Orthodox Christians eventually led to the end of Ottoman domination in the late 19th century. But even after the Ottomans left, many people in this region continued practicing Islam, as their families had been doing for centuries. These people constitute an ethnic group called "Bosniaks," and many of them are still practicing Muslims today (following the Sunni branch of the Muslim faith). Most Bosniaks are Slavs—of the same ethnic stock as Croats and Serbs—and look pretty much the same as their neighbors; however, some Bosniaks have ancestors who married into Turkish families, and they may have some Turkish features.

The actions of a small but attention-grabbing faction of Muslim extremists have burdened Islam with a bad reputation in the Western world. But judging Islam based on Osama bin Laden and al-Qaeda is a bit like judging Christianity based on the Oslo gunman and the Ku Klux Klan. Visiting Mostar is a unique opportunity to get a taste of a fully Muslim society, made a bit less intimidating because it wears a more-familiar European face.

Here's an admittedly basic and simplistic outline (written by

with the colorfully painted facades double as galleries for local artists. The artists live and work upstairs, then sell their work right on this street. Pop into the *atelier d'art* ("Đul Emina") on the right to meet Sead Vladović and enjoy his impressive iconographic work (daily 9:00-20:00). This is the most touristy street in all of Bosnia-Herzegovina, so don't expect any bargains. Still, it's fun. As you stroll, check out the fine views of the Old Bridge.

• *Continue uphill. After the street levels out, about halfway along the street on the left-hand side, look for the entrance to the...*

▲Koski Mehmed-Pasha Mosque (Koski Mehmed-Paša Džamija)

Mostar's Bosniak community includes many practicing Muslims. Step into this courtyard for a look at one of Mostar's many

a non-Muslim) designed to help travelers from the Christian West understand a very rich but often misunderstood culture that's worthy of respect:

Muslims, like Christians and Jews, are monotheistic. They call God "Allah." The most important person in the Islamic faith is Muhammad, Allah's most important prophet, who lived in the sixth and seventh centuries A.D.

The "five pillars" of Islam are the same among Muslims in Bosnia-Herzegovina, Turkey, Iraq, Indonesia, the US, and everywhere else. Followers of Islam should:

1. Say and believe, "There is only one God, and Muhammad is his prophet."

2. Pray five times a day, while facing Mecca. Modern Muslims explain that it's important for this ritual to include several elements: washing, exercising, stretching, and thinking of God.

3. Give to the poor (one-fortieth of your wealth, if you are not in debt).

4. Fast during daylight hours through the month of Ramadan. Fasting is a great social equalizer and helps everyone to feel the hunger of the poor.

5. Visit Mecca. This is interpreted by some Muslims as a command to travel. Muhammad said, "Don't tell me how educated you are, tell me how much you've traveled."

Good advice for anyone, no matter what—or if—you call a higher power.

MOSTAR AND NEARBY

mosques. This mosque, dating from the early 17th century, is notable for its cliff-hanging riverside location, and because it's particularly accessible for tourists. But Mostar's other mosques share many of its characteristics—much of the following information applies to them as well.

Cost and Hours: 4 KM to enter mosque, 4 KM more to climb minaret, daily April-Oct 9:00-18:00, until 19:00 at busy times, Nov-March 9:00-15:00; if it seems crowded with tour groups, you can enter a very similar mosque later on this walk instead.

Touring the Mosque: The **fountain** *(šadrvan)* in the courtyard allows worshippers to wash before entering the mosque, as directed by Islamic law. This practice, called ablution, is both a literal and a spiritual cleansing in preparation for being in the presence of Allah. It's also refreshing in this hot climate, and the sound of running water helps worshippers concentrate.

The **minaret**—the slender needle jutting up next to the dome—is the Islamic equivalent of the Christian bell tower, used to call people to prayer. In the old days, the *muezzin* (prayer leader) would climb the tower five times a day and chant, "There is only one God, and Muhammad is his prophet." In modern times, loud-speakers are used instead. Climbing the minaret's 89 claustropho-bic, spiral stairs is a memorable experience, rewarding you at the top with the best views over Mostar—and the Old Bridge—that you can get without wings (entrance to the right of mosque entry).

Because this mosque is accustomed to tourists, you don't need to take off your shoes to enter (but stay on the green car-pet), women don't need to wear scarves, and it's fine to take pho-tos inside. Near the front of the mosque, you may see some of the small, overlapping rugs that are below this covering (reserved for shoes-off worshippers).

Once **inside,** notice the traditional elements of the mosque. The niche *(mihrab)* across from the entry is oriented toward Mecca (the holy city in today's Saudi Arabia)—the direction all Muslims face to pray. The small stairway *(mimber)* that seems to go nowhere is symbolic of the growth of Islam— Muhammad had to stand higher and higher to talk to his growing following. This serves as a kind of pulpit, where the cleric gives a speech, similar to a sermon or homily in Christian church services. No priest ever stands on the top stair, which is symbolically reserved for Muhammad.

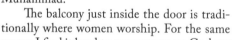

The balcony just inside the door is tradi-tionally where women worship. For the same reason I find it hard to concentrate on God at yoga classes, Muslim men decided prayer would go better without the enjoyable but problematic distraction of bent-over women between them and Mecca. These days, women can also pray on the main floor with the men, but they must avoid physical contact.

Muslims believe that capturing a living creature in a painting or a sculpture is inappropriate. (In fact, depictions of Allah and the prophet Muhammad are strictly forbidden.) Instead, mosques are filled with ornate patterns and Arabic calligraphy (of the name "Muhammad" and important prayers and sayings from the Quran). You'll also see some floral and plant designs, which you'd never see in a more conservative, Middle Eastern mosque.

Before leaving, ponder how progressive the majority of Mostar's Muslims are. Most of them drink alcohol, wear modern European clothing (you'll see virtually no women wearing head scarves or men with beards), and almost never visit a mosque to pray. In so many ways, these people don't fit our preconceived notions of Islam...and yet, they consider themselves Muslims all the same.

The mosque's **courtyard** is shared by several merchants. When you're done haggling, head to the terrace behind the mosque for the best view in town of the Old Bridge.

• *Just beyond this mosque, the traffic-free cobbles of the Old Town end. Take a right and leave the cutesy tourists' world. Walk up one block to the big...*

▲▲New Muslim Cemetery

In this cemetery, which was a park before the war, every tomb is dated 1993, 1994, or 1995. As the war raged, more exposed

cemeteries were unusable. But this tree-covered piece of land was relatively safe from Croat snipers. As the casualties mounted, locals buried their loved ones here under cover of darkness. Many of these people were soldiers, but some were civilians. Strict Muslim graves don't display images of people, but here you'll see photos of war dead who were young, less-traditional members of the Muslim community. The fleur-de-lis shape of many of the tombstones is a patriotic symbol for the nation of Bosnia. The Arabic squiggles are the equivalent of an American having Latin on his or her tombstone—old-fashioned and formal.

• *Go up the wide stairs to the right of the cemetery (near the mosque). At #4 on the right, just before and across from the bombed-out tower, you'll find the...*

Museum of Herzegovina (Muzej Hercegovine)

This humble little museum is made worthwhile by a deeply moving **film**, rated ▲▲, that traces the history of the town through its Old Bridge: fun circa-1957 footage of the diving contests; harrowing scenes of the bridge being pummeled, and finally toppled, by artillery; and a stirring sequence showing the bridge's reconstruction and grand reopening on that day in 2004—with high-fives, Beethoven's *Ode to Joy*, fireworks, and more divers.

The museum itself displays fragments of this region's rich history, including historic photos and several items from its Ottoman period. There are sparse English descriptions, but without a tour guide the exhibits are a bit difficult to appreciate. Topics include the Turkish period, Herzegovina under the Austro-Hungarian

Empire, village life, and local archaeology. One small room com-memorates the house's former owner, Dzemal Bijedić, who was Tito's second-in-command during the Yugoslav period until he was killed in a mysterious plane crash in 1977. (If Bijedić had lived, many wonder whether he might have succeeded Tito...and suc-ceeded in keeping Yugoslavia together.)

Cost and Hours: 5-KM museum entry includes 12-minute film, no narration—works in any language, ask about "film?" as you enter; Mon-Fri 9:00-14:00, Sat 10:00-12:00, closed Sun; Bajatova 4—walking up these stairs, it's the second door that's marked for the museum, under the overhanging balcony, www.muzej hercegovine.com.

• *Backtrack to where you left the Old Town. Notice the* **Tepa Market**, *with locals buying produce, in the area just beyond the pedestrian zone. Now walk (with the produce market on your left) along the lively street called* **Braće Fejića**. *(There's no sign, but the street is level and busy with cafés.) You're in the "new town," where locals sit out in front of boisterous cafés sipping coffee while listening to the thumping beat of distinctly Eastern-sounding music.*

Stroll down this street for a few blocks. At the palm trees (about 50 yards before the minaret—look for sign to Ottoman House*), you can side-trip a block to the left to reach...*

▲Bišćević Turkish House (Bišćevića Ćošak)

Mostar has three traditional Turkish-style homes that are open for tourists to visit. The Bišćević House is the oldest, most inter-esting, and most convenient for a quick visit, but two others are described at the end of this listing. Dating from 1635, the Bišćević House is typical of old houses in Mostar, which mix Oriental style with Mediterranean features.

Cost and Hours: 4 KM, daily March-Oct 8:00-19:00 or 20:00, Nov-Feb 9:00-15:00—but can close unexpectedly, Bišćevića 13.

Touring the House: First you'll step through the outer (or animals') garden, then into the inner (or family's) garden. This inner zone is surrounded by a high wall—protection from the sun's rays, from thieves...and from prying eyes, allowing women to take off the veil they were required to wear in public. Enjoy the geometrical patters of the smooth river stones in the floor (for example, the five-sided star), and keep an eye out for the house's pet turtles. It's no coincidence that the traditional fountain *(šadrvan)* resembles those at the entrance to a mosque—a reminder of the importance of running water in Muslim culture. The little white building is a kitchen—cleverly located apart from the house so that the heat and smells of cooking didn't permeate the upstairs living area.

Buy your ticket and take off your shoes before you climb up the wooden staircase. Imagine how a stairway like this one could be pulled up for extra protection in case of danger (notice that this one has a "trap door" to cover it). The cool, shady, and airy living room is open to the east—from where the wind rarely blows. The overhanging roof also prevented the hot sun from reaching this area. The loom in the corner was the women's workplace—the carpets you're standing on would have been woven there. The big chests against the wall were used to bring the dowry when the homeowner took a new wife. Study the fine wood carving and the heavy stonework of the roof.

Continue back into the main gathering room *(divanhan)*. This space—whose name comes from the word "talk"—is designed in a circle so people could face each other, cross-legged, for a good conversation while they enjoyed a dramatic view overlooking the Neretva. The room comes with a box of traditional costumes—great for photo fun. Put on a pair of baggy pants and a fez and really lounge.

Other Turkish Houses: If you're intrigued by this house, consider dropping by Mostar's two other Turkish houses. The **Muslibegović House** (Muslibegovića Kuća) feels newer because it dates from 1871, just a few years before the Ottomans left town. This homey house—which also rents out rooms to visitors (see "Sleeping in Mostar," later)—has many of the same features as the Bišćević House. If they're not too busy, Sanela or Gabriela can give you an English tour (4 KM, mid-April-mid-Oct daily 10:00-18:00, closed to visitors off-season, just two blocks uphill from the Karađozbeg Mosque at Osman Đikića 41, tel. 036/551-379, www.muslibegovichouse.com). To find it, go up the street between the Karađozbeg Mosque and the cemetery, cross the busy street, and continue a long block uphill on the alley. The wall with the slate roof on the left marks the house.

The **Kajtaz House** (Kajtazova Kuća), hiding up a very residential-feeling alley a few blocks from the Old Bridge, feels lived-in because it still is (in the opposite direction from most of the other sights, at Gaše Ilića 21).

• *Go back to the main café street and continue to the...*

▲Karađozbeg Mosque (Karađozbegova Džamija)

The city's main mosque was completed in 1557, the same year work began on the Old Bridge. This mosque, which welcomes visitors,

feels less touristy than the one back in the Old Town. Before entering the gate into the complex, look for the picture showing the recent war damage sustained here. You'll see that this mosque has most of the same elements as the Koski Mehmed-Pasha Mosque (described earlier), but some of these decorations are original. Across the street is another cemetery with tombstones from that terrible year, 1993.

Cost and Hours: 4 KM to enter mosque, 4 KM more to climb minaret, daily May-Sept 9:00-19:30, Oct-April 10:00-15:00. Inside the mosque, either stay on the green carpet or remove your shoes.

• *Now continue into modern, urban Mostar along the street in front of the Karađozbeg Mosque. This grimy, mostly traffic-free street is called...*

▲Braće Fejića

Walking along the modern town's main café strip, enjoy the opportunity to observe this workaday Bosniak town. You'll see the humble offices of the ragtag B&H Airlines; a state-run gambling office taxing its less-educated people with a state lottery; and lots of cafés that serve drinks but no food. People generally eat at home before going out to nurse an affordable drink. (Café ABC has good cakes and ice cream; the upstairs is a popular pizza hangout for students and families.)

At the small mosque on the left, obituary announcements are tacked to the outer wall, listing the bios and funeral times for locals who have recently died. A fig tree grows out of the mosque's minaret, just an accident of nature illustrating how that plant can thrive with almost no soil (somehow, the Bosniaks can relate). Walking farther, look up to see a few ruins—still ugly nearly two decades after the war. There's a messy confusion about who owns what in Mostar. Surviving companies have no money. Yugo Bank, which held the mortgages, is defunct. No one will invest until clear ownership is established. Until then, the people of Mostar sip their coffee and rip up their dance clubs in the shadow of these jagged reminders of the warfare that wracked this town not so long ago.

Near the end of the pedestrian zone, through the parking lot on the right, look for the building with communist-era reliefs of 12th-century Bogomil tomb decor—remembering the indigenous culture that existed here even before the arrival of the Ottomans.

When you finally hit the big street (with car traffic), head left one block to the big **Masala Square** (literally, "Place for Prayer").

The Dawn of War in Mostar

Mostar was always one of the most stubbornly independent parts of the former Yugoslavia. It had one of the highest rates of mixed-ethnicity marriages in all of Bosnia-Herzegovina. In the early 1990s, Mostar's demographics were proportioned more-or-less evenly—about 35 percent of its residents were Bosniaks, 34 percent Croats, and 19 percent Serbs. But this delicate balance was shattered in a few brutal months of warfare.

On April 1, 1992, Bosnia-Herzegovina—led by Muslim president Alija Izetbegović—declared independence from Yugoslavia. Very quickly, the Serb-dominated Yugoslav People's Army moved to stake their claim on territory throughout the country, including the important city of Mostar. On April 3, Serb forces occupied the east end of town (including the Ottoman Old Town), forcing many residents—predominantly Croats and Bosniaks—to hole up in the western part of the city. Meanwhile, Serbian and Croatian leaders were secretly meeting to divvy up Bosnian territory, and by early May, they'd agreed that Croatia would claim Mostar. Several weeks later, when the joint Croat-Bosniak forces crossed back over the river, the Serb forces mysteriously withdrew from the city (having been directed to capitulate), and retreated to the mountaintops above town, where they watched...and waited. The Croats and Bosniaks, believing they'd achieved peace, began putting their city back together. During this time, some factions also rounded up, tortured, and killed Serbs still living in Mostar. Many Bosniaks moved back to their homes on the east side of town, but, rather oddly, many of the Croats who had previously resided there instead stayed in the west—in many cases, moving into apartments vacated by Serbs who had fled.

On May 9, 1993—the Yugoslav holiday of "Victory over Fascism Day"—Mostarians were rocked awake by the terrifying sounds of artillery shells. Croat military forces swept through the city, forcibly moving remaining Bosniaks from the west part of town into the east. Throughout that summer, Bosniak men were captured and sent to concentration camps, while the Croats virtually sealed off the east side of town—creating a giant ghetto with no way in or out. The long and ugly siege of Mostar had begun.

Historically this was where pilgrims gathered before setting off for Mecca on their hajj. This is a great scene on balmy evenings, when it's a rendezvous point for the community. The two busts near the fountain provide perfect goal posts for budding soccer stars.

• *For a finale, you can continue one block more out onto the bridge to survey the town you just explored. From here, you can backtrack to linger in the places you found most inviting. Or you can venture into...*

Western (Croat) Mostar

Most tourists stay on the Bosniak side of town. For a complete look at this divided city, consider a stroll to the west. While there are few attractions here, and it's not particularly pretty—it feels like any dreary mid-size Balkan city—it provides an interesting contrast to the Muslim side of town.

Crossing the river and Bulevar, the scarred husks of destroyed buildings begin to fade away, and within a block you're immersed in concrete apartment buildings—making it clear that, when the city became divided, the Muslims holed up in the original Ottoman Old Town, while the Croats claimed the modern Tito-era sprawl. The relative lack of war damage (aside from a few stray bullet holes) emphasizes that it was the Croats laying siege to the Muslims of Mostar. Looking at a map, you'll notice that many streets on this side of town are named for Croatian cities (Dubrovačka, Splitska, Vukovarska) or historical figures (Kralja Tomislava, for the duke who first united the Croats in the 10th century). This side of town also has several remnants of Habsburg rule (including genteel buildings that look like they'd be at home in Vienna, and fine boulevards lined with plane trees). A few of these streets converge at the big roundabout called the Rondo, where *Centar* signs pointedly direct traffic *away* from the (Bosniak) Old Town. Also notice the many road signs pointing toward Široki Brijeg—a Bosnian Croat stronghold. A block toward the Old Town from the Rondo, notice the big cemetery with Muslim tombstones from the early 1990s. These are the graves of those killed during the first round of fighting, when the Croats and Bosniaks teamed up to fight the Serbs. You'll also notice some glitzy new shopping centers and more pizza and pasta restaurants than *ćevapčići* joints (in other words, even the food over here is more Croatian than Bosnian).

Nightlife in Mostar

Be sure to enjoy the local scene after dark in Mostar. Though the town is touristy, it's also a real urban center with a young population riding a wave of raging hormones. The meat market in the

courtyard next to the old Turkish bathhouse near the TI is fun to observe. The Old Bridge is a popular meeting place for locals as well as tourists (and pickpockets). A stroll from the Old Bridge down the café-lined Braće

Fejića boulevard, to the modern Masala Square at the far end of town (described earlier), gives a great peek at Mostarians socializing away from the tourists.

Ali Baba is an actual cave featuring a fun, atmospheric, and youthful party scene. Order a cocktail or try a Turkish-style hub-

bly-bubbly (*šiša*, SHEE-shah). Ask to have one of these big water pipes fired up for you and choose your flavored tobacco: apple, cappuccino, banana, or lemon (20 KM per pipe per group, 8-KM cocktails, open late daily; look for low-profile, cave-like entrance along Coppersmiths' Street, just down from the Old Bridge—watch for "Open Sesame" sign tucked down a rocky alley).

Oscar Nightclub is a caravanserai for lounge lizards—an exotic world mixing babbling streams, terraces, lounge chairs, and big sofas where young and old enjoy 5-10-KM cocktails and *šiša* (10 KM will last you about 40 minutes; June-Aug open "non-stop," closed Sept-May, up from the Old Bridge on Onešćukova street, near the Crooked Bridge at the end of the pedestrian zone).

Sleeping in Mostar

The Bristol and Ero are big, full-service hotels, but a bit farther from the charming Old Town. The rest are small, friendly, accessible, affordable guest houses in or very near the Old Town. Many hotels and pensions in town promise "parking," but it's often street parking out front—private lots are rare. Mostar's Old Town can be very noisy on weekends, with nightclubs and outdoor restaurants rollicking into the wee hours. If you're a light sleeper, consider Villa Fortuna and the Muslibegović House, which are quieter than the norm.

$$$ The **Muslibegović House,** a Bosnian national monument that also invites tourists in to visit during the day, is in an actual

Turkish home dating from 1871. The complex houses 10 homey rooms and two suites, all of which combine classic Turkish style (elegant and comfortable old beds, creaky wooden floors with colorful carpets, lounging sofas; guests remove shoes at the outer door) with modern comforts (air-con, free Wi-Fi, flatscreen TVs). Situated on a quiet residential lane just above the bustle of Mostar's main pedestrian drag and Old Town zone, this

Sleep Code

($1 = about 1.40 KM, €1 = about $1.40, country code: 387, area code: 036)

S = Single, **D** = Double/Twin, **T** = Triple, **Q** = Quad, **b** = bathroom. Unless otherwise noted, prices include breakfast.

Rates: If I list two rates separated by a slash, the first is for peak season (June-Sept), and the second is for off-season (Oct-May).

Price Ranges: To help you sort easily through these listings, I've divided the accommodations into three categories based on the price for a double room with bath during peak season:

$$$ Higher Priced—Most rooms €70 or more.
$$ Moderately Priced—Most rooms between €40-70.
$ Lower Priced—Most rooms €40 or less.

Prices can change without notice; verify the hotel's current rates online or by email. For other updates, see www.ricksteves.com/update.

MOSTAR AND NEARBY

is a memorable experience (Sb-€55, Db-€90/€75, "pasha suite"-€105, includes a tour of the house, closed Nov-Feb, 2 blocks uphill from the Karađozbeg Mosque at Osman Đikića 41, tel. 036/551-379, www.muslibegovichouse.com, muslibegovichouse@gmail .com; Taž, Sanela, and Gabriela).

$$$ Hotel Bristol is the only business-class place near central Mostar. Its 47 rooms don't quite live up to their four stars, but the location is handy, overlooking the river a 10-minute walk from the heart of the Old Town (Sb-€42, Db-€76, apartment-€90, extra bed-€16, air-con, elevator, free Internet access and Wi-Fi, some street noise, limited parking, Mostarskog Bataljona, tel. 036/500-100, fax 036/500-502, www.bristol.ba, info@bristol.ba).

$$$ Hotel Ero, a 20-minute walk north of the Old Town, is a good big-hotel option, with 91 fine rooms and a professional staff. This was one of the only big buildings in the center not damaged during the war, since it hosted journalists and members of the international community and was therefore off-limits (Sb-€51, Db-€86, suite-€110, air-con, elevator, free Wi-Fi, some traffic noise, ulica Dr. Ante Starčevića, tel. 036/386-777, fax 036/386-700, www.ero.ba, hotel.ero@tel.net.ba).

$$ Hotel Kriva Ćuprija ("Crooked Bridge"), by the bridge of the same name, is tucked between waterfalls in a picturesque valley a few steps from the Old Bridge. It's an appealing oasis with five rooms, four apartments, and a restaurant with atmospheric outdoor seating (Sb-€39, Db-€65, apartment-€75, extra bed-€18, 10 percent discount on rooms and food with this book, can be noisy, air-con, free Wi-Fi, free parking, call to reconfirm if arriving after 19:00, enter at Onešćukova 23 or Kriva Ćuprija 2, tel. 036/550-953, mobile 061-135-286, www.motel-mostar.ba, info@motel-mostar.ba, Sami). Their second location—**Hotel Kriva Ćuprija II**—offers 10 modern rooms with a business-class vibe in a Habsburg-style building overlooking the river from a drab urban street, about 200 yards to the south (same prices, discount, amenities, and contact information as main hotel; some traffic noise, Maršala Tita 186, next to the Lučki Bridge, reception tel. 036/554-125).

$$ Pansion Čardak, run by sweet Suzana and Nedžad Kasumović, has four rooms sharing a kitchen and Internet nook in a stone house set just back from the bustling Crooked Bridge area (Db-€50/€45, Tb-€75/€60, Qb-€90/€75, cash only, no breakfast, air-con, free Wi-Fi, free parking, Jusovina 3, tel. 036/578-249, mobile 061-385-988, www.pansion-cardak.com, info@pansion -cardak.com).

$$ Pansion Nur, run by Feđa, a relative of Suzana and Nedžad (above), also has four rooms and a shared kitchen (twin Db-€40/€35, Db-€50/€40, Tb-€70/€60, suite-€80/€70, cash only, no breakfast, air-con, free Wi-Fi, free parking, Jusovina 8b, tel. 036/580-296, mobile 062-160-872, www.pansion-nur.com, info @pansion-nur.com).

$$ Villa Anri, a bit more hotelesque than other pensions in Mostar, sits a block farther from the bustle near the Bulevar. The stony facade hides seven rooms (five with balconies) combining old Herzegovinian style and bright colors. The big draw is the rooftop terrace, shared by two rooms, which enjoys grand views over the Old Bridge area (Db-€60/€50, Db with grand terrace-€70/€60, Tb-€85/€70, Tb with grand terrace-€100/€80, Qb-€110/€90, cash only, air-con, free Wi-Fi, free parking, Braće Đukića 4, tel. 036/578-477, www.villa-anri-mostar.ba, villa.anri@gmail.com).

$$ Motel Emen has six modern, sleek rooms overlooking a busy café street a few cobbled blocks from the Old Bridge (Sb-€50, Db-€70, bigger Db with balcony-€80, all rooms €10 less Oct-May, air-con, free Internet access and Wi-Fi, free parking, Onešćukova 32, tel. 036/581-120, www.motel-emen.com, info@motel-emen .com).

$ Villa Fortuna is an exceptional value, located in a nondescript urban neighborhood a few minutes' walk farther away from the Old Bridge. Owners Nela and Mili Bijavica rent eight tasteful, modern rooms above the main office of Fortuna Tours. The courtyard in front offers free, secure parking, and in back there's a pleasant garden with a traditional Herzegovinian garden cottage

(Sb-€30, Db-€40, apartment-€80, these prices if you book direct, breakfast-€5, non-smoking, air-con, free Wi-Fi, Rade Bitange 34, tel. & fax 036/580-625, mobile 063-315-017, www.villafortuna .ba, villa_fortuna@bih.net.ba). Fortuna Tours can also put you in touch with locals renting rooms and apartments.

$ **Villa Botticelli,** overlooking a charming waterfall garden just up the valley from the Crooked Bridge, has five colorful rooms (Sb-€30, Db-€40, Tb-€60, breakfast-€3, air-con, free Wi-Fi, Muje Bjelavca 6, enter around back along the alley, mobile 063-809-658, www.villabotticelli.com, botticelli@bih.net.ba, Snježana and Zoran).

Eating in Mostar

Most of Mostar's tourist-friendly restaurants are conveniently concentrated in the Old Town. If you walk anywhere that's cobbled, you'll stumble onto dozens of tempting restaurants charging the same reasonable prices and serving rustic, traditional Bosnian food. In my experience, the menus at most places are virtually identical—though quality and ambience can vary greatly. As eateries tend to come and go quickly here, and little distinguishes these places anyway, don't be too focused on a particular spot. Grilled meats are especially popular. Another specialty is *dolma*—a pepper stuffed with minced meat, vegetables, and rice. On menus, look for the word *domaća*—"homemade." Sarajevska beer is on tap at most places.

On the Embankment, with Old Bridge Views

For the best atmosphere, find your way into the several levels of restaurants that clamber up the riverbank and offer perfect views of the Old Bridge. In terms of the setting, this is the most memorable place to dine in Mostar—but be warned that the quality of the food along here is uniformly low, and prices are relatively high (figure 8-15 KM for a meal). If you want a good perch, it's fun and smart to drop by earlier in the day and personally reserve the table of your choice.

To reach two of the most scenic eateries, go over the Old Bridge to the west side of the river, and bear right on the cobbles until you get to the old Turkish bathhouse (with the copper domes on the roof). To the right of the bathhouse is the entrance to a lively courtyard surrounded with cafés. Continuing toward the river from the courtyard, stairs lead

Enter the Dragon

The city's oddest monument is a testament to how reconcili-ation can come about in strange and unexpected ways. In the early 2000s, idealistic young Mostarians formed the Urban Movement of Mostar, which searched for a way to connect the still-feuding Catholic and Muslim communities. As a symbol of their goals, they chose Bruce Lee, the deceased kung-fu movie star, who is beloved by both Croats and Bosniaks for his characters' honorable struggle against injustice. A life-size bronze statue of Lee was unveiled with fanfare in November 2005 in Veliki Park. Unfortunately, soon after, the statue was damaged. Whether or not the vandalism was ethnically moti-vated is unclear, but many locals hope the ideals embodied in the statue will continue to bring the city together.

down to several riverfront terraces belonging to two different res-taurants: **Teatar,** a bit closer to the bridge, has unobstructed views and lower-quality food, while **Babilon** has slightly better (but still not great) food and nearly as good views. Poke around to find your favorite bridge panorama before settling in for a drink or a meal.

Two other places (including a pizzeria) are a bit closer to the bridge—to reach these, look for the alley on the left just before the bridge tower.

Near the Old Bridge

While they lack the Old Bridge views, these places are just as cen-tral as those listed above, and serve food that's generally a step up. The first three places are in the atmospheric Old Town, while the last one is in the modern part of town.

Restoran Hindin Han is pleasantly situated on a woody terrace over a rushing stream. It's respected locally for its good cooking and fair prices (big 12-16-KM salads, 7-13-KM grilled dishes, 12-20-KM fish and other main dishes, Sarajevsko beer on tap, daily 11:00-24:00, Jusovina 10, tel. 036/581-054). To find it, walk west from the Old Bridge, bear left at the Šadrvan restaurant, cross the bridge, and you'll see it on the left.

Šadrvan ("Fountain"), situated smack-dab in the cen-ter of the tourist zone, where cobbled paths converge near the Old Bridge, is undoubtedly touristy. But it also has fine service, good food, and pleasant outdoor seating under a tree around its namesake fountain. This is also a good place to nurse a "Bosnian coffee"—like Turkish coffee, unfiltered, with "mud" in the bot-tom of the cup (7-10-KM vegetarian options, 10-15-KM pastas, 7-20-KM main dishes, daily 7:00-23:00, Jusovina 11, tel. 036/579-057).

Ima Dana ("Someday") is woven into a tangle of terraces over a rushing little stream facing the Crooked Bridge, with good food and a pleasant riverside setting (7-10-KM pizzas and pastas, 7-18-KM meat and fish meals, daily 11:00-24:00, on Jusovina street at the end of the Crooked Bridge, head waiter Miro's mobile is 061-529-408).

Local Alternative in the New Town: **Saray** is an untouristy, nondescript little eatery just uphill from the Karađozbeg Mosque in the modern part of town. They have a basic menu of cheap and very tasty grilled meats—specializing in the classic *ćevapčići* (little sausage-shaped meat patties)—and outdoor seating overlooking a playground that offers good people- and kid-watching while you eat (4-10-KM grilled meat dishes, big 6-7-KM salads, daily 9:00-17:00, Karađozbegova 3, mobile 062-062-301).

Mostar Connections

By Bus

Not surprisingly for a divided city, Mostar has two different, autonomous bus terminals, each served by different companies. Mostar's **main bus station** (called "Autobusna Stanica") is on the east/Bosniak side of the river, about a 15-minute walk north of the Old Town (for details, see "Arrival in Mostar," earlier). Most buses you're likely to take use this station; for information on the other station (on the west/Croat side of town), see the end of this section.

Schedules and Tickets: At the main station, two primary companies (one Bosniak, one Croat) operate independent offices, providing schedule information and tickets only for their own buses. Because the companies refuse to cooperate, there's no single information or ticket office for all Mostar buses—so it's essential to visit both companies to know your options before buying tickets. (You may be lucky and encounter a helpful person in one office who'll clue you in on options at the other, but don't count on it—they're just as likely to pretend the other company doesn't exist.) As you face the bus station, near the left end is the Bosniak company **Autoprevoz** (tel. 036/551-900, www.autoprevoz-bus.ba); they also sell tickets for a few other companies (including Eurolines and Bogdan Bus). Near the right end is the Croat-owned **Globtour** (tel. 036/318-333, www.globtour.com), which sells tickets only for its own buses. Local and regional connections (not listed below) are operated by Mostar Bus, whose buses depart from across the street from the main bus station (www.mostarbus.ba).

Tracking down reliable **schedule** information in Mostar is tricky, but you can start by checking the websites listed above, then calling or visiting both companies at the station to confirm your options and buy tickets. While this may sound intimidating, it's workable—just be sure to double-check your plans. Note that buses to seasonal destinations (such as along the Dalmatian Coast) run more frequently in peak season, roughly June through mid-September. The prices I've listed are estimates; it can depend on the company.

From Mostar's Main Bus Station to: Međugorje (6-7/day, 40 minutes, all operated by Globtour, 4-5 KM), **Sarajevo** (at least hourly, 2.5 hours, several different companies—check with both offices to know all your options, 20 KM), **Zagreb** (4/day on Globtour, 1/day on Autoprevoz, 8-9.5 hours, includes a night bus, 45 KM), **Split** (2/day with Globtour, 2-3/day with Autoprevoz, 4-4.5 hours, plus 1 night bus with Eurolines/Autoprevoz, 20-30 KM), **Dubrovnik** (2/day with Globtour, 1/day with Eurolines/Autoprevoz—or 3/day in summer, 4-5 hours, 25-30 KM). The important Dubrovnik connection is tricky: Most days, all Dubrovnik buses depart early in the day, making an afternoon return from Mostar to Dubrovnik impossible. In summer, however, Eurolines adds two more departures each day—including a handy 17:30 departure, which makes day-tripping from Dubrovnik workable (tickets sold at Autoprevoz office). Globtour also runs a handy bus to Montenegro's **Bay of Kotor** (departs Mostar at 7:00, arrives at Kotor at 12:30 and Budva at 13:30, then returns the same day).

From Mostar's West/Croat Bus Station: A few additional buses, mostly to Croatian destinations and to Croat areas of Bosnia-Herzegovina, depart from the west side of town. These use a makeshift "station" (actually a gravel lot behind a gas station) on Vukovarska street, called "Kolodvor." It's about a 15-minute walk due west of the main bus station. Most buses using the Kolodvor station are operated by the Euroherc company. In addition to one daily bus apiece to **Zagreb, Split,** and **Sarajevo,** this station has several departures to **Metković** (at the Croatian border, with additional connections to Croatian destinations; 8/day) and to **Međugorje** (7/day Mon-Fri, 3/day Sat, none Sun, 5 KM). Additionally, some Croat buses leave from a bus stop near the Franciscan Church. But since the connections from this side are sparse, the location is inconvenient, and the "station" is dreary, I'd stick with the main bus station and ignore this option unless you're desperate.

By Train

Mostar is on the train line that runs from Ploče (on the Croatian coast between Split and Dubrovnik) to Zagreb, via Mostar and Sarajevo. This train—which leaves from next to the main bus station—generally runs once daily, leaving **Ploče** soon after 6:00 in the morning, with stops at **Mostar** (1.75 hours), **Sarajevo** (4.25 hours), and **Zagreb** (13.5 hours; bus is faster). Going the opposite direction, the train leaves Zagreb at about 9:00 in the morning. There's also a night train connection running in both directions along the same track (leaving Ploče northbound at 16:25, arriving in Mostar at 18:35, Sarajevo at 20:59, and Zagreb at 6:44; and southbound leaving Zagreb at 21:24, arriving in Sarajevo at 6:39 and Mostar at 9:31). Train info: tel. 036/550-608.

Route Tips for Drivers: From Dubrovnik to Mostar

You have two ways to drive between Dubrovnik and Mostar: easy and straightforward along the coast, or adventurous and off the beaten path through the Herzegovinian mountains. I've narrated each route as you'd encounter it driving from Dubrovnik to Mostar, but you can do either one in reverse—just hold this book upside-down.

The Main Coastal Road

The vast majority of traffic from Dubrovnik to Mostar follows the coastal road north, then cuts east into Bosnia. Because this is one of the most direct routes, it can be crowded (allow about 2.5 hours). It's also a bit inconvenient, as you have to cross the border three times (into and out of Bosnia at Neum, and into Bosnia again at Metković).

Begin by driving north of Dubrovnik, passing some of the places mentioned in the Near Dubrovnik chapter: **Trsteno** (with its arboretum), and **Ston** and **Mali Ston** (with a mighty wall and waterfront restaurants, respectively). After passing the Ston turn-off, you'll see the long, mountainous, vineyard-draped **Pelješac Peninsula** across the bay on your left.

Soon you'll come to a surprise border crossing, at **Neum**. Here you'll cross into Bosnia-Herzegovina—then, six miles later, cross back out again.

You won't be back in Croatia for long. Just north of Neum, the main coastal road jogs away from the coast and around the striking **Neretva River Delta**—the extremely fertile "garden patch of Croatia," which produces a significant portion of Croatia's fruits and vegetables. The Neretva is the same river that flows under Mostar's Old Bridge upstream—but in Metković, it spreads out into 12 branches as it enters the Adriatic, flooding a vast plain and creating a bursting cornucopia in the middle of an otherwise rocky and arid region. Enjoying some of the most plentiful sunshine on the Croatian coast, as well as a steady supply of water for irrigation, the Neretva Delta is as productive as it is beautiful.

At the Neretva Delta, turn off for the town of **Metković**;

at the far end of that town, you'll cross the border into **Bosnia-Herzegovina,** then continue straight on the main road (M17) directly into Mostar. As you drive, you'll see destroyed buildings and occasional roadside memorials bearing the likenesses of fresh-faced soldiers who died in the recent war.

Along the way are a few interesting detours: In Čapljina, you can turn off to the left to reach **Međugorje**. If you stay on the main road, keep your eyes peeled soon after the Čapljina turnoff for a mountaintop castle tower (on the right side of the road), which marks the medieval town of **Počitelj**. With extra time, just before Mostar (in Buna), you can detour a few miles along the Buna River into **Blagaj**.

Approaching **Mostar** on M17, you'll pass the airport, then turn left at your first opportunity to cross the river. After crossing the bridge, bear right onto Bulevar street, and continue on that main artery for several blocks (passing several destroyed buildings). At the street called Rade Bitange (just after the giant church bell tower), turn right to find the public parking lot (2 KM/hour, 10 KM/8 hours)—less than a 10-minute walk from the Old Bridge. Be warned that signage is poor; if you get lost, try asking for directions to "Stari Most" (STAH-ree most)—the Old Bridge.

Rugged-but-Scenic Backcountry Journey through Serb Herzegovina

While the coastal route outlined above is the most common way to connect Dubrovnik to Mostar, I enjoy getting out of the tourist rut by twisting up the mountains behind Dubrovnik and cutting across the scenic middle of Herzegovina. (If you're traveling by road between Dubrovnik and Split at another point in your trip, you'll see the coastal road anyway—so this alternative helps you avoid the rerun.) This route feels much more remote, but the roads are good and the occasional gas station and restaurant break up the journey. I find this route particularly interesting because it offers an easily digestible taste of the **Republika Srpska** part of Herzegovina—controlled by the country's Serb minority, rather than its Bosniak and Croat majority. You'll see Orthodox churches and monasteries, the Cyrillic alphabet, and various symbols of the defiantly proud Serb culture (such as the red, white, and blue flag with the four golden C's). You can't get a complete picture of the former Yugoslavia without sampling at least a sliver of Serb culture. (Because this road goes through the Serbian part of Herzegovina, it's not popular among Bosniaks or Croats—in fact, locals might tell you this road "does not exist." It does.) If you want a little taste of Republika Srpska, consider just day-tripping into Trebinje—especially on Saturday, when the produce market is at its liveliest.

The first step is to climb up into the mountains and the charming market town of Trebinje. From there, two different roads lead to Mostar: via Stolac or via Nevesinje. If you take the Stolac route, the whole journey from Dubrovnik to Mostar takes about as long as the coastal road (and potentially even faster, thanks to the light traffic and lack of an extra border). The Nevesinje route takes a good hour longer than the Stolac route, and immerses you in an even more remote landscape.

Dubrovnik to Trebinje: From Dubrovnik, head south toward Cavtat, the airport, and Montenegro. Shortly after leaving Dubrovnik, watch for—and follow—signs on the left directing you to *Brgat Gornji*. (Signage completely ignores the large Serb town of Trebinje, just past this obscure border village.) As you drive through the border into Bosnia-Herzegovina, notice the faint remains of a long-abandoned old rail line cutting sharp switchbacks up the hill. This once connected Dubrovnik to Mostar and Sarajevo. The charred trees you may see are not from the war, but from more recent forest fires.

Carry on across the plateau, where you may begin to notice Cyrillic lettering on signs: You've crossed into the Republika Srpska. About 20 minutes after the border, you'll come upon **Trebinje** (Требиње)—a pleasant and relatively affluent town with a leafy main square that hosts a fine Saturday market. Trebinje is a good place to stretch your legs, get some Bosnian Convertible Marks (ATMs are scattered around the town center),  and maybe nurse a coffee while people-watching on the main square. Overlooking the town from its hilltop perch is the striking Orthodox Church of Nova Gračanica, built to resemble the historically important Gračanica Monastery in Kosovo. If you have time, drive up to the church's viewpoint terrace for great views over Trebinje and the valley, and step inside the church to immerse yourself in a gorgeously vibrant world of Orthodox icons.

From Trebinje, you have two options for getting to Mostar: The faster route via Stolac, or the very rugged slower route via Nevesinje.

Stolac Route: As you enter Trebinje, after crossing the river, follow signs for *Mostar* and *Ljubinje*. Follow the Trebišnjica River into a high-altitude karstic basin, where waterwheels power a primitive irrigation system. From here, the river flows down to the coast—providing hydroelectric power for Dubrovnik—before detouring south and emptying into the sea near Herceg Novi, Montenegro...one river, three countries, in just a few miles. This area is blanketed with vineyards and dotted with old monasteries. Passing the village of Mesari ("Butchers"), you'll also see flocks of sheep. In this part of the Balkans, Croats were traditionally the city-dwellers, while Serbs were farmers. There used to be sheep like these in the pastures near Dubrovnik, but when the Serbs left during the war, so did the sheep.

The large field you're driving along is called **Popovo Polje** ("Priests' Field"). Because it floods easily, the canal was built to remove floodwater. Pull over at one of the humble, slate-roofed Orthodox chapels by the road. In the cemeteries, many of the gravestones are from 1991—when soldiers from this area joined the war effort against Dubrovnik.

At the fork, carry on straight to Ljubinje. Climbing up into the mountains, you'll see garbage along the side of the road—an improvised dump in this very poor land, where a fractured government struggles to provide even basic services. Twisting up through even higher mountains, you'll wind up in the town of **Ljubinje** (Љубиње). In this humble burg, roadside stands with *med* signs advertise homegrown honey. The partially built houses are not signs of war damage (the war didn't reach here); it's a form of "savings" in the Balkans, where people don't trust banks: Rather than deposit money in an account, they spend many years gradually adding on to a new house.

Continuing toward Mostar, you'll pass through more desolate countryside to the town of **Stolac** (Столац); the town's defiant mosque minaret tells you that you've crossed from Serb territory into Bosnia's Muslim-Croat Federation. Stolac is home to some fascinating history, and worth a stroll if you have the time. Leaving Stolac, keep an eye out (on the left) for its interesting **necropolis**—a cluster of centuries-old traditional Bosnian tombstones (worth a quick photo-op stop).

Past Stolac, you'll soon pop out at an intersection with the main road between Mostar and the coast. From here, turn right to head into **Počitelj**, then the turnoff for **Blagaj** and on to **Mostar.** (If you want to go to **Međugorje** turn left here, then turn right once you get to Čapljina.) For arrival tips in Mostar, see the end of the driving directions above.

Nevesinje Route: This longer, more remote, middle-of-nowhere adventure takes about an hour longer than the Stolac route. But if you're adventurous, it's a fun ride. From Trebinje, drive north toward **Bilećko Lake**—a vast, aquamarine lake you'll see on your right (the Vikiovac Restaurant offers a great viewpoint). Then you'll go through the town of **Bileća** (Билећа), turning west at the gloomy industrial town of **Gacko** (Гацко, with a giant coal mine), and onward to the humble but proud little town of **Nevesinje** (Невесиње). From Nevesinje, it's a quick drive up over the mountains, then down into Mostar—passing spectacular views of Herzog Stjepan's imposing castle over the town of Buna. Follow signs on into Mostar.

Near Mostar

While Mostar has its share of attractions, there's also plenty to see within a short drive. Ideally try to splice one or two of these stops into your trip between Mostar and the coast (see my "Route Tips for Drivers," earlier, for tips on linking them up).

Blagaj

Blagaj (BLAH-gai, rhymes with "pie") was the historical capital of this region until the arrival of the Ottomans. This is the site

of a mountain called Hum, which is topped by the ruins of a hilltop castle that once belonged to Herzog ("Duke") Stjepan, who gave Herzegovina its name. Deep in Blagaj is an impressive cliff face with a scenic house marking the source of the Buna River. The building, called the Tekija, is actually a former monastery for Turkish dervishes (an order that emphasizes poverty and humility, famous for the way they whirl in a worshipful trance); inside is a modest museum with the graves of two important dervishes. Today the area is surrounded by gift shops and a big restaurant with fine views over the river and cliff.

Blagaj is easiest to see on the way to or from Mostar—just turn off from the main road and follow the Buna River to the big parking lot.

Počitelj

Počitelj (POTCH-ee-tell) is an artists' colony filled with a compelling mix of Christian and Muslim architecture. Ideally situated

right along the main Mostar-to-Croatia road, it's one of the most popular rest stops for passing tour buses, so it's hardly undiscovered. But it's still worth a stop for its dramatically vertical townscape and beautifully restored Ottoman architecture.

Park your car and hike across the riverstone cobbles to the open square at the base of town, with a handy restaurant, lots of gift shops, and aggressive vendors. The multidomed building is an old hammam (bathhouse). Then hike up the steep stairs (dodging costumed vendors, and enjoying fine aerial views on those hammam domes) to reach the **mosque.** It's free to enter (women must cover their heads). The interior is bigger, though not necessarily better decorated, than the mosques in downtown Mostar. A photo on the porch shows the building circa 1993, destroyed to its foundation.

Continue up the stairs behind the mosque, which lead steeply all the way up to the **fortress,** which was originally built in the 15th century by Hungarian King Mátyás Corvinus (who pushed

the Ottomans back, briefly reclaiming some territory—including this region—for the forces of Christian Europe). There's virtually nothing to see inside (the stairs inside the tower are extremely steep and narrow—tread carefully), but the views are sensational. The best views are from the flat terrace out front. It's clear just how strategic this location is, with perfect views up and down the Neretva Valley, constricted as it is here between steep cliffs.

Stolac

One of the most historic spots in Herzegovina, Stolac (STOH-lats) was a cradle of early Balkan civilization. Unless you're fascinated by archaeology, Stolac isn't worth a long detour—but since it's on the way between Mostar and Dubrovnik (on the back-roads route), consider stopping off if you have a little time to spare.

About 15,000 to 16,000 years ago—long before the Greeks or Romans arrived in this region—the Illyrians (ancestors of today's Albanians) lived in this area's caves, where they left behind some drawings. On a hill above the modern town are the overgrown remains of the once-fearsome dry-stone Illyrian fortress that watched over this strategic road in the third and fourth centuries B.C. The Romans were later supplanted by the local Bogomil civilization, an indigenous Christian society. Stolac's most impressive attraction dates from this era: On the outskirts of town (on the road toward Mostar), you'll find a **necropolis** with a bonanza of giant tombstones called *stećak*s (from the 13th-15th centuries), engraved with evocative reliefs. Soon after these were erected, the Ottomans arrived, and conversions to Islam followed.

Archaeological treasures aside, today's Stolac is a workaday village with little tourism—trudging along, largely oblivious to the ancient treasures embedded all around. The town was particularly hard-hit during the recent war, when it was taken over by Croat forces and its majority Muslim residents forced to flee to Mostar. Today the war crimes tribunal in The Hague has an entire division devoted to "Stolac Crimes"—at least 80 civilians were killed here. The mosque and surrounding area were completely leveled; it's now rebuilt, and the town's population is divided evenly between Croats and Bosniaks. Tension still hangs heavy in the air. Local Croats have erected crosses in front of several buildings in town, and the main square features a giant monument engraved with the names of Croats killed in the fighting here. In a recent soccer match between the Croatian and Turkish national teams, local Bosniaks backed the Turks...and things got very tense.

If you're interested in learning more, it's well worth hiring local guide **Sanel Marić** to show you around. Sanel is an industrious young man who works for a local organization that strives to help the people of Stolac transcend the scars of the recent war. He can both show you some of the ancient sights around town, and fill you in on recent events (€30 for a tour around town, mobile 061-071-830, sanell_m@yahoo.com).

Međugorje

Međugorje is an unassuming little village "between the hills" (as its name implies) that ranks with Lourdes, Fátima, and Santiago de Compostela as one of the most important pilgrimage sites in all of Christendom. To the cynical non-Catholic, it's just a strip of crassly commercial hotels, restaurants, and rosary shops leading up to a dull church, all tied together by a silly legend about a hilltop apparition. But if you look into the tear-filled eyes of the pilgrims who've journeyed here, it's clear that to some, this place offers much more than what you see on the surface. Strolling through the grounds, you can hear the hushed sounds of prayer whispering through the bushes.

For true believers, Međugorje represents a once-in-a-lifetime opportunity to tread on sacred soil: a place where, over the last three decades, the Virgin Mary has appeared to six local people. Even though the Vatican has declined to recognize the apparitions, that doesn't stop hundreds of thousands of Catholics from coming here each year. More than 30 million pilgrims have visited Međugorje since the sightings began—summer and winter, war (which didn't touch Međugorje) and peace, rain and shine. People make the trek here from Ireland, Italy, Germany, Spain, the US, and just about anywhere else that has Catholics.

MOSTAR AND NEARBY

Planning Your Time

Unless you're a pilgrim (or think you might be a pilgrim), skip Međugorje—it's an experience wasted on nonbelievers. (The only "attractions" are an unexceptional modern church, a couple of hilltop hikes, and pilgrim-spotting.)

If you do go, the easiest way is to take a day-trip excursion from the Dalmatian Coast (sold from Split, Dubrovnik, and Korčula). By public bus, you can day-trip into Međugorje from Split, but not from Dubrovnik. Consider spending the night here, or sleep in Mostar two nights and day-trip into Međugorje.

Orientation to Međugorje

(country code: 387; area code: 036)

Međugorje (MEDGE-oo-gor-yeh, sometimes spelled "Medju-gorje" in English) is basically a one-street town—most everything happens in the half-mile between its post office (where the bus

Međugorje Mary

What compels millions to flock to this little village in the middle of nowhere? The official story goes like this: On the evening of June 24, 1981, two young women were gathering their sheep on the hillside above Mostar. They came across a woman carrying a baby who told them to come near. Terrified, they fled, only to realize later that this might have been a vision of the Virgin Mary. They returned the next night with some friends and saw the apparition again.

In the nearly three decades since, six different locals (including the two original seers) claim to have seen the vision, and some of them even say they see it regularly to this day. They also say that Mary has given them 10 secrets—predictions of future events that will portend Judgment Day. Written on a piece of parchment, these are kept safely at the home of one of the seers. They have said they will reveal each of these secrets, 10 days before the event occurs, to the local parish priest, who will then alert the world.

But official representatives of the Vatican are not among the believers. According to Catholic law, such visions must be "certified" by the local bishop—and the one around here didn't buy it. One cause for suspicion is that the six seers, before witnessing the visions, were sometimes known to be troublemakers. (In fact, they later admitted that they went up the hill that fateful night not to chase wayward sheep, but to sneak a smoke.) One investigator even suggested that they invented the story as a prank, only to watch it snowball out of control once they told it to the local priest. After decades of reluctance, in mid-2010 the Vatican formed a commission to determine whether to officially endorse this "miracle." (For now, priests are allowed to accompany pilgrimages to Međugorje, but not to *lead* them.)

Whether or not the story is true is, to a certain extent, beside the point—that people *believe* it's true is why they come here.

stop is) and the main church, St. James (Crkva Sv. Jakova). On the hills behind the church are two trails leading to pilgrimage sites. Many travel agencies line the main strip; at any of these, you can find a room, rent a car, hire a local guide, buy ferry tickets for Croatia, and use the Internet.

By the way, Međugorje is clearly a "Croat" sight. While this may seem odd (after all, you're in Bosnia-Herzegovina, not

Croatia), remember that any Catholic from the former Yugoslavia is called a Croat. Virtually every local person you'll meet in Međugorje is, strictly speaking, a Bosnian Croat.

Sights in Međugorje

The center of pilgrim activity is **St. James' Church** (Crkva Sv. Jakova), which was built before the apparitions. The exterior and interior are both pretty dull, but that doesn't stop pilgrims from worshipping here at all times of day (inside and outside). The inside, like the outside, is modern and monochromatic—with a soothing yellow color, and modern stained-glass windows lining the nave. Out in front of the church are posted maps that are useful for getting oriented, and a white statue of the Virgin Mary that attracts a lot of attention from pilgrims. Outside, along the left side of the church, notice the long row of multilingual confessional booths—each one marked with the language spoken by the priest inside, who stands at the ready.

As you face the church, you'll see two trails leading up to the hills. Behind and to the left of the church is **Apparition Hill** (at Podbrdo), where the sightings occurred (a 1-mile hike, topped by a statue of Mary). Directly behind the church is the **Great Hill** (Križevac, or "Cross Mountain"), where a giant hilltop cross, which predates the visions, has become a secondary site of pilgrimage (1.5-mile hike). Note that the paths up to the hilltops are embedded with rocks. If you wonder why they don't make it easier to climb up, remember that an act of pilgrimage is supposed to be challenging. In fact, pilgrims often do one or both of these hikes barefoot, as a sign of penitence.

Around back of the church is a makeshift amphitheater with benches, used for outdoor services. Beyond that is a path, lined with scenes from the life of Jesus. Farther along, on the right, is a giant statue of the **Resurrected Savior** (Uskrsli Spasitelj), also known as the "Weeping Knee." While the elongated, expressionistic sculpture—exemplifying Christ's suffering—is inherently striking, the eternal dampness of its right knee attracts the most attention from pilgrims. Miraculously (or not), it's always wet—go ahead and touch

the spot that's been highly polished by worshippers and skeptics alike.

Believers and nonbelievers both appreciate the parade of

kitsch that lines the **main street** leading up to the church. While rosaries are clearly the big item, you can get basically anything you want stamped with Catholic imagery (Mary is particularly popular, for obvious reasons).

Sleeping in Međugorje

The main street has dozens of hotels and pensions to accommodate pilgrims.

$ Hotel Martin, well-run by Martin Ilić, is set back slightly from the main road. With 45 comfortable, modern rooms—all with balconies—it's an easy choice (Db-€44, cash only, air-con, elevator, tel. 036/651-541, fax 036/651-505, www.martin.ba, martin.ilic@tel.net.ba). Don't confuse this with the Pension Martin, much farther out of town.

Eating in Međugorje

The main street is lined with straightforward, crank-'em-out eateries catering to tour groups. For something a little more atmospheric and fun, head for **Gardens Restaurant** (near the post-office end of the main drag). The ground-floor bar, which feels a bit like a transplanted British pub, serves only drinks; you can order tasty international cuisine in the classy dining room upstairs, and the namesake garden terrace out back. Somewhat youthful, but still respectable, it's a nice place to unwind at the end of a long pilgrimage (8-13-KM pastas and pizzas, 14-22-KM main courses, daily 10:00-23:00, Antunovića 66, tel. 036/650-499, www.clubgardens.com).

Sleeping and Eating near Međugorje

Considering how drab the town itself is, if you're determined to sleep or eat near Međugorje, you might as well do it at a pleasant new facility just outside town (leaving town, follow signs for *Split/Ljubuški*, and look for it on the left between warehouses). **Herceg Etno Selo** (Herceg Ethno Village) is a completely artificial but undeniably appealing faux-village of brand-new but old-looking Bosnian dry-stone buildings wedged between industrial areas and office parks. With slate roofs, inviting ponds, playgrounds, a vineyard, a small farm, and a big amphitheater, this sprawling complex includes 50 buildings, housing a restaurant, a big hotel, gift shops, and more. Designed as a retreat center for church groups on pilgrimage, it's a restful place. If Epcot had a low-rent "Croat Herzegovina" pavilion, it would look a lot like this—completely artificial but utterly charming. The industrial-sized, smoky restaurant has a menu of very well-executed Bosnian and Croatian food (6-15-KM starters, 13-25-KM main dishes), while the hotel has 71 rooms (Db-€82, Tromeđa bb, tel. 036/653-400, www.etno-herceg .com, info@etno-herceg.com).

UNDERSTANDING YUGOSLAVIA

Americans struggle to understand the complicated breakup of Yugoslavia—especially when visiting countries that rose from its ashes. Here's an admittedly oversimplified, as-impartial-as-possible history to get you started. (For a longer version, see www.ricksteves.com/yugo.)

For starters, it helps to have a handle on the different groups who've lived in the Balkans—the southeastern European peninsula between the Adriatic and the Black Sea, stretching from Hungary to Greece. The Balkan Peninsula has always been a crossroads of cultures. The Illyrians, Greeks, and Romans had settlements here before the Slavs moved into the region from the north around the seventh century. During the next millennium and a half, the western part of the peninsula—which would become Yugoslavia—was divided by a series of cultural, ethnic, and religious fault lines.

The most important influences were three religions: Western Christianity (i.e., Roman Catholicism, first brought to the western part of the region by Charlemagne and later reinforced by the Austrian Habsburgs), Eastern Orthodox Christianity (brought to the east from the Byzantine Empire), and Islam (in the south, from the Ottomans).

Two major historical factors made the Balkans what they are today: The first was the split of the Roman Empire in the fourth century A.D., dividing the Balkans down the middle between Roman Catholic (west) and Byzantine Orthodox (east)—roughly along today's Bosnian-Serbian border. Then the Ottoman victory at the Battle of Kosovo Polje (1389) began five centuries of Islamic influence in Bosnia-Herzegovina and Serbia, further dividing the Balkans into Christian (north) and Muslim (south).

Because of these and other events, several distinct ethnic identities emerged. Confusingly, the major "ethnicities" of Yugoslavia are all South Slavs—they're descended from the same ancestors and speak closely related languages, but they practice different religions. Roman Catholic South Slavs are called **Croats** or **Slovenes**; Orthodox South Slavs are called **Serbs** or **Montenegrins**; and Muslim South Slavs are called **Bosniaks**

Yugoslav Succession

AUSTRIA HUNGARY

ITALY
Ljubljana ⊛
Slovene
SLOVENIA
⊛ Zagreb
CROATIA
Hungarian
VOJVODINA
Novi Sad ⊛
ROMANIA

BOSNIA-
• Banja Luka
HERZEGOVINA
⊛ Belgrade
SERBIA

Adriatic Sea
Serbo-Croatian
Knin •
Sarajevo ⊛

ITALY

MONTE-
NEGRO
⊛ Podgorica
Priština ⊛
KOSOVO

Albanian

BULGARIA

⊛ Skopje
MACEDONIA

ALBANIA

GREECE

100 Kilometers
100 Miles

- Former Yugoslavia Border
- Current Border
- Province within Serbia
- **Slovene** Language
- "Serbian Krajina" (Serb-Controlled Croatia 1991-1995)
- Republika Srpska (Serb territory in Bosnia-Herz.)

(whose ancestors converted to Islam under the Ottomans). The region is also home to several non-Slavic minority groups, including **Hungarians, Albanians,** and others. The groups overlapped a lot—which is exactly why the eventual breakup of Yugoslavia was so contentious.

The Kingdom of Yugoslavia ("Land of the South Slavs"—*yugo* means "south") was first formed after the Austro-Hungarian Empire fell at the end of World War I. It was an arbitrary union of the various, mostly Slavic groups of southeast Europe. But from the very beginning, the different ethnicities struggled for power within the new Yugoslavia. This continued through the interwar period, until the region was occupied by the Nazis during World War II.

At the end of World War II, the rest of Eastern Europe was "liberated" by the Soviets, but the Yugoslavs regained their independence on their own, as their communist Partisan Army forced out the Nazis. After the short but rocky Yugoslav union between the World Wars, it seemed that no one could hold the southern

Slavs together in a single nation. But there was one man who could, and did: Communist Party president and war hero Josip Broz, better known as Tito. With a Slovene for a mother, a Croat for a father, a Serb for a wife, and a home in Belgrade, Tito was a true Yugoslav. Tito had a compelling vision that this fractured union of the South Slavs could function.

Tito's new incarnation of Yugoslavia aimed for a more equitable division of powers. It was made up of six republics, each with its own parliament and president: **Croatia** (mostly Catholic), **Slovenia** (mostly Catholic), **Serbia** (mostly Orthodox; also included the "autonomous provinces" of **Kosovo** and **Vojvodina**), **Bosnia-Herzegovina** (the most diverse—mostly Muslim Bosniaks, but with very large Croat and Serb populations), **Montenegro** (mostly Orthodox—a sort of a Serb/Croat hybrid), and **Macedonia** (with about 25 percent Muslim Albanians and 75 percent Orthodox Macedonians). Each republic managed its own affairs...but always under the watchful eye of president-for-life Tito, who said that the borders between the republics should be "like white lines in a marble column."

Tito's Yugoslavia was communist, but it wasn't Soviet communism. Despite strong pressure from Moscow, Tito refused to ally himself with the Soviets—and therefore received good will (and $2 billion) from the United States. Tito's vision was for a "third way," in which Yugoslavia could work with both East and West, without being dominated by either. While large industry was nationalized, Tito's system allowed for small businesses. This experience with a market economy benefited Yugoslavs when Eastern Europe's communist regimes eventually fell.

After Tito died in 1980, it did not take long for his union to unravel. In the late 1980s, squabbles broke out in the autonomous province of Kosovo between the Serb minority and the ethnic-Albanian majority. Serbia, led by Slobodan Milošević, annexed Kosovo—causing other republics (especially Slovenia and Croatia) to fear that he would gut their nation to create a "Greater Serbia," instead of a friendly coalition of diverse Yugoslav republics. Over the next decade, Yugoslavia broke apart, with much bloodshed.

Slovenia declared independence from Yugoslavia on June 25, 1991. After 10 days of fighting and fewer than a hundred deaths, they were granted their freedom. But the situation in other republics—which were far more ethnically diverse—was not so simple.

In April 1990, a historian named Franjo Tuđman won Croatia's first free elections. Tuđman invoked the spirit of the last group that led an "independent" Croatia—the Ustaše, who had ruthlessly run Croatia's puppet government under the Nazis (and had killed many Serbs in their concentration camps). The 600,000 Serbs living in Croatia began to rise up.

By the time Croatia formally declared its independence (also on June 25, 1991), it was already embroiled in the beginnings of a bloody war. Croatia's Serb residents immediately declared their own independence from Croatia. The Serb-dominated Yugoslav National Army swept in, supposedly to keep the peace between Serbs and Croats—but it soon became obvious that they were there to support the Serbs.

Fighting raged through the region. In a surprise move, the Yugoslav National Army even attacked the tourist resort of Dubrovnik. By early 1992, the Serbs had gained control over the parts of inland Croatia where they were in the majority, and a tense ceasefire began. Then, in 1995, the Croats swept back through Serb territory to reclaim it for Croatia. During this period, both the Serbs and the Croats carried out "ethnic cleansing"—systematically removing an ethnic group from a territory, by displacing or killing them. Finally, the 1995 Erdut Agreement brought peace.

Bosnia-Herzegovina declared its independence from Yugoslavia four months after Croatia and Slovenia did. But Bosnia-Herzegovina was even more diverse than Croatia, as it was populated predominantly by Muslim Bosniaks (mostly in the cities) but also by large numbers of Serbs and Croats (many of them farmers).

At first, the Bosniaks and Croats teamed up to fight against the Serbs. But even before the first wave of fighting had subsided, Croats and Bosniaks turned their guns on each other. A bloody war raged for years between the three groups: the Serbs led by Radovan Karadžić (with support from Serbia proper), the Croats (with support from Croatia proper), and—squeezed between them—the internationally recognized Bosniak government, led by President Alija Izetbegović, who desperately worked for peace.

Bosnia-Herzegovina was torn apart. Even the many mixed families were forced to choose sides. If you had a Serb mother and a Croat father, you were expected to pick one ethnicity or the other—and your brother might choose the opposite. As families and former neighbors trained their guns on each other, proud and beautiful cities such as Sarajevo and Mostar were turned to rubble, and people throughout Bosnia-Herzegovina lived in a state of constant terror.

Finally, in 1995, the Dayton Peace Accords carefully divided Bosnia-Herzegovina among the different ethnicities. And today—following the peaceful declarations of independence in Montenegro (2006) and Kosovo (2008)—there are seven countries where once was a single, united Yugoslavia. While tension still exists, the region is peaceful, stable, and welcoming to visitors.

Travelers to this region quickly realize that the vast majority of people they meet here never wanted these wars. And so finally

UNDERSTANDING YUGOSLAVIA

comes the inevitable question: Why did any of it happen in the first place?

Explanations tend to gravitate to two extremes. Some observers consider this part of the world to be inherently warlike—a place where deep-seated hatreds and age-old ethnic passions unavoidably flare up. Others believe that this theory is an insulting oversimplification. Sure, animosity has long simmered in the Balkans, but the conflict broke out because of the single-minded, self-serving actions of a few selfish leaders who exploited existing resentments to advance their own interests. It wasn't until Milošević, Karadžić, Tuđman, and others expertly manipulated the people's grudges that the country fell into war.

Many of the people you'll meet here are eager to tell you their own story. But keep in mind that everyone in the former Yugoslavia seems to have a slightly different version of events. A very wise Bosniak told me, "Listen to all three sides—Muslim, Serb, and Croat. Then decide for yourself what you think."

UNDERSTANDING YUGOSLAVIA

PRACTICALITIES

This section covers just the basics on traveling in Croatia (for much more information, see *Rick Steves' Croatia & Slovenia*). You can find free advice on specific topics at www.ricksteves.com/tips.

This book also includes destinations that are in different countries: Bosnia-Herzegovina and Montenegro. You'll find practicalities about traveling in each of those places (such as the local currency and telephone tips) in their chapters.

Money

Croatia uses a currency called the kuna: 5 Croatian kunas (kn) = about $1. A kuna is broken into 100 smaller units, called lipas. To roughly convert Croatian kunas into dollars, double the amount and drop the final zero (e.g., 5 kn = about $1; 70 kn = about $14; 200 kn = about $40).

The standard way for travelers to get kunas is to withdraw money from a cash machine (called a *bankomat* in Croatia) using a debit or credit card, ideally with a Visa or MasterCard logo. Before departing, call your bank or credit-card company: Confirm that your card will work overseas, ask about international transaction fees, and alert them that you'll be making withdrawals in Europe.

To keep your valuables safe, wear a money belt. But if you do lose your credit or debit card, report the loss immediately to the respective global customer-assistance centers. Call these 24-hour US numbers collect: Visa (410/581-9994), MasterCard (636/722-7111), and American Express (623/492-8427).

Phoning

Smart travelers use the telephone to reserve or reconfirm rooms, reserve restaurants, get directions, research transportation connections, confirm tour times, phone home, and lots more.

To call Croatia from the US or Canada: Dial 011-385 and

then the phone number, minus its initial zero. (The 011 is our international access code, and 385 is Croatia's country code.)

To call Croatia from a European country: Dial 00-385 followed by the phone number, minus its initial zero. (The 00 is Europe's international access code.)

To call within Croatia: If you're dialing within an area code, just dial the local number; but if you're calling outside your area code, you have to dial both the area code (which starts with a 0) and the local number.

To call from Croatia to another country: Dial 00 followed by the country code (for example, 1 for the US or Canada), then the area code and number. If you're calling European countries whose phone numbers begin with 0, you'll usually have to omit that 0 when you dial.

Tips on Phoning: To make calls in Croatia, your best bet is to buy a prepaid phone card to insert into public phone booths. Sold locally at newsstands, these are reasonable for calls within Croatia (and work for international calls as well, but can be expensive). I'd skip the international phone cards (which work with a scratch-to-reveal PIN code), as they are less common and save less money in Croatia than in other countries. Most of my recommended accommodations are rooms in private homes *(sobe)* that lack phones; if your hotel does have a phone, making local calls from your room can be affordable, but long-distance and international calls are pricey—always ask the rates before you dial. A mobile phone—whether an American one that works in Croatia, or a European one you buy when you arrive—is handy, but can be pricey. For more on phoning, see www.ricksteves.com/phoning.

Emergency Telephone Numbers in Croatia: To summon the **police,** dial 92. For **medical emergencies,** dial 112. For passport problems, call the **US Embassy** (in Zagreb, tel. 01/661-2200, after business-hours tel. 01/661-2400, consular services tel. 01/661-2300) or the **Canadian Embassy** (in Zagreb, tel. 01/488-1200). For other concerns, get advice from your hotel.

Croatian Accommodations

For most travelers, Croatian hotels are a bad value; instead, I focus my recommendations on what locals call "private accommodations": a rented apartment *(apartman)* or a room in a private home *(soba,* pronounced SOH-bah; plural *sobe,* SOH-bay). Private accommodations offer travelers a characteristic and money-saving alternative for a fraction of the price of a hotel.

Generally the more you pay for your *soba,* the more privacy and amenities you get: private bathroom, TV, air-conditioning, kitchenette, and so on (though telephones are rare). Apartments are bigger and cost more than *sobe,* but they're still far cheaper than hotels. The prices for private accommodations generally fluctuate with the seasons, and stays of fewer than three nights usually come with a 20–50 percent surcharge (though this is often waived outside of peak season).

For the *sobe* listed in this book, **always book direct.** You can reserve most *sobe* in advance by email or by phone. Since the best-value *sobe* understandably book up early, reservations are highly recommended. Email the *sobe* host with the following key pieces of information: number and type of rooms; number of nights; date of arrival; date of departure; and any special requests. (For a sample form, see www.ricksteves.com/reservation.) Use the European style for writing dates: day/month/year. For example, for a two-night stay in July, you could request: "1 double room for 2 nights, arrive 16/07/13, depart 18/07/13."

Some *sobe* hosts may ask for your credit-card number to secure the reservation (though you'll pay in cash when you're there). Other hosts might ask you to mail or wire money to them as a deposit; to avoid bank fees, it's better to mail a check or travelers check than to wire money. If the *sobe* host's request seems too complicated for you, reserve elsewhere.

If you like to travel without reservations, during most of the year you'll have no problem finding *sobe* as you go (though late July and August are the exceptions). Locals hawking rooms meet each arriving boat and bus. Be sure you understand exactly where the room is located (i.e., within easy walking distance of the attractions) before you go to take a look. You can also keep an eye out for rooms as you walk or drive through town—blue *sobe* and *apartmani* signs are everywhere.

As a last resort, enlist the help of a travel agency to find you a room—but you'll pay 10–30 percent extra (to search from home, try www.dubrovnikapartmentsource.com).

Eating

Croatian food has a distinct Mediterranean flavor; you'll enjoy locally produced wine, olive oil, and *pršut* (air-dried ham, similar to prosciutto). The budget standby is pizza and pasta. For a splurge, try seafood: fish, scampi, mussels, squid, octopus, and more. Prices for fish dishes are listed either by the kilogram (1,000 grams) or by the 100-gram unit; figure about a half-kilo, or 500 grams—that's about one pound—for a large portion. Try the octopus salad, a flavorful mix of octopus, tomatoes, onions, and spices.

You'll find similar fare in Bosnia-Herzegovina and Montenegro, but there you're also likely to come across some pan-Balkan elements. One staple is phyllo dough pastries—both honey-drenched baklava and its savory cousin, *burek* (stuffed with cheese, meat, or spinach). But the big item is grilled meat: *ćevapčići* (cheh-VAHP-chee-chee), grilled minced meat shaped like a sausage link; *pljeskavica* (plehs-kah-VEET-suh), grilled minced meat shaped like a patty; and *ražnjići* (RAZH-nyee-chee), skewered grilled steak similar to a shish kebab. Any kind of meat goes perfectly with the eggplant/red-pepper condiment called *ajvar* (EYE-var).

Good service is relaxed (slow to an American). You won't get the bill until you ask for it: *"Račun?"* (RAH-choon). To tip at restaurants that have a waitstaff, round up the bill 5 to 10 percent if you're happy with the service.

Transportation

Since Dubrovnik has no train access, you'll generally get around by car, bus, or boat.

By Car: A car is a headache to drive and park in Dubrovnik, but is the most convenient way to side-trip to this book's other destinations. You can arrange a short-term rental on the fly in Dubrovnik (ask any travel agency), or—often cheaper—reserve it in advance from the US (several big rental-car companies have offices in Dubrovnik). For tips on your insurance options, see www.ricksteves.com/cdw. Bring your driver's license; it's also recommended to carry an International Driving Permit (IDP), available at your local AAA office ($15 plus two passport-type photos, www.aaa.com). As you approach any town, follow the signs to *Centar* (usually also signed with a bull's-eye symbol). Follow this book's parking advice, and get additional tips from your hotelier. If you want someone else to do the driving, hire a local driver (listed on page 145).

By Bus: If you lack a car, buses are the best way to connect most of the destinations in this book (and beyond). Confusingly, a single bus route can be operated by a variety of different companies, making it difficult to find comprehensive timetables; confirm schedules with a local TI or bus station (or try www.libertasdubrovnik.com). For popular routes during peak season, drop by the station to buy your ticket a few hours—or even days—in advance to ensure getting a seat (ask the bus station ticket office or the local TI how far ahead you should arrive). You'll pay about $2 per bag to stow your luggage under the bus.

By Boat: Slow car ferries and speedy catamarans inexpensively shuttle tourists between major coastal cities and quiet island villages. The big ferries are operated by the national boat company, Jadrolinija (www.jadrolinija.hr). Walk-on passengers riding these boats don't need reservations, but drivers will want to line up their cars in advance (get advice locally about how early you need to arrive). A faster, private catamaran called *Nona Ana*—which takes only passengers (no cars)—also connects Dubrovnik to nearby islands (www.gv-line.hr). Because space is limited on this boat, it's smart to show up 30–60 minutes before departure time.

Helpful Hints

Time: Croatia uses the 24-hour clock. It's the same through 12:00 noon, then keep going: 13:00, 14:00, and so on. Croatia, like most of continental Europe, is six/nine hours ahead of the East/West Coasts of the US.

Business Hours: Business hours can fluctuate wildly, based on demand—shops are open long hours daily in summer, but might be closed entirely in winter. Most businesses close on Sundays.

Holidays and Festivals: Croatia celebrates many holidays, which can close sights and attract crowds (book hotel rooms ahead). For information on holidays and festivals, check Croatia's website: http://us.croatia.hr. For a simple list showing major—though not all—events, see www.ricksteves.com/festivals.

Numbers and Stumblers: What Americans call the second floor of a building is the first floor in Europe. Europeans write dates as day/month/year, so Christmas is 25/12/13. Commas are decimal points and vice versa—a dollar and a half is 1,50, and there are 5.280 feet in a mile. Croatia uses the metric system: A kilogram is 2.2 pounds; a liter is about a quart; and a kilometer is six-tenths of a mile.

Resources from Rick Steves

This Snapshot guide is excerpted from *Rick Steves' Croatia & Slovenia,* which is one of more than 30 titles in my series of guidebooks on European travel. I also produce a public television series, *Rick Steves' Europe,* and a public radio show, *Travel with Rick Steves.* My website, www.ricksteves.com, offers free travel information, a Graffiti Wall for travelers' comments, guidebook updates, my travel blog, an online travel store, and information on European railpasses and our tours of Europe. If you're bringing a mobile device on your trip, you can download free information from Rick Steves Audio Europe, featuring podcasts of my radio shows, free audio tours of major sights in Europe, and travel interviews about Croatia (via www.ricksteves.com/audioeurope, iTunes, or the Rick Steves Audio Europe free smartphone app).

Additional Resources

Tourist Information: http://us.croatia.hr
Passports and Red Tape: www.travel.state.gov
Packing List: www.ricksteves.com/packlist
Cheap Flights: www.skyscanner.net
Airplane Carry-on Restrictions: www.tsa.gov/travelers
Updates for This Book: www.ricksteves.com/update

How Was Your Trip?

If you'd like to share your tips, concerns, and discoveries after using this book, please fill out the survey at www.ricksteves.com/feedback. Thanks in advance—it helps a lot.

PRACTICALITIES

Croatian Survival Phrases

When using the phonetics, pronounce ī / Ī as the long I sound in "light."

English	Croatian	Phonetics
Hello. (formal)	Dobar dan.	DOH-bahr dahn
Hi. / Bye. (informal)	Bog.	bohg
Do you speak English?	Govorite li engleski?	GOH-voh-ree-teh lee EHN-glehs-kee
Yes. / No.	Da. / Ne.	dah / neh
I (don't) understand.	(Ne) razumijem.	(neh) rah-ZOO-mee-yehm
Please. / You're welcome.	Molim.	MOH-leem
Thank you (very much).	Hvala (ljepa).	HVAH-lah (LYEH-pah)
Excuse me. / I'm sorry.	Oprostite.	oh-PROH-stee-teh
problem	problem	proh-BLEHM
No problem.	Nema problema.	NEH-mah proh-BLEH-mah
Good.	Dobro.	DOH-broh
Goodbye.	Do viđenija.	doh veed-JAY-neeah
one / two	jedan / dva	YEH-dahn / dvah
three / four	tri / četiri	tree / CHEH-teh-ree
five / six	pet / šest	peht / shehst
seven / eight	sedam / osam	SEH-dahm / OH-sahm
nine / ten	devet / deset	DEH-veht / DEH-seht
hundred / thousand	sto / tisuća	stoh / TEE-soo-chah
How much?	Koliko?	KOH-lee-koh
local currency	kuna	KOO-nah
Write it?	Napišite?	nah-PEESH-ee-teh
Is it free?	Da li je besplatno?	dah lee yeh BEH-splaht-noh
Is it included?	Da li je uključeno?	dah lee yeh OOK-lyoo-cheh-noh
Where can I find / buy...?	Gdje mogu pronaći / kupiti...?	guh-DYEH MOH-goo PROH-nah-chee / KOO-pee-tee
I'd like / We'd like...	Želio bih / Željeli bismo...	ZHEH-lee-oh beeh / ZHEH-lyeh-lee BEES-moh
...a room.	...sobu.	SOH-boo
...a ticket to ___.	...kartu do ___.	KAR-too doh
Is it possible?	Da li je moguće?	dah lee yeh MOH-goo-cheh
Where is...?	Gdje je...?	guh-DYEH yeh
...the train station	...željeznička stanica	ZHEH-lyehz-neech-kah STAH-neet-sah
...the bus station	...autobusna stanica	OW-toh-boos-nah STAH-neet-sah
...the tourist information office	...turističko informativni centar	TOO-ree-steech-koh EEN-for-mah-teev-nee TSEHN-tahr
...the toilet	...vece (WC)	VEHT-SEH
men	muški	MOOSH-kee
women	ženski	ZHEHN-skee
left / right	lijevo / desno	LEE-yeh-voh / DEHS-noh
straight	ravno	RAHV-noh
At what time...	U koliko sati...	oo KOH-lee-koh SAH-tee
...does this open / close?	...otvara / zatvara?	OHT-vah-rah / ZAHT-vah-rah
(Just) a moment.	(Samo) trenutak.	(SAH-moh) treh-NOO-tahk
now / soon / later	sada / uskoro / kasnije	SAH-dah / OOS-koh-roh / KAHS-nee-yeh
today / tomorrow	danas / sutra	DAH-nahs / SOO-trah

In a Croatian Restaurant

I'd like to reserve…	Rezervirao bih…	reh-zehr-VEER-ow beeh
We'd like to reserve…	Rezervirali bismo…	reh-zehr-VEE-rah-lee BEES-moh
…a table for one / two.	…stol za jednog / dva.	stohl zah YEHD-nog / dvah
Non-smoking.	Za nepušače.	zah NEH-poo-shah-cheh
Is this table free?	Da li je ovaj stol slobodan?	dah lee yeh OH-vī stohl SLOH-boh-dahn
Can I help you?	Izvolite?	EEZ-voh-lee-teh
The menu (in English), please.	Jelovnik (na engleskom), molim.	yeh-LOHV-neek (nah EHN-glehs-kohm) MOH-leem
service (not) included	posluga (nije) uključena	POH-sloo-gah (NEE-yeh) OOK-lyoo-cheh-nah
cover charge	couvert	KOO-vehr
"to go"	za ponjeti	zah POHN-yeh-tee
with / without	sa / bez	sah / behz
and / or	i / ili	ee / EE-lee
fixed-price meal (of the day)	(dnevni) meni	(duh-NEHV-nee) MEH-nee
specialty of the house	specijalitet kuće	speht-see-yah-LEE-teht KOO-cheh
half portion	pola porcije	POH-lah PORT-see-yeh
daily special	jelo dana	YEH-loh DAH-nah
fixed-price meal for tourists	turistički meni	TOO-ree-steech-kee MEH-nee
appetizers	predjela	PREHD-yeh-lah
bread	kruh	krooh
cheese	sir	seer
sandwich	sendvič	SEND-veech
soup	juha	YOO-hah
salad	salata	sah-LAH-tah
meat	meso	MAY-soh
poultry	perad	PEH-rahd
fish	riba	REE-bah
seafood	morska hrana	MOHR-skah HRAH-nah
fruit	voće	VOH-cheh
vegetables	povrće	POH-vur-cheh
dessert	desert	deh-SAYRT
(tap) water	voda (od slavine)	VOH-dah (ohd SLAH-vee-neh)
mineral water	mineralna voda	MEE-neh-rahl-nah VOH-dah
milk	mlijeko	mlee-YEH-koh
(orange) juice	sok (od naranče)	sohk (ohd NAH-rahn-cheh)
coffee	kava	KAH-vah
tea	čaj	chī
wine	vino	VEE-noh
red / white	crno / bijelo	TSEHR-noh / bee-YEH-loh
sweet / dry / semi-dry	slatko / suho / polusuho	SLAHT-koh / SOO-hoh / POH-loo-soo-hoh
glass / bottle	čaša / boca	CHAH-shah / BOHT-sah
beer	pivo	PEE-voh
Cheers!	Živjeli!	ZHEE-vyeh-lee
More. / Another.	Još. / Još jedno.	yohsh / yohsh YEHD-noh
The same.	Isto.	EES-toh
Bill, please.	Račun, molim.	RAH-choon MOH-leem
tip	napojnica	NAH-poy-neet-sah
Delicious!	Izvrsno!	EEZ-vur-snoh

INDEX

INDEX

Audio Europe

RICK STEVES AUDIO EUROPE

Rick's free app and podcasts

The FREE Rick Steves Audio Europe™ app for iPhone, iPad, iPod Touch and Android gives you self-guided audio tours of Europe's top museums, sights and historic walks—plus hundreds of tracks filled with cultural insights and sightseeing tips from Rick's radio interviews—all organized into geographic-specific playlists.

Let Rick Steves Audio Europe™ amplify your guidebook. This free app includes self-guided audio tours for all the most important museums and historical walks in London, Paris, Rome, Venice, Florence, Athens, and more.

With Rick whispering in your ear, Europe gets even better.

Thanks Facebook fans for submitting photos while on location! From top: John Kuijper in Florence, Brenda Mamer with her mother in Rome, and Alyssa Passey with her friend in Paris.

Find out more at ricksteves.com

Start your trip at

Free information and great gear to

▸ Plan Your Trip

Browse thousands of articles and a wealth of money-saving tips for planning your dream trip. You'll find up-to-date information on Europe's best destinations, packing smart, getting around, finding rooms, staying healthy, avoiding scams and more.

▸ Eurail Passes

Find out, step-by-step, if a railpass makes sense for your trip—and how to avoid buying more than you need. Get free shipping on online orders

▸ Graffiti Wall & Travelers Helpline

Learn, ask, share—our online community of savvy travelers is a great resource for first-time travelers to Europe, as well as seasoned pros.

Rick Steves' Europe Through the Back Door, Inc.

Rick Steves

www.ricksteves.com

Rick Steves guidebooks are published by Avalon Travel,
a member of the Perseus Books Group.

NOW AVAILABLE:
eBOOKS, APPS & BLU-RAY

eBOOKS

Most guides are available as eBooks from Amazon, Barnes & Noble, Borders, Apple, and Sony. Free apps for eBook reading are available in the Apple App Store and Android Market, and eBook readers such as Kindle, Nook, and Kobo all have free apps that work on smartphones.

RICK STEVES' EUROPE DVDs

10 New Shows 2011–2012
Austria & the Alps
Eastern Europe
England & Wales
European Christmas
European Travel Skills & Specials
France
Germany, BeNeLux & More
Greece & Turkey
Iran
Ireland & Scotland
Italy's Cities
Italy's Countryside
Scandinavia
Spain
Travel Extras

BLU-RAY

Celtic Charms
Eastern Europe Favorites
European Christmas
Italy Through the Back Door
Mediterranean Mosaic
Surprising Cities of Europe

PHRASE BOOKS & DICTIONARIES

French
French, Italian & German
German
Italian
Portuguese
Spanish

JOURNALS

Rick Steves' Pocket Travel Journal
Rick Steves' Travel Journal

APPS

Select Rick Steves guides are available as apps in the Apple App Store.

PLANNING MAPS

Britain, Ireland & London
Europe
France & Paris
Germany, Austria & Switzerland
Ireland
Italy
Spain & Portugal

Rick Steves books and DVDs are available at bookstores and through online booksellers.

ABOUT THE AUTHORS

RICK STEVES

Since 1973, Rick Steves has spent 100 days every year exploring Europe. Rick produces a public television series *(Rick Steves' Europe)*, a public radio show *(Travel with Rick Steves),* and an app and podcast *(Rick Steves Audio Europe);* writes a bestselling series of guidebooks and a nationally syndicated newspaper column; organizes guided tours that take over ten thousand travelers to Europe annually; and offers an information-packed website (www.ricksteves.com). With the help of his hardworking staff of 80 at Europe Through the Back Door—in Edmonds, Washington, just north of Seattle—Rick's mission is to make European travel fun, affordable, and culturally enlightening for Americans.

CAMERON HEWITT

Cameron Hewitt grew up listening to the Polish nursery rhymes of his grandfather, Jan Paweł Dąbrowski. Today, Cameron researches and writes guidebooks for Rick Steves. For this book, he has spent countless hours tracking down Dubrovnik's best *sobe*, disentangling Balkan history, and raving about the friendliest locals in Europe. When he's not on the road, Cameron lives in Seattle with his wife Shawna.

Avalon Travel
a member of the Perseus Books Group
1700 Fourth Street
Berkeley, CA 94710

Text © 2012 by Rick Steves
Cover © 2012 by Avalon Travel. All rights reserved.
Maps © 2012 by Europe Through the Back Door
Printed in Canada by Friesens. First printing May 2012.

Portions of this book were originally published in *Rick Steves' Eastern Europe* ©
2012, 2011, 2009, 2007, 2006, 2005, 2004 by Rick Steves and Cameron Hewitt.

For the latest on Rick's lectures, guidebooks, tours, public radio show, and public television
series, contact Europe Through the Back Door, Box 2009, Edmonds, WA, 98020, 425/771-
8303, fax 425/771-0833, www.ricksteves.com, rick@ricksteves.com.

ISBN 978-1-61238-196-1

Europe Through the Back Door Reviewing Editors: Jennifer Madison Davis,
    Cameron Hewitt
ETBD Editors: Suzanne Kotz, Cathy McDonald, Tom Griffin, Gretchen Strauch,
    Cathy Lu
ETBD Managing Editor: Risa Laib
Avalon Travel Senior Editor & Series Manager: Madhu Prasher
Avalon Travel Project Editor: Kelly Lydick
Copy Editor: Patrick Collins
Proofreader: Janet Walden
Indexer: Stephen Callahan
Production & Typesetting: McGuire Barber Design
Cover Design: Kimberly Glyder Design
Graphic Content Director: Laura VanDeventer
Maps & Graphics: David C. Hoerlein, Laura VanDeventer, Lauren Mills, Twozdai Hulse,
    Chris Markiewicz, Kat Bennett, Mike Morgenfeld, Brice Ticen
Photography: Cameron Hewitt, Rick Steves, David C. Hoerlein, Rhonda Pelikan,
    Pat O'Connor
Cover Photo: Town Walls © Cameron Hewitt

Want More Eastern Europe?
Maximize the experience with Rick Steves as your guide

Guidebooks
Rick's Eastern Europe guide makes side-trips smooth and affordable

Planning Maps
Use the map that's in sync with your guidebook

Rick's DVDs
Preview where you're going with 3 shows on Croatia and Slovenia

Free! Rick's Audio Europe™ App
Hear Eastern Europe travel tips from Rick's radio shows

Small-Group Tours
Including the Best of the Adriatic

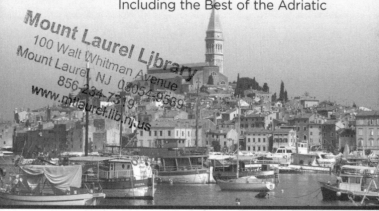

Mount Laurel Library
100 Walt Whitman Avenue
Mount Laurel, NJ 08054-9539
856-234-7319
www.mtlaurel.lib.nj.us

For all the details, visit ricksteves.com